Yale Studies in English, 189

Pablo Picasso, *Portrait of Gertrude Stein,* 1906, oil on canvas, 39⅜ x 32 inches. (Courtesy of Metropolitan Museum of Art, New York. Bequest of Gertrude Stein, 1946.)

EXACT RESEMBLANCE
TO
EXACT RESEMBLANCE:

THE LITERARY PORTRAITURE
OF GERTRUDE STEIN

Wendy Steiner

New Haven and London   Yale University Press

1978

Grateful acknowledgment is made to The Estate of Gertrude Stein for use of material from the G. Stein collection at the Beinecke Rare Book and Manuscript Library, Yale University.

Grateful acknowledgment is also made to the following:

Random House, Inc., for permission to quote from the following copyrighted works of Gertrude Stein: *The Geographical History of America, The Autobiography of Alice B. Toklas, Everybody's Autobiography, Portraits and Prayers,* and *Lectures in America.*

Harcourt Brace Jovanovich, Inc., for permission to reprint excerpts from *The Making of Americans* by Gertrude Stein, copyright 1934 by Harcourt Brace Jovanovich, Inc., copyright © 1962 by Alice B. Toklas.

The Hogarth Press for permission to reprint from *Composition as Explanation* by Gertrude Stein.

Association pour la Diffusion des Arts Graphiques et Plastiques for permission to reproduce *The Man from Touraine* by Juan Gris, © 1978, A.D.A.G.P., Paris.

Designed by John O. C. McCrillis and set in IBM Baskerville type. Printed in the United States of America by The Alpine Press, Inc., South Braintree, Mass.

Published in Great Britain, Europe, Africa, and Asia (except Japan) by Yale University Press, Ltd., London. Distributed in Australia and New Zealand by Book & Film Services, Artarmon, N.S.W., Australia; and in Japan by Harper & Row, Publishers, Tokyo Office.

Library of Congress Cataloging in Publication Data

Steiner, Wendy, 1949–
    Exact resemblance to exact resemblance.
    (Yale studies in English ; 189)
    Bibliography: p.
    Includes index.
    1. Stein, Gertrude, 1874–1946—Criticism and interpretation. 2. Characters and characteristics in literature. I. Title. II. Series.
PS3537.T323Z8267   818'.5'209   78-6917
ISBN 0-300-02165-8

Contents

Illustrations

Preface

The words that immediately come to mind in connection with Gertrude Stein are bohemianism, idiosyncrasy, incomprehensibility. As William Gass puts it, she was "an eccentric, dilettante, and gossip, madwoman, patron, genius, tutor, fraud, and queer—the Mother Goose of Montparnasse." Each of these titles indicates a critical position that has been taken in regard to Stein: that she is a cultural curiosity at the center of a brilliant era in the arts, a trifler with literature and the occult, a mere tutor to the great, or alternately the most significant force in modern literature. There is a grain of truth, of course, in each of these views, although certainly Stein's most successful creation was her extraordinary image. However, in this book I shall be little concerned with such sweeping characterizations. Instead, I shall claim that Stein was a writer with a training in psychology and philosophy that made her uniquely attentive to modernist problems. From this point of view a detailed exploration of her self-conscious, programmatic work is a way of recovering a train of thought that gave rise to some of the most important literature and painting of our century.

Such a study necessitates a limited focus, for Stein's writing is so diverse and frequently so difficult that an examination in depth would exceed the bounds of a single volume, and perhaps of most readers' patience. An obvious strategy, then, is to concentrate on Stein's portraits, a group of texts written throughout her career, short enough in themselves to be exhaustively analyzed, and designated by Stein herself as central to her theory of art.

The scope of the topic, however, is not as limited as it might at first appear. In fact, it seems to open out in all directions—toward the history of the literary portrait, toward the relation between painted and literary portraiture, toward 'cubist writing' and Jamesian psychology and genre theory, and most of all toward the inherent contradiction in the portrait genre itself: the literary imitation of an individual. This definitional paradox (it *is* a paradox, as chapter 1 explains) lies at the heart of all of Stein's writing and accounts for the continuing revision and experimentation that mark her artistic career. The same paradox, I would add, reveals some of the most difficult issues in nonfictional art in general.

The present book, then, is an attempt at explaining Stein's theoretical framework, at making several of her portraits and theoretical works accessible to readers, and at showing the cultural relevance of her writing. What this book is not is an apology for Stein. Though I am anxious to point out the logic of her artistic activity, I am far from claiming that art succeeds by virtue of the logic of its program; and Stein's program, we shall discover, is not perfect even in its logic. Nevertheless hers is an extraordinarily interesting literary evolution, its very failures providing new insights into both the verbal and the visual arts.

I have had much kind assistance in this project. Richard Bridgman, whose *Gertrude Stein in Pieces* is the best treatment of Stein's work to date, has pointed out errors in my manuscript and offered me encouragement. Donald Gallup has given me invaluable advice regarding the Stein manuscripts at the Beinecke Rare Book Library of Yale University. Meyer Schapiro painstakingly and constructively went over the chapter on Stein and the cubists; many of his suggestions have been incorporated into the text. Thomas Whitaker generously supported this study and supplied much helpful criticism and advice. And Charles Feidelson directed it in its beginnings as a doctoral dissertation and provided an example of scholarship and humanity that I will always remember. I am grateful also to the Canada Council for financing the graduate studies that led to this book, and to the A. Whitney Griswold Fund for covering the costs of typing and copying the manuscript. And most of all, I would like to thank my husband, Peter, who gave me his name, and thus made possible a study by Steiner on Stein.

I wish to express my thanks to Jiří Kolář, who created the collage and crumplage that decorate the dust jacket of this book. His work and that of other concrete artists are perhaps the most direct tribute to Stein's importance.

1

The Literary Portrait: History and Theory

For portrait is a curious bastard of art, sprung on the one side from a desire which is not artistic, nay, if anything, opposed to the whole nature and function of art: the desire for the mere likeness of an individual.

Vernon Lee, *Euphorion*

One wonders whether even the bemused writer of this description of portraiture knew how curious this "bastard of art" could become in the hands of a writer like Gertrude Stein. The following depiction of Georges Hugnet, for example, represents the culmination of her efforts in literary portraiture:

George Hugnet

George and Genevieve.
Geronimo with a with·whether they thought
    they were with whether.
Without their finding it out. Without. Their
    finding it out. With whether.
George whether they were about. With their
    finding their whether it finding it out
    whether with their finding about it out.
George with their finding it with out.
George whether their with their it whether.
Redoubt out with about.
With out whether it their whether with out doubt.
Azure can with out about.
It is welcome welcome thing.
George in are ring.
Lain away awake.
George in our ring.
George Genevieve Geronimo straightened it out
    without their finding it out.
Grammar makes George in our ring which Grammar
    make George in our ring.

> Grammar is as disappointed not is as grammar is
>   as disappointed.
> Grammar is not as Grammar is as disappointed.
> George is in our ring. Grammar is not is
>   disappointed. In are ring.
> George Genevieve in are ring.
>
> [*Portraits and Prayers*]

Stein herself termed "George Hugnet" and a number of her other works "portraits," discussing them as a separate and central genre in her essay "Portraits and Repetition." Knowing this, the reader would seem to have found a context for the difficult text above. But perhaps not. For this opaque piece of writing seems even more unyielding when set within the ancient and stolid tradition of character writing. What has it to do with Theophrastan type-portraits, with the rhetorical exercises of *ethopoeia* or *prosopopoeia*, with the character sketches of seventeenth-century historians and later society scribblers, with the epiphanic anecdotes of Carlyle and others of the nineteenth century? Why should one of the most radically experimental writers of the twentieth century work out her ideas within such a conservative and secondary genre? And how, if this was indeed her aim, could she arrive at a *portrait* in the form of "George Hugnet"?

These questions, which the following chapters will attempt to answer, have relevance beyond "George Hugnet" and even Stein herself. For portraiture is a genre that epitomizes many of the problems posed in modernist art. It is traditionally considered a mimetic genre, so that its practitioners are forced to interpret the meaning of mimesis in literature. As a result, portraiture falls within the twentieth-century conflict marked by realism and naturalism on one hand, and stream of consciousness, surrealism, and archetypal literature on the other—a minute faithfulness to accepted categories of meaning versus a direct chronicling of mental process, in whatever guise that process is understood to exist. To achieve such a correspondence, the portraitist must subject language to a technical analysis more normal to linguists than to artists. For under what circumstances could the structure of language come to simulate the world?

Moreover, the 'world' at issue in the portrait—individual identity—lies at the very center of modernist concerns. Explored in the theories of William James, Bergson, Freud, and so many others, the location of the self in an alienated, mechanized world is the theme of countless works of art in our century. Identity must be defined by the artist before he can take the first step in portraiture, and in try-ing to effect this capturing of human essence, the portraitist collides with the same problems in perception explored by Gestalt psychol-ogy and phenomenology. How can the subject be known apart from the perceiver, and what mental properties of the perceiver necessar-ily color his view of the portrait subject? Is physical sensation a reflection of the stimulus or the receiver? With the spectre of an inescapable solipsism before him, the modern portraitist is faced with a seemingly doomed project.

Many of these difficulties in literary portraiture, moreover, arise because of its conceptual dependence upon its counterpart in the graphic arts. As a result, the literary portrait is an open invitation to the kind of interartistic experimentation characteristic of early twen-tieth-century writing. The connection between the two arts was con-sciously exploited in verbal portraits by such 'painterly' writers as Cummings, Williams, and Max Jacob—the two latter, like Stein, often termed "cubist writers." But what is the effect of translating a set of visual norms into literature? How 'commutative' in fact are the two arts?

The tendency to experiment with portraiture results, too, from its structure. The portrait is severely limited in length, usually non-narrative, traditionally a prose form, and frequently written in group-ings or collections. It began in ancient times as a stylistic exercise, and continued in this function throughout the Middle Ages. Thus, it easily lends itself to stylistic experiment, to the modernist focusing on language itself.

However, in direct contrast to this tendency, the portrait pushes outward to refer to reality. This factor—the actuality of the portrait subject—made the portrait a prime exhibit in the early Structuralist polemics against Formalism, since here was a vital aspect of a text which could not be considered in an "immanent approach."[1] The

1. For example, V. Zirmunskij dissented from certain militant members of the Russian Formalist School, saying, "the construction of the portrait is not totally determined by the formal, compositional plan: it is connected with the natural structure of the human face, with the denotational meaning of the artistic work" ("K voprosu o 'formal'nom metode,'" *Voprosy teorii literatury* [Leningrad, 1928], p. 168). In the same way, the structuralists of the Prague Linguistic Circle often used the portrait as an illustration of the importance of the referential aspect of the artistic sign. J. Mukarovský states that "there is, finally, a branch of painting and sculpture which is entirely artistic, but which nevertheless contains an oscillation between communicative and self-centered functions. This is the portrait, which is simultaneously a depiction of a person that we judge by criteria of truth and an artistic construction without an obligatory relation to reality. In this respect the portrait differs functionally from a painting that is not a portrait even though the latter may copy the ap-pearance of its model realistically" (*Estetická funkce, norma a hodnota jako sociální fakty* [Prague, 1936], p. 15).

portrait is drawn, then, toward both an art for art's sake aesthetics
and a call for documentary reference in art. It makes the modernist
issue of self-reflexiveness versus reference stand out in high relief.

Stein's part in all of this is rather interesting. For she is also used
as an exhibit of both modernist hermeticism and primitivist realism.
This paradox is directly tied to the schizophrenia of the genres she
employed, and to the limitations in our understanding of what self-
enclosure and direct reference mean in art. Stein herself appears to
have understood them quite well, and her writing was a careful
working out of these notions. It is the contention of this book that
her theories were in fact employed in her artistic creation, that the
systematic character of her work is undeniable, and that an examination of the theories and system, particularly in connection with
portraiture, is useful in achieving an appreciation of Stein's writing
as literature. The configuration of modernist concerns which I have
outlined here was precisely what Stein investigated and attempted
to resolve, strange as it may seem, in portraits like "George Hugnet."

As I have suggested, the need for a 'resolution' or even a 'solution'
for the portrait is not a mere figure of speech, and the history of
Stein's struggles with this recalcitrant genre is long and painful. It is
a kind of object-lesson in the relation between artistic theory and
practice, and stands as an emblem of modernist aspirations and their
so frequent frustration. Just how demanding the portrait genre is,
however, becomes apparent only under close scrutiny, as does the
ingenuity which Stein exercised in meeting its demands. Thus, before
discussing Stein's theories and works and their relation to the visual
arts, I shall spend this chapter investigating, theoretically and histor-
ically, what in fact a portrait is. This excursus, though ranging far in
time and sensibility from the twentieth-century avant garde, will pre-
pare us for that very sensibility and, in particular, for texts like
"George Hugnet."

As noted above, the portrait as a genre involves a number of apparent contradictions. Most importantly, it is both a work of art and
a document. It posits a subject with a unique, actual essence; it is
one of the very few arts of the particular. And this is the fact that
the quotation heading this chapter registers with such emphasis: the
paradox of the co-presence in portraiture of two different and normally antagonistic sets of norms—the aesthetic and the specifically
referential. The tension between general reference and aesthetic
closure is present to a degree in all literature, although it is particularly problematic in the modern period. But in the portrait, the pull

toward representation is extreme, for the work not only points to general realms of meaning, but attempts to render a specific, existent element of reality, a single human being. Thus, the portrait poses the general artistic problem of the aesthetic versus the referential as an overt conflict: it represents a real person whose actuality it announces through its title and through 'individualizing' detail; at the same time, it presents itself as a work of art—framed, highly structured, of interest 'in itself.' The fact that neither a mug-shot nor an allegorical painting, neither a police description nor a play of humors is a portrait, indicates that the co-presence of artistry and reference to specific reality is essential to the portrait genre.

The centripetal thrust of the portrait's aesthetic properties and the centrifugal thrust of its documentary nature create a very special response in its audience. We can see it exploited in the earliest portraiture, in ancient funerary masks and statues which aimed at both a representation of the dead one and a direct experience with him through the work; the portrait was a magical preservation of the departed. The modern obituary is also an attempt to keep the dead one 'before our eyes' or 'in our thoughts.' And a remnant of this feeling can be seen in Donald Stauffer's statement that the biographer is a "necromancer" whose art is necessary for "trafficking with the dead," for making a life which is past appear before us as if it were happening. Portrait silhouettes and miniatures also create this magical presence, putting a loved one, whether dead or absent, constantly and intimately in touch with the wearer of his likeness. And more practically, portraits or photographs of officials are used in public places such as courts of law and post offices to summon up the authority of the official, to endow the place with his characteristics.

This ability of the portrait to 'render its subject present' is, in fact, its most central characteristic. It is a consequence of the special claim of the genre to render reality, to make us feel the actuality and immediacy of the subject. R. G. Collingwood makes just this point in defining portraiture and other arts of the particular: "the true definition of representative art is not that the artifact resembles an orginal . . . but that the feeling evoked by the artifact resembles the feeling evoked by the original . . . When a portrait is said to be like the sitter, what is meant is that the spectator, when he looks at the portrait, 'feels as if' he were in the sitter's presence."[2]

As Collingwood presents it then, the portrait, like all works of art, is a sign; this sign need not be iconic or mimetic—that is, the actual

2. R. G. Collingwood, *The Principles of Art* (New York, 1958), pp. 76ff.

material of the sign vehicle need not be similar to its referent—but it must make the perceiver feel as if he were in the referent's presence. Though this presence is only illusory, the creation of immediacy in portraiture, particularly painted portraiture, aims at diminishing the distinction between portrait and subject. The portrait tries to 'render present' its subject by replacing him or by creating a necessary linkage between itself and him. We shall call this the indexical function of portraiture, using the terminology of the semiotician C. S. Peirce.[3] Indexical signs, unlike icons or symbols, indicate the specificity, imminence, presence, actuality of objects; the index finger points at something, for example, or the demonstrative pronoun takes the place of a word and simultaneously 'points' to it. Indexes are necessary components of reality statements—that is, one cannot identify an object in reality without an index—'*this* house' rather than 'house.' As a kind of index, then, the portrait functions to identify, to point attention to, to render present, to make one aware of someone as an existent person.

One feature of the portrait structure especially supports its ability to create immediacy. This is its use of title and name, both of which are standard examples of the index; for a name has no class meaning but simply points to a particular person. Further, although it is normally one of the unique possessions of an individual, in the portrait the same name is applied to two objects (since very often the work is not called 'A Portrait of X' but simply 'X'). In this case the name is a homonym, and a motivated one at that. The implication is that the portrait and the subject are equivalent, that the portrait can in a sense be substituted for the subject, be a surrogate for him. And even when a portrait title is in the form, 'A Portrait of X,' the title is stressing the relation between the work and its subject, an indexical relation.

Moreover, a name is a special case of an index in that it always has the same referent. Many indexes, such as pronouns, constantly change their referents from context to context, but the name, regardless of context, refers to one and only one person. It is this quality that the portrait aims at too—the evocation of its subject across time and space. The portrait in its pure indexical function, then, would function as a name, an immediate evocation of an individual.

3. C. S. Peirce. *Collected Papers,* vol. 4 (Cambridge, Mass., 1966), pp. 359–61. The terms 'indexical' along with 'iconic' and 'symbolic' are categories of signs designating particular relations between their sign vehicles and referents. The indexical sign is existentially related to its referent, the iconic sign is similar to its referent, and the symbol is related to its referent through a social convention.

Rather than operating indexically, however, many portraits are merely informational. The great burst of portraiture during the seventeenth century, for example, resulted from a widespread interest in history-writing. Its "first and at all times its chief purpose . . . was to show to later ages what kind of men had directed the affairs and shaped the fortunes of the nation."[4] Painted portraiture as well could serve this informational function. For example, Herbert Furst claims that Flemish paintings, especially portraits, grew out of the influence of "illuminated document, which makes them even in purpose a kind of literal document." He concludes: "in point of fact portrait painting was in the northern conception a document of evidence rather than a work of art."[5] This statement indicates the fundamental tension in portraiture between information and artistry: the informational function tends to weaken the text's impact as a work of art.

A third function of portraiture is the evaluation of the subject. Caricature, for example, exaggerates one aspect of a person to imply a judgment of him. Epideictic oratory, with its two divisions of *laus* and *vituperatio*, presents the individual as a multiplicity of details which can be used either to prove his virtue or fault. Here the raw data of character are manipulated within different value systems in order to produce a portrait that supports an ideology rather than merely presenting an individual as such. The saint's life, though not a portrait proper, is a similarly value-laden structure, and ethical motivation has long been a primary stimulus to portraiture. For example, Clarendon writes that "the celebratinge the memory of eminent and extraordinary persons, and transmittinge ther greate virtues for the imitation of posterity [is] . . . one of the principle endes and dutyes of History" (Smith, p. 71), and his history-writing, as a result, is a patchwork of portraits.

It might be argued that there can be no description without evaluation, in that any description places an object within a culturally determined world in which values are all-pervasive. In such a view, the intent to create pure individuation without reference to categories of value is misguided, in that it calls for a complete isolation of the subject from his world and a suspension of the normal modes of reference of the medium in which he is depicted. This drastic program would appear impossible to realize, and yet anyone interested in purely indexical portraiture as Gertrude Stein was, would have to take it into account.

4. David Nichol Smith, *Characters of the Seventeenth Century* (Oxford, 1918), p. x.
5. Herbert Furst, *Portrait Painting: Its Nature and Function* (London, 1927), pp. 38–39.

The entire history of conceiving individuality has contributed to this elusiveness of 'pure individuality.' Aristotle set the pattern here through his contention that all the actions of the soul were perceptible in the body, and that the nature of a particular soul was echoed in its body. "In a sense, the 'Aristotelian' portrait has remained the definitive conception for the Western imagination ever since. Its theoretical basis—the principle that the true character of a man is revealed in his physical conformation—was rejected by some later ages, but it could not be forgotten."[6] Seemingly, the individuality of a person's appearance is a sure means of distinguishing him from every other person. It is simply a matter of making his appearance "speak," of presenting it in such a way as to reveal the "inner man."

The problem, however, is that the usual means of effecting this body/soul correspondence is the vast array of conventional associations (stereotypes) that have grown up throughout history between the appearance and the spirit, associations that inevitably involve values. This investing of sense data with values can be seen equally in fictional and 'actual' portraiture. For example, Alice Colby points out that descriptions in medieval French romance are highly stylized, especially for heroes and heroines.[7] It is usual to find a heroine described as blond, blue-eyed, with a large, white forehead, slender body, and well-parted braids. One of the commonest *topoi* is that Nature has had some personal hand in endowing the heroine with these favors. Now, since a heroine was also beautiful by convention, and since these particular traits keep reappearing in connection with heroines, Miss Colby reasons that these were the accepted traits of beauty. In fact, the sequence, 'She was beautiful—she had blond hair, blue eyes, etc.,' is a virtual tautology. Further, physical beauty here directly implies inner perfection, so that we are being propelled from a set of empirical data to an assessment of spiritual qualities.

It is interesting to see that the force of such conventions had not greatly dissipated even in the Renaissance. For John Hayward describes Queen Elizabeth in the following way: "She was a Lady upon whom nature had bestowed and well placed many of her fairest favours; of stature meane, slender, streight, and amiably composed; of such state in her carriage, as every motion of her seems to beare majesty: her haire was enclined to pale yellow, her fore-head large

6. James D. Breckenridge, *Likeness: A Conceptual History of Ancient Portraiture* (Evanston, 1968), p. 130.

7. Alice M. Colby, *The Portrait in Twelfth-Century French Literature* (Geneva, 1965).

and faire, a seemly seat for Princely grace. . . ."[8] What is interesting here is not only the persistence of the particular elements of beauty from the Middle Ages to the Renaissance, but their transposition from romance to ceremonial portraiture. Elizabeth is a monarch, and thus is to be assessed in terms of her majesty. She is also a woman. The trick, then, is to prove her majesty (which, after all, had previously been associated with specifically masculine traits) by a demonstration of her excellence in an established feminine value system. Though a slender waist and blond hair had never been associated with majesty or "Princely grace," they were equated with excellence in the mythic-romantic feminine sphere and hence were capable of suggesting excellence in a queen-monarch.

We are coming perilously close in such depictions to a portraiture according to type, for the body/soul correspondence, with its conventional value-laden associations, tends to generalize rather than individuate its subjects. Elizabeth, for example, is almost presented as the type of the monarch-heroine. And indeed, the rediscovery of the Theophrastan or type portrait was the most important stimulus to literary portraiture in the Renaissance. It was a highly structured representation of a moral, social, or professional type as it would be manifested in a single hypothetical person, and as such, it is precisely the opposite of what one would expect in a portrait of an individual.[9] Yet the Aristotelian conception of character, as we have seen, leads inevitably to a merging of the individual with a type, and thus contains a clear contradiction.

A further characteristic of both painted and literary portraiture intensifies this difficulty. Both habitually conceive of the individual not as a being at one arbitrary moment of his existence, but as an essence beyond the accident of the moment. In a few Renaissance self-portraits the use of a mirror did lead to a 'distorted' portrait of the artist as he saw himself at the moment of painting (small, distant

8. Sir John Hayward, "Queen Elizabeth," *Portraits in Prose,* ed. Hugh Macdonald (New Haven, 1947), p. 15.

9. Theophrastan portraits begin by naming and defining the quality to be depicted, e.g., "'Garrulity is the delivering of talk that is irrelevant or long and unconsidered.' After the definition comes the main development, the list of actions and speeches that are typical of a victim of the quality under consideration. The picture is built up entirely of details of what the man does or says, usually in apparently random order, as seen or heard by an impersonal observer" (Benjamin Boyce, *The Theophrastan Character in England to 1642* [Cambridge, Mass., 1947], pp. 5–6). Imitations of Theophrastan portraits became very popular in the seventeenth century, the most famous of which were the characters by Hall, Overbury, and Earle.

head and oversized, near hands), without any correction based on knowledge of his appearance gained at other moments. These experiments, however, were not the rule. The much more common tendency was to portray the individual in some 'characteristic' attitude or context, as is evident in the Renaissance use of background and decorative detail. This detail was supplemented by the inscriptions common in Renaissance portraiture, which served not only a poetic but also an informational purpose, supplying the name or family of the sitter (Furst, p. 71). And "onomatopoetic symbolism" or *imprese* were also used to identify him, as when Leonardo painted a juniper tree behind a girl, Genevra (Juniper). Allegorical or mythological trappings came into play, for example, in portraits of Elizabeth I surrounded by the hunting equipment of Diana or other emblems of virginity. This generalizing of character was a gradual development in Renaissance painting:

> The historian can see that, on the whole, the individual entity was absorbed more and more in the totality of the figure. . . . First the face, the uncurtained portion of the body, a sort of shop-window, against a neutral background; then the bust together with the hands, sticking up over the edge of the frame; then the half-figure, with talking hands; then the three-quarter length, finally the whole figure. First the personality dissolved out of its locality and surroundings; later as something indigenous to the spot, since landscape-background or domicile or interior is developed along with it. The more the figure becomes visible as a whole, the more solidly entrenched the sitter seems in his station, his profession, his social class, and the more his local and temporal ties will govern the impression.[10]

The influence of Aristotelian decorum here, directing that the speech, dress, and actions of a subject be suitable to his character, thus drove portraiture toward a conceptual rather than an immediately descriptive treatment of its subjects. This was as true of literary as of painted portraiture. For the *descriptio* prescribed a list of *topoi* for the portrait that had little to do with the moment of portraiture: race, citizenship, family, wondrous events at the moment of birth, early up-bringing, education, body, soul, profession, deeds; relatives, friends, riches, household, fortune; length of life, kind of death, and events after death (Colby, p. 91). Not only are many of these characteristics constant throughout the subject's life, but they are all

---

10. Max Friedländer, *Landscape Portrait Still-Life* (New York, 1963), pp. 236–37.

value contexts, even 'name' sometimes functioning in this way. In
fact, there is here a two-member hierarchy of values: not only is
societal rank or degree of wealth a measure in a particular context,
but other characteristics can determine how well or badly the individual fills these measures (i.e., not only to be a "modern Major-
General" but to be "*the very model* of a modern Major-General").
This use of detail in portraiture militates against the accidental and
prescribes an aesthetic program for the work: "No design in portraiture can be beautiful unless it is relevant to the sitter, because in
portraiture irrelevance is ugliness" (Furst, p. 140).

The rejection of the accidental in portraiture is of tremendous importance, for as a result the presentation of the subject in the painting or character sketch does not correspond to any actual moment
of time in his life, where accidentality and irrelevance are omni-
present. The portraitist is not one giving a direct report of his perceptions, but one presenting the conclusions of much thought and
careful judgment, so that the portrait represents a mental fabrication
and not an existent being as immediately perceived. These facts,
normative in all portraiture, are striking for an art of the particular,
the individual, the directly representational. They amount to an
implicit contradiction within the claims of the genre, but one which
remained virtually unnoticed until Stein began her experimentation.

This contradiction concerns not only the treatment of the individual—his reduction to a mere type or a total abstraction—but the
other essential factor in portraiture, the mode in which the subject
is signified. For if the subject as presented is utterly disjoint from the
actual appearances of the living person in space and time, the portrait cannot be indexical. It is loosed from specific space-time co-
ordinates. Thus, if it is a painting, it becomes a purely iconic sign,
an imitation of an idea of a person without reference to a concrete,
actual presence.[11] We have insisted, however, in agreement with Collingwood, that iconicity is inessential to portraiture, that a portrait
must first and foremost function to 'render present,' to evoke an
existent being. When this immediacy is ignored, as happen so frequently, the work is indistinguishable from representations of imaginary people or even idealized types, unless external information is
supplied.

But with iconicity dominant in painting, literary portraitists considered their work 'imitations' as well, even though the abstraction

11. Peirce states that "An *Icon* is a Representamen whose Representative Quality is a
Firstness of it as a First. . . . A sign by Firstness is an image of its object and, more strictly
speaking, can only be an *idea*" (*Collected Papers,* vol. 2 [Cambridge, Mass., 1960], p. 157).

of the subject made their mode of representation primarily symbolic, in Peirce's sense of the word. That is, a description of a person 'as he really is' was often confused with a rendering that was physically *like* him. In the first case, the use of language is symbolic in that words are related to their referents through a socially agreed upon convention; in the second, words refer through the similarity of their physical organization to that of their referent, as in the onomatopoeia. The *accuracy* of the rendering in both cases involves indexical factors (see note 3).

Stein's innovations in portraiture consisted both in adjusting her concept of her subject to what could be directly imitated in the verbal medium, and, in her later works, in divorcing the treatment of individuality from any evocation of type. She was thus attempting an indexical-iconic portraiture in writing, so that her portrait program was really that of painted portraiture, and grew directly out of the traditional assumption that a portrait is an "imitation of an individual." In a fundamental respect, she was overturning the norms of her medium, in which a portrait can be effected, at best, through indexical-symbolic means.

The reason for the traditional association between portraiture and iconicity is that in painting, imitation can be a powerful means of creating immediacy. The resemblance between the sign vehicles and referents of iconic signs suggests the possibility of an equation between them; that is, the greater the similarity between the sign vehicle and its referent, the more one tends to think of the sign vehicle *as* the referent. This lack of interposition or mediacy creates the impression of immediacy in a visual sign, the direct presence of the subject.

Verbal portraiture initially used iconic techniques for the same purpose. The ancestors of the literary portrait, the *figurae sententiarum* of *ethopoeia* and *prosopopoeia*, are truly imitations of individuals. "Quintilian explained *ethopoeia* merely as the orator's imitation of another person's character or habits ('imitatio morum alienorum'). *Prosopopoeia* is almost the same thing, but with a dramatization of the person as well as the giving of his words" (Boyce, p. 27). "*Prosopopoeia* aims not to be objective but to reveal the thoughts as well as character of the speaker (who may be a living man, a man summoned up from the shades, an historical or fictitious figure, an inanimate object, a state or a nation), and it presents the speech of an individual" (p. 28). In both these figures, the subject is presented through an imitation, an icon, of his speech, and the particularity, the individuality of that speech manifests the individuality of the subject.

More importantly, however, the *prosopopoeia* attempts an immediacy of presentation. It is a dramatic enactment of its subject, a living presentation of his speech and mannerisms. The *prosopopoeia* is the one literary form of the portrait in which indexicality and iconicity are compatible, and, as we shall see, it was not until Stein that anyone again achieved a verbal equivalent of an existent person—a true literary imitation of an individual. Stein's portraiture, I shall claim, is an attempt at fulfilling an ancient program for literature in which the factors of immediacy, imitation, and individuation were to be compatible.

However, a great many techniques for rendering the individual—symbols, word-plays (juniper and Genevra), mythological allusions, and metonymic associations—have little to do with iconic representation. The juniper/Genevra example, or that of Elizabeth and Diana, are quite 'literary' in the sense that they work through the association of words or ideas rather than by some physical resemblance between sign vehicles and referents.

In literature, moreover, the usual notion of mimesis confuses the issue thoroughly. If we think about the normal usage of the word, as exemplified in Auerbach's *Mimesis*, we discover that while implying a similarity of sign vehicle to referent, it is used when a referent coincides with a notion of reality: the 'world' pictured in the work is consistent with the world in which we live, and the referents of the words used are the referents which they usually have in normal speech. Such "mimetic" writing is seen in opposition to the flights of romanticism and the "gibberish" of abstractionism. Thus, "mimetic" is often applied where "realistic," "true," or even "normative" would be appropriate; there is no mimesis proper, no iconicity, in such cases. And clearly, the written art work does not normally resemble its referent; at best it provokes some ideas that seem similar to ideas provoked by the original in reality. Therefore, the mimetic program that the written portrait inherited from painting seems an impossibility for it. Writing can never be iconic of a visual object in the same way that painting can.

This is not to say that one cannot find iconic elements in written portraits. For example, the following sentences from Nicholas Harpsfield's portrait of Thomas More are obviously structurally imitative of their meaning:

Then, as he was no tall man, so was he no notable lowe and little

> man; all the partes of his body were in as good proportion and
> congruance as a man would wishe. His skinne was somewhat
> white, and the colour of his face drewe rather to whiteness than
> to paleness, farre from rednes, saving that some little thinne
> redde sparkles everywhere apered. His heare was blackishe yeal-
> lowe, or rather yelowe blackishe. . . . [Macdonald, p. 7]

The formal balancing of negated extremes in corresponding clauses,
followed by the positing of the mean in a third weighted clause,
grammatically renders More's rejection of extremes in favor of the
golden mean. Nevertheless, the passage from which these sentences
are taken cannot as a whole be formally compared to More or to
any aspect of him. The medium of the written portrait is normally
not iconic of its subject.

It was apparently not until the eighteenth century, however, that
the mimetic capability of writing was questioned. In *The Mirror and
the Lamp*, Abrams shows that that century developed a new awareness of the way the different media render their subjects. "In 1789
. . . Thomas Twining confirmed [the] distinction between arts whose
media are 'iconic' (in the later terminology of the Chicago semiotician, Charles Morris), in that they resemble what they denote, and
those which are significant only by convention."[12] Among literary
phenomena only two were considered mimetic by Twining: dramatic
poetry, in that it imitates speech, and the isolated figure of onomatopoeia in the rest of literature. By implication, the proper imitative
subject of writing can be only speech.

On the other hand, there is a much older and much more emphatic
denial of the mimetic possibilities of *painting*. Saint John the Evange-
list said: "the portrait is like me, yet not like me but like my fleshly
image, for if this painter desireth to draw the very me in a portrait,
he will need more than colors and things that are seen with the eye.
This that thou hast done is childish and imperfect. Thou hast drawn
a dead likeness of the dead" (Breckenridge, p. 268). Aside from the
conventional Christian objection that the flesh and the spirit are
utterly dissimilar, John is claiming that "colors and things that are
seen with the eye" are incapable of rendering or resembling the true
man. The medium itself is being declared inadequate, and the inadequacy, as in Twining's discussion of writing, results from the
nature of the subject which the medium attempts to render. Painting is seen as capable of imitating only "dead" or static subjects,

12. M. H. Abrams, *The Mirror and the Lamp* (Oxford, 1953), p. 14.

while the true man is quick, volatile. Similarly, writing can imitate *only* volatile activity—speech (and perhaps thought)—rather than any of the other possible aspects of man's nature.

Lessing, perhaps more definitively than anyone before him, formulated the difference between the mimetic properties of the two media:

> I reason thus: if it is true that painting and poetry in their imitations make use of entirely different means or symbols—the first, namely of form and colour in space, the second of articulated sounds in time—if these symbols indisputably require a suitable relation to the thing symbolized, then it is clear that symbols arranged in juxtaposition can only express subjects of which the wholes or parts exist in juxtaposition; while consecutive symbols can only express subjects of which the wholes or parts are themselves consecutive.
>
> Subjects whose wholes or parts exist in juxtaposition are called bodies. Consequently, bodies with their visible properties are the particular subjects of painting.
>
> Subjects whose wholes or parts are consecutive are called actions. Consequently, actions are the peculiar subject of poetry.[13]

The clearest implication of this statement for portraiture is that if both the written and the painted portrait are to be imitations having the same subject—the individual—this subject must be conceived in different ways in each art: in painting as a static object, an appearance, or a configuration of qualities; in writing as a speaking, thinking, acting being. Secondly, a written imitation of the physical appearance of a subject (a temporal sequence for a spatial juxtaposition) is a virtual impossibility. As Lessing points out, Homer never describes Helen, but merely repeats over and over again that she is beautiful. Hence the tautological nature of descriptions in writing, where appeals to sense data seem to by-pass any sensory evocation, ending simply as value-laden implicates of an abstract characteristic such as beauty.

However, this clarification of the possibilities of the two media was largely ignored by portraitists, who continued to treat the individual as a configuration of unique, timeless characteristics. The static nature of this definition made it impossible for the written portrait to be mimetic, and at the same time the actuality and

13. "Laokoon," *Lessing's Prose Works*, ed. Edward Bell (London, 1913), p. 91.

specificity of the portrait subject forced painting to resort to non-iconic techniques. Thus, painted portraits often seem like intellectual puzzles, while written portraits read like dull lists of character traits.

Even though the written portrait seldom availed itself of a dynamic conception of the individual, however, many portraits did end up with a dynamic subject. For though their declared subject was the individual of their title, their actual subject was the process of arriving at a judgment of him. We saw earlier that the conceptual status of the individual implied a process of observation and judgment by the portraitist. If the data of empirical observation, because of their value-laden contents, inevitably implied certain conclusions, the written portrait could become the occasion for the argument from datum to trait. It could be the record of the solution to a problem of knowledge, as is apparent in the following definition of the form: "A character must be short; and it must be entire, the complete expression of a clear judgment" (Smith, p. li). This judgment in portraiture proper is often spoken of as an induction, an argument from empirical data to abstract 'character.' The Theophrastan character, in contrast, is deductive, beginning with a general trait that marks a type, and working backward to reveal the acts, speech, and physical characteristics by which the trait is manifested. "A man who is such-and-such habitually acts as follows" (Boyce, p. 78).

However, this distinction is more a matter of theory than of fact, since many portraits of individuals are as deductive as type-portraits, simply plugging in the individual as the minor premise in an old, conventional sort of syllogism. For example, when Caesar says, "Yond Cassius has a lean and hungry look;/He thinks too much: such men are dangerous," he is providing both the major and minor premises (in reverse order), and his unstated conclusion—that Cassius is dangerous—is simply the result of a deduction. With all the Aristotelian 'major premises' associating data with character generalizations, this method of reasoning is extremely common in written portraiture, and leads, as we have seen, to a non-individualizing portrait. In contrast, the more individualizing a portrait attempts to be, the more its judgment should resemble an induction.

We might note too that the temporal unfolding of the written portrait allows the stages in its argument to be presented as such, while in painted portraiture, though a similar "argument" is in progress, the argument itself is not present in the work of art. It is perhaps part of the experience of the work, but not explicitly present in the painting. One of the literary portrait's chief differences from the

painted portrait then is that it can be an overt process of argumentation or interpretation with an important mimetic potential. The more
'inductive' it is—the more it provides evidence rather than conclusions
—the more mimetic it will be of the portraitist's process of thought
spurred by perceptions of the subject.

In the portraiture of 'conclusions' the most common literary technique is the list. We have already seen this in physical description,
and much the same factors are present in the listing of character
traits. Most frequently found are the verbs "to be" and "to have" in
their timeless modes (e.g., "being naturally of a cheerfull and pleasant humour" ["Thomas Hobbes," Macdonald, p. 98]). Traits come
trooping one after another in a catalogue: "Falkeland, a person of
such prodigious partes of learninge and knowledge, of that inimitable
sweetnesse and delight in conversation, of so flowinge and obliginge a
humanity and goodnesse to mankinde. . ." ("Lord Falkeland," Smith,
p. 71). That these characteristics are value-laden is clear, not only because of conventional societal values for knowledge or humanity, but
also because of the laudatory tone of the "such"es and "so"s, and of
"prodigious" and "inimitable." This is again the "very model of a
modern Major-General" situation, a doubly value-laden context.

Further, in such portraits the ordering of the attributes is arbitrary.
There is no sense in which a logical development of ideas is plotted
here, nor is the order determined by any temporality essential to the
individual. This group of traits floating around the center of the subject, his name, is an essential feature of the Theophrastan character
as well, so that conventional portraits of individuals imitate even
structurally the type-portrait.

There is good reason for this, as Benjamin Boyce explains by associating arbitrary ordering with the Senecan prose style of the seventeenth century: "'every period, every sentence almost, is independent,
and may be taken asunder, transposed, postponed, anticipated, or
set in any new order, as you fancy'" (Boyce, pp. 181–82). He ar-
gues that this arbitrary order destroys any sense of chronological
sequence, and hence of connection between the work and a concrete
subject. Without this 'Senecan' arbitrariness, "a narrative tends to
suggest an individual person on a particular day, whereas the Character should evoke any typical man of the group at any typical moment.
The chronological order emphasizes the man; the Character-writer
wishes to high light the essence of the man, which in any non-sequen-
tial order of events would still govern and form him." The ordering
of the elements of an abstract essence is indeterminate; the existent

person, however, is utterly determined (and determining) as to both the temporal and conceptual ordering of his make-up. To render his nature in an apparently arbitrary order is to deny his individuality, to reduce him to an abstract generalization.

Thus the arbitrary ordering characteristic of so many portraits of conclusions frees the text from any internal reflection of its referent. This loosening of the relation between form and referent in 'Senecan' portraits inevitably focuses attention on the text itself, making it a self-determined, independent entity. Description in general and portraiture in particular frequently involve this aestheticizing tendency; their sequence, much more than that in narrative or argumentation proper, becomes a realm of free play. Here we see explicitly the mutual exclusivity of the aesthetic and the specifically referential. As soon as the portraitist neglects an indexical possibility it is appropriated for an aesthetic counter-effect.

This observation is reflected in the fact that in Stein's first period of portraiture, her thorough-going typologizing of character was matched by extreme arbitrariness of order. She developed a style built programmatically on the repetition and rearrangement of sentence segments: "They stayed there and were gay there, not very gay there, just gay there. They were both gay there, they were regularly working there both of them cultivating their voices there, they were both gay there.[14] This play with order freed her subjects from all specificity, generalizing them to the most basic level of their collective 'being.' However, Stein deliberately abandoned this style when she decided to depict her subjects as 'pure individuals.'

The dividing of the subject into this arbitrarily ordered list of character traits is, moreover, the first step toward synecdoche, for the person is made recognizable, identifiable, as a collection of these parts. The next step is simply to argue that one or more of them characterize the whole. This process is most visible in the eighteenth-century "ruling passion," a concept consciously embraced as a means of catching the "essential man" from the midst of his accidental diversity. "The ruling principle will strongly mark the general character. See how endlessly the human face is diversified, by the combination of a few simple elements: while, in a general sameness, some prominent striking turn of feature stamps the particular character of countenance. Now it is the seizing this characteristic distinctive mark, and producing it to light, which reflects the true image of the individual:

14. "Miss Furr and Miss Skeene," *Geography and Plays* (Boston, 1922), p. 17.

This omitted, or unskilfully taken off, the particular man is lost, in the vague resemblance of the thing at large."[15]

One of the most interesting discussions of the process of arriving at such a general characteristic occurs in Alexander Pope's "Epistle to Cobham." Its "Argument" might serve as a summary of the traits of conventional portraiture, for it systematically discards any approach to characterization that does not identify the individual with a (Theophrastan) type. The poetic climax of this reasoning reads:

> Manners with Fortunes, Humours turn with Climes,
> Tenets with Books, and Principles with Times.
>   Judge we by Nature? Habit can efface,
> Int'rest o'ercome, or Policy take place:
> By Actions? those Uncertainty divides:
> By Passions? these Dissimulation hides:
> Opinions? they still take a wider range:
> Find, if you can, in what you cannot change.
>   Search then the Ruling Passion: There, alone,
> The Wild are constant, and the Cunning known;
> The Fool consistent, and the False sincere;
> Priests, Princes, Women, no dissemblers here.
> This clue once found, unravels all the rest,
> The prospect clears, and Wharton stands confest.
>
> [ll. 166–79]

In the description of Wharton that follows Pope might as well be portraying the Avaricious Man. We have here a demonstration of the fact that in its extreme position, the conventional portrait becomes almost a type-portrait. For the only way that actions can be seen as revelatory in any sense is through the prism of the ruling passion.

The opposite tendency in portraiture—the inductive or evidential mode—is epitomized by biography, which attempts a complete individuation of its subject through voluminous, chronologically and causally ordered, factual detail. Indeed, David Nichol Smith explains the switch of interest from portraiture to biography in the eighteenth century as related specifically to a desire for more concrete detail: "When the facts of a man's life, his works, and his opinions claimed detailed treatment, the fashion of the short character had passed" (Smith, p. ix).

15. Donald Stauffer, *The Art of Biography in Eighteenth-Century England* (Princeton, 1941), p. 326.

the aged, bent man creates this sense of strength in the narrator of the poem through their very contrast, the rough, rustic Wordsworth of the dinner table gives a sense of reassurance to the more urbane Carlyle.

The process of argumentation from act to trait that the reader follows in this anecdote, even though it may end in a 'ruling passion'— e.g., countrified earthiness—is not experienced as the usual enthymeme. Instead, the reader is left with an emblem of Wordsworth that remains a value in and of itself, regardless of any interpretations of it.

In addition, Carlyle has employed an important and problematic possibility in portraiture—the immediacy created by the portraitist's reaction to his subject. Carlyle says that the sight of Wordsworth was "comforting and amusing to me who felt like him but could not eat raisins." Because of the "symbolical" character of the whole passage, eating raisins suggests involvement in simple, natural objects of the senses. The author could not "eat raisins," although he felt sympathy with one who did, and this kind of admiration tempered by distance or inadequacy (a symbolic extension perhaps of Carlyle's notorious inability to digest rich foods) is characteristic of the reaction of Carlyle to his subject. He describes himself as physically "far off" at the table from Wordsworth; he is not really sure what the raisins are at first—"some portion of what I judged to be raisins"—and he uses the word "gnawing," suggesting a point in sympathy beyond which he cannot go.

This inclusion of the portraitist as one of the 'characters' of the portrait is a latent source of ambiguity which Stein found enormously important. Who in fact is the subject of the portrait: the apparent subject or the portraitist himself? In "George Hugnet," where the referential aspects of the text are almost totally suppressed, we must take it upon faith that the portrait is in fact about its ostensible subject and not a recording of Stein's random thoughts. The development of Stein's portraiture, which we shall witness later, demonstrates that when the perceiver's role is dominant in a mimetic program, the object of perception seems correspondingly reduced, perhaps necessarily lost sight of altogether in a faithful rendering of the perceiver's thought process.

Aside from anecdotes, nouns of agency, and characteristic acts, portraits focusing on actions rather than traits have one very powerful technique available, although it was used more frequently in biography. This is the direct speech of the subject, and is thought to have entered biography by way of drama. The possibilities of characteristic speech were exploited to their full by Boswell, who peppered his great biography with Johnsonian periods. As Stein put it, " . . . Boswell conceived himself as an audience an audience achieving recognition at one and the same time that Johnson achieved recognition of the thing he Johnson was saying, Johnson was saying those things as if he were writing those things that is achieving recognition of the thing while the thing was achieving expression and Boswell by the intensity of his merging himself in the immediacy of Johnson achieved recognition as Johnson himself was doing."[18]

It is clear that a whole new mimetic range in portraiture is opened up by the idea of characterizing a subject through his own speech, since speech is one of those processes which the written word can truly imitate. With this possibility we have the final condition for a literary "imitation of an individual." We are back, in fact, at the *prosopopoeia*, but one with a necessarily existent subject and a written, rather than oral, presentation. We are close to the dramatic monologue as well, a fictional forerunner of the Steinian portrait. If the individual is conceived as a dynamic speaker or thinker and if the portrait renders this characteristic speech or thought, then we have a mode of portraiture in which the full capacity of literary language to imitate a human being would be tested, in which literary mimesis would be logically consistent with that in the visual arts. Moreover, if the portraitist is the one who speaks the words of his subjects or thinks their thoughts, the boundary between perceiver and perceived becomes even more tenuous than in the anecdote. The portraitist must not only observe the subject; he must enact him. The difficulties of such a demand go far in explaining Stein's final disillusion not only with portraiture but with all indexical art depending on a mimetic program.

But this is to anticipate the argument of the chapters to come. Stein took up the portrait at the historical point where biography, eighteenth-century aesthetics, and the dramatic monologue had sufficiently clarified the issues of portraiture and the properties of language to make an imitation of an individual seem like a viable and interesting undertaking. The fact that she was drawn to such a literary program is hardly surprising, given her education and inclinations. She claimed an early love for English grammar and especially for the parsing of sentences, thus manifesting a technical interest in the medium of language essential to anyone attempting verbal mimesis. Her

18. Lecture 4, *Narration* (Chicago, 1935), p. 60.

major in college and her research area afterward was psychology, and her teacher, William James, led her to conceptions of character types, of the self as thought process, of time as a mental category, and of language as an exact expression of thought. This scientific approach to character conception received practical expression, moreover, in her experiments in the psychology laboratories at Radcliffe and Johns Hopkins.

Stein's later experience in Paris amid the most formidable avant-garde painters of the day—Picasso, Matisse, Gris—made her sensitive to the relations between painting and literature. And if we are to believe her account in "Pictures," she was concerned from her youth onward with the issue of mimesis. She says that she loved to look away from the paintings in the Louvre to the scenes through the windows there, creating a visual counterpoint of framed art and framed reality.[19] Over and over in her writing she worries over the question of resemblance and reference in art. Does an artist need a model? What difference does it make to the viewer if the painting looks like a part of reality? Such questions were tailor-made for the paradox of portraiture, with its insistence on both artistry and immediate, specific reference. The issues of mimesis, of character conception, of time in art, of language become tangible as a medium, of type versus individual, and of painting and literature as analogues were thus part of Stein's intellectual and experiential make-up. They led inevitably to portraiture,·and in addition, to her essentially modernist art.

Yet the obstacles in the path of a modernist portraiture are enormous, as the following statement by Irving Howe suggests. "A pre-Freudian psychology, rationalistic and empirical, . . . assumes that character is marked by continued and knowable traits, and that our conduct is explainable through categories of thought. We are inclined, at this moment in the twentieth century, to discount this sort of psychology: it does not make sufficient allowance for the irrational; it blots out the chaos of the unconscious, it overestimates the coherence and accessibility of the psyche."[20] This statement sweeps aside the entire tradition of character depiction in portraiture as we have presented it and suggests that the easy distinction between

19. *Lectures in America* (New York, 1975), p. 70. "I always like, as well as liked looking out of windows in museums. It is more complete, looking out of windows in museums, than looking out of windows anywhere else."

20. "Martin du Gard: The Novelty of Goodness," *The Decline of the New* (New York, 1963), pp. 48–49.

portraitist and subject, between reference and self-reference is an illusion. The alienation of the modernist artist only exacerbates this problem. For with the absence of individual patrons or a special class cultivating taste and encouraging certain forms of art, the artist's sense of whom he is writing for and of who he is for others disintegrates, and the dependable framework of values we have seen throughout the history of portraiture disappears. As Stein said, " I write for myself and strangers," demonstrating both the isolation and negative definition of audience which colored her writing. If one identifies strongly enough with one's role as artist, it is a small step to make audience a symbol of anyone with whom one interacts. The portraitist then becomes an explorer in utterly unknown waters.

Thus, in the early years of the twentieth century, the traditional approach to portraiture was completely out of touch with the issues and sensibility of the day. With this in mind, the revolutionary quality of "George Hugnet" perhaps may be more easily understood. Perhaps, indeed, we might see it as a fulfilment of the following musings of Ortega y Gasset:

> A traditional painter painting a portrait claims to have gotten
> hold of the real person when, in truth and at best, he has set
> down on his canvas a schematic selection, arbitrarily decided
> on by his mind, from the innumerable traits that make a living
> person. What if the painter changed his mind and decided to
> paint not the real person but his idea, his pattern, of the person?
> Indeed, in that case the portrait would be the truth, and failure
> would no longer be inevitable. In foregoing to emulate reality
> the painting becomes what it authentically is: an image, an un-
> reality. [21]

True, but in such a case is the painting still a portrait? The desire to tell the strict "truth," to put upon the canvas or page an exact copy of what is in the mind, by-passes reality and leads quite predictably, we shall argue, to such a nonrepresentational work as "George Hugnet." This paradox, unwittingly foretold by Ortega, was demonstrated rather tragically by Stein in a process of experimentation that began with more or less conventional assumptions about portraiture and proceeded closer and closer to the "truth." Stein's unwillingness

21. "The Dehumanization of Art," in *The Idea of the Modern in Literature and the Arts,* ed. Irving Howe (New York, 1967), p. 91.

either to "fail" in Ortega's sense or to leave the represented object behind led her finally to an open contradiction.

However, the very doggedness of her attempt makes her writing a kind of testing ground for modernist assumptions concerning art. How far can literature conform to a program derived from painting? To what degree can literature be mimetic, in the absolute sense of the word? Is it indeed possible to capture an element of reality in art or is one confined within a perceiver's consciousness? Are people, finally, knowable?

In the chapters that follow, we shall trace the line of theory and experiment that culminated in "George Hugnet," and see the implications of this development for the rest of Stein's works and for modernist art in general. Chapter 2 will discuss Stein's theory of portraiture, which involves such modernist notions as stream of consiousness, automatic writing, duration, the "specious present," creative genius, simultaneity, synesthesia, and "pure art." This theorizing was supplemented by a continuous process of practical experimentation resulting in the extraordinary texts analyzed in chapter 3. Chapter 4 takes up the comparison between Stein's literary techniques and cubism in painting, exploring the extent to which the common twentieth-century analogy between painting and literature in fact applies and how far it explains the difficulties encountered in modernist writing. And chapter 5 demonstrates the leading position held by the portrait within Stein's array of genres until the logic of her program forced her toward complete self-reflexiveness, an unwilling, personal/literary theorizing. The unusual clarity with which these matters are focused in Stein's writing makes her works valuable; not only have they an undeniable aesthetic appeal, but they are documents of one of the most intensely experimental periods in literary history.

2

The Steinian Portrait: The History of a Theory

It is possible that there are some writers who write very largely with ... [a] sense of a language as such, so that their effects would be almost out of reach of analysis. Racine always seems to me to write with the whole weight of the French language, to remind one always of the latent assumptions of French, in a way that I am not competent to analyse in any case, but that very possibly could not be explained in intelligible terms. Dryden is a corresponding English figure in this matter; Miss Gertrude Stein, too, at this point, implores the passing tribute of a sigh. To understand their methods one might have to learn a great deal about the mode of action of language which is not yet known, and it might always be quicker to use habit than analysis, to learn the language than to follow the explanation.

William Empson, *Seven Types of Ambiguity*

Empson's assessment of Stein is one of the most flattering by any major critic. That her work reveals an extraordinary insight into the English language, however, is a conclusion apparent to anyone who troubles to take her work seriously. Equally apparent, unfortunately, is the accompanying hopelessness of explaining this insight, of forcing our response beyond the "passing tribute of a sigh."

But here Stein herself can help us. She leaves clues everywhere—in short asides, in full-length theoretical treatises, in references to her great teacher, William James, and finally, in the development of her writing itself, a development that can be accounted for only by the presence of "leading ideas." Stein's works are clearly the result of a dynamic program of theory, experimentation, discovery, and new theory.

This is a point which cannot be too much stressed. The experience of reading Stein—of really reading her—with the assumption that her words are worth taking seriously, is striking in its coherence. Her theoretical writings are still the best critical guide to her literary texts, and document a system that went through logical and identifiable stages. Some critics dismiss these writings as rationalizations after the fact, arguing that by the mid-twenties Stein was desperately

A condensed version of this chapter has appeared as "The Steinian Portrait," *Yale University Library Gazette* (July 1975), pp. 30–40.

trying to legitimize her work to the public. But whatever her motivation for producing the essays, they are valid critical discussions and should be treated as such. Moreover, much of the theorizing that we shall look at was written concurrently with the works described, so there is no gap in time between the two at all.

The relation of Stein's theories to her literary practice brings us to the two cruxes of Stein scholarship. First, do Stein's writings really fall within the program she outlines? And secondly, even if they do, does that make them art? To the first question, I offer the evidence presented in the following chapters, which is so overwhelming that there can be little doubt that Stein's work is animated by a conscious program.

The second question I would prefer ultimately to leave to the reader. If he subscribes to a notion of artistic response as foregrounded experience, Stein's extraordinary writing surely would be termed aesthetic and probably artistic too. If textual complexity is a literary value, then the analyses of chapter 3 should demonstrate Stein's worth. If a humanistic orientation is the *sine qua non* of art, then Stein's relentless exploration of interpersonal knowledge should qualify her as an artist. And if the relation of the work to contemporary norms of art is the criterion, Stein's special connection with cubism and experimental literature places her squarely within the vital artistic movements of her day. But most arguments for value affect the reader only insofar as they coincide with his own ideas about Stein. Surely after all the tirades and gush that have constituted Steinian scholarship until the recent past it is more important to understand her work than to sit in judgment on it. The judgment comes anyway.

This chapter, then, is an attempt to set out as fully as possible Stein's theories of portraiture. By presenting the theory first I hope to dramatize its contrast to Stein's literary practice, to show at once how faithfully she tried to follow out her ideas and at the same time how stubbornly the problems she addressed eluded a satisfactory solution in practice.

Moreover, we shall see that these ideas are a direct response to the historical definitions of portraiture discussed in chapter 1. As a result, the order followed here is dictated by the two parts of the portrait problem—the conceptualization of the individual (including the mode of his temporality) and the role of mimesis in his depiction. The reader should keep in mind the fact that concepts of character and mimetic techniques are important in other literary genres than the portrait, and that the texts of Stein's from which the following theoretical statements are drawn are often concerned with writing in general rather than merely with portraiture. Thus, this chapter is not only a treatment of Stein's notions of character and mimesis as they apply to portraiture, but also a background to the discussion of the whole of Stein's oeuvre in chapter 5.

The theoretical categories for much of Stein's thinking about the individual stem from William James's psychology, which she encountered at Radcliffe. Though she pursued these ideas in directions foreign to James, the similarity between their concepts of the individual is so striking that it must be considered. For James, the basic notion of the human being is clear: "*to think ourselves as thinkers*. This attention to thought as such, and the identification of ourselves with it rather than with any of the other objects which it reveals, is a momentous and in some respects a rather mysterious operation."[1] The implications of such a notion are particularly momentous for portraiture, for it should be obvious that this conception is dynamic and synecdochic, identifying the individual with an essential process.

If the human being is a thinker, James finds that his identity is based on a special feature of thought. Thought has two ways of 'knowing' its objects, either through "acquaintance" or through "knowledge-about." James describes these two modes as follows: "the difference between those [states of mind] that are mere 'acquaintance,' and those that are 'knowlege-*about*' . . . is reducible almost entirely to the absence or presence of psychic fringes or overtones. Knowledge *about* a thing is knowledge of its relations. Acquaintance with it is limitation to the bare impression which it makes" (pp. 258–59). A person can know himself, or any other person for that matter, in either of these two ways, and this has great relevance to what we have called 'rendering present,' the indexical function in portraiture. If a portrait is written as a conventional physical description or an enumeration of parts, then its purpose is to provide information—"knowledge about" its subjects. However, the attempt to present the subject with immediacy, to render him present, is an attempt to create "acquaintance" with him as a simple point in a perceiver's awareness. Indeed, when James gives examples of words which create acquaintance, he relies exclusively on indexes: "The minimum of grammatical subject, of objective presence, of reality known about, the mere beginning of knowledge, must be named by the word that says the least. Such a word is the interjection,

1. William James, *The Principles of Psychology* (New York, 1890), p. 296.

as *lo! there! ecco! voilà!* or the article or demonstrative pronoun introducing the sentence, as *the, it, that*" (p. 222). All these words express the reality, presence, immediacy of their referents. They are an epitome of the portrait function. One would expect, then, that acquaintance would be the mode of knowledge which Stein's portraits would try to create.

James, however, considered knowledge-about the mode underlying identity:

> The possibility of two such knowledges depends on a fundamental psychical peculiarity which may be entitled '*the principle of constancy in the mind's meanings*,' and which may be thus expressed: '*The same matters can be thought of in successive portions of the mental stream, and some of these portions can know that they mean the same matters which the other portions meant.*' One might put it otherwise by saying that '*the mind can always intend, and know when it intends, to think of the Same.*'
>
> This *sense of sameness* is the very keel and backbone of our thinking. We saw . . . how the consciousness of personal identity reposed on it, the present thought finding in its memory a warmth and intimacy which it recognizes as the same warmth and intimacy it now feels. [p. 459]

Since knowledge of sameness involves "mental fringes" which link sames together, it appears that identity is knowledge about the self, a recognition of a sameness among distinct impressions. Comparison and memory are thus essential factors in identity. As James says, identity "*is exactly like any one of our other perceptions of sameness among phenomena. It is a conclusion grounded either on the resemblance in a fundamental respect, or on the continuity before the mind, of the phenomena compared*" (p. 334). And again, "*Resemblance among the parts of a continuum of feelings* (especially body feelings) experienced along with things widely different in all other regards, *thus constitutes the real and verifiable 'personal identity' which we feel*" (p. 336).

Probably because of James's influence, resemblance and memory were essential components of Stein's conception of identity as well, at least in its earlier stages. She was to describe identity as "recognition, you know who you are because you and others remember anything about yourself . . . I am I because my little dog knows me."[2] Stein experimented with this notion for some time in depictions of people, and eventually discovered that such a concept, based on knowledge-about and hence description, was inappropriate to portraiture. Because of this she developed a new concept—entity—which came closer to the possibilities of acquaintance. However, the path from her first learning of James's ideas to the mature development of her own notion was rather complex, and should be considered in some detail.

The first theoretical statement from Stein on the subject appeared in a pair of articles written by Leon Solomons and Stein to present the results of their experiments at Radcliffe. The two articles, "Normal Motor Automatism" (Solomons)[3] and "Cultivated Motor Automatism" (Stein),[4] attempted to describe the behavior of subjects who were induced by various means to write, while having their attention diverted by some other stimulus. The experiment aimed at exploring an aspect of the 'secondary personality,' a concept in great currency at the time in the explanation of the strange, 'uncharacteristic,' 'impersonal' behavior of hysterical patients. James himself uses the 'fact' of the secondary personal self to support his contention that "thought is always part of a personal consciousness" (p. 225).

Solomons and Stein set out to demonstrate that the secondary personality also functions in non-hysterical subjects, and they did indeed show that a large percentage of people, including themselves, were capable of automatic behavior. Their articles, largely ignored by psychologists, became a goldmine for disparaging critics who portrayed Stein as an entranced writer, unintelligible because she was transcribing the incoherencies of a disordered aspect of the mind.

Stein later pointed out a more interesting aspect of this research.

> I was supposed to be interested in their [the student subjects'] reactions but soon I found that I was not but instead that I was enormously interested in the types of their characters that is what I even then thought of as the bottom nature of them, and

2. Gertrude Stein, "What Are Master-Pieces and Why Are There So Few of Them," *What Are Masterpieces* (Los Angeles, 1940), p. 84.

3. *Psychological Review* (September 1896), reprinted in pamphlet form with "Cultivated Motor Automatism" and entitled "Motor Automatism" (New York, 1969).

4. *Psychological Review* (May 1898); see n. 4.

when in May 1898 I wrote my half of the report of these experiments I expressed these results as follows: In these descriptions
it will be readily observed that habits of attention are reflexes of
the complete character of the individual.[5]

The fact that the individuals involved were being discussed within
certain general categories—suggestibility, level of fatigue—which is of
course the case in any scientific description, no doubt led Stein to
consider "the complete character of the individual" in terms of
groupings or types of character. In the above passage she even equates
"the types of characters" with "the bottom nature of them," and
here the singular of "nature" is, I think, significant. The essence of a
person is a shared essence.

The actual typology which had thus far emerged in her thinking
was, unfortunately, not very inspired. Indeed, it seems incredible
that a budding psychologist, even one at the end of the nineteenth
century, could categorize people in this way:

Type I. This consists mostly of girls who are found naturally in
literature courses and men who are going in for law. The type is
nervous, high-strung, very imaginative, has the capacity to be
easily roused and intensely interested. . . .

Type II. is very different from Type I., is more varied, and
gives more interesting results. In general, the individuals, often
blonde and pale, are distinctly phlegmatic. If emotional, decided-
ly of a weakish sentimental order. They may be either large,
healthy, rather heavy and lacking in vigor, or they may be what
we call anaemic and phlegmatic. Their power of concentrated
attention is small. They describe themselves as never being held
by their work; they say that their minds wander easily . . . the
feeling of having been there before is very common with them.
. . . They are often fatalistic in their ideas. They indulge in day-
dreams, but not those of a very stirring nature. As a rule they
don't seem to have *bad* tempers—are rather sullen. Many of them
are hopelessly self-conscious and rather morbid. ["Cultivated
Motor Automatism," pp. 29-30]

That Stein identified Type II as a significant segment of the

5. "The Gradual Making of The Making of Americans," *Lectures in America* (New York, 1975 [1935]), p. 138.

approximately one hundred Radcliffe students she observed is either
testimony to a sorry state among the students of the day or proof
of Stein's amazing capacity for sweeping generalization. She lumps
into a single type subjects with exactly opposite characteristics—the
large, healthy with the anaemic, phlegmatic. And later in the same
article she acknowledges that there are great individual variations
among the subjects and that not all of them share all the traits of
the type. In spite of this, the two types appear to have some cognitive value for her.

In this typology the conventional relation between observable
traits—appearance, activities—and generalizations about character is
radically altered. An exception to this is the reference to "girls who
are found naturally in English courses"—rather like wild-fowl in
marshy lakes—as being sensitive and imaginative; no doubt this assumption will rest unchallenged till the end of time. However, the
other observed traits are grouped together strictly on the basis of the
results of the experiment; that is, where students were responsive or
prone to be more or less affected by fatigue, their other observed
traits were taken into account as identifying responsiveness or fatigue by association. Any similarities that could be found among
subjects were then grouped and declared to be, in a sense, elements
of a syndrome, a collection of factors which in conjunction could
indicate the presence of some more general trait—Type I-ness, for
example. This method not only does away with much of the storehouse of conventionalized character implications, as one would expect of a quasi-scientific procedure, but it permits in addition a very
dynamic kind of interplay between the new implicates and implications. Not every element of the syndrome need be present for the
conclusion to be indicated, so that a different configuration of
elements in each person can still indicate a single essential type. This
dynamism of type-individual relations was to become one of the most
important problems in Stein's portraiture.

By the time that Stein was writing *The Making of Americans*, approximately ten years later, the crudeness of these categories had
disappeared, but she was still using a scheme of two basic categories:

> There are then two kinds of women, those who have dependent
> independence in them, those who have in them independent de-
> pendence inside them; the ones of the first of them always some-
> how own the ones they need to love them, the second kind of
> them have it in them to love only those who need them, such of

them have it in them to have power in them over others only
when these others have begun already a little to love them,
others loving them give to such of them strength in domination.
There are then these two ways of loving there are these two ways
of being when women have loving in them, as a bottom nature
to them. . . . [p. 118]

These two types are used for any women Stein deals with in the
book, and for men as well, for the configuration of associated
traits within each of the two types is extremely broad.

Stein's mode of naming the two types, independent dependence
and dependent independence, implies character as an interplay of a
pair of inverse traits, the dominance of either determining the type.
The fact that there is tension between the two opposing traits within any person (although seemingly for Stein one or the other is
fundamentally dominant) suggests an essentially dynamic condition
of the character. And further, the simplicity of the difference between the two types—simple opposition—immediately allows for the
comparison and contrasting of people within each of the two types
and between them. Categories such as Type I and Type II, with their
multiplicity of disorganized sub-characterisitics, do not permit this,
since they imply no relation to each other but that of the arbitrary
sequence, I, II.

Stein's system works on the basis of comparison, and of contrast
as well, for her typology was certainly not an attempt to deny individuality. As she says,

> Every one then is an individual being. Every one then is like
> many others always living, there are many ways of thinking of
> every one. . . .
> Every one is one inside them, every one reminds some one of
> some other one who is or was or will be living. [p. 212]

A graphic image of this comparing and contrasting can be seen in
Stein's manuscript notes for an early portrait of Isadora Duncan,
"Orta or One Dancing."[6] Stein sets up the following table of corres-
pondences to chart the changes in her subject:

6. Stein's manuscripts are housed in the Yale Collection of American Literature (YCAL)
housed in the Beinecke Rare Books and Manuscripts Library at Yale University, Donald
Gallup curator.

Alma ~~Davray~~

like Nadelman relation of ideas to impulse to
temperament to morality.

Isadora,	youth	resemblance.	Ada.
"	adult	"	Mary and Lewis.
"	maturity	"	Bird.
"	complete maturity	"	Alice Ullman.

Go on to Ivette Gilbert and so forth. [See figure 1.]

This scheme indicates both the importance of comparison in her
early understanding of character and the thoroughgoing connected-
ness she saw in all aspects of character, from "ideas to impulse to
temperament to morality."

On the basis of the differences and similarities she observed among
people, Stein developed a simulation of a scientific typology of genus,
species, sub-species: "There are two kinds of them, there are many
kinds of these kinds of them, there are many kinds in each one of the
many kinds of each kind of them" (*The Making of Americans*, 1934 ed.,
p. 230). This systemization was pushed even further in Stein's remarkable stated intention of classifying every person in terms of his type, and
of describing every possible type and relation among types:

> sometime then there will be a history of each one, of all the
> kinds of them, of all the ways any one can know them, of all
> the ways each one is inside her or inside him, of all the ways
> anything of them comes out from them. [p. 125]

> More and more then this will be a history of every kind and the
> way one kind is connected with the other kind of them. . . .
> [p. 126]

Stein even predicted the elaboration of a special typology of children, for "they have then their own system of being resembling"
(p. 213).[7]

---

7. It may very well be that some of the stimulus for the categories here came from William
James's *Varieties of Religious Experience*. When Stein says, for example, that of the two
types of people, "the first have resisting as the fighting power in them, the second have at-
tacking as their natural way of fighting" (*ibid.*, p. 133), she may be alluding to James's
categories of the saint and the soldier. F. Scott Taylor has suggested to me that *Fernhurst*
is based on James's typology of religious varieties.

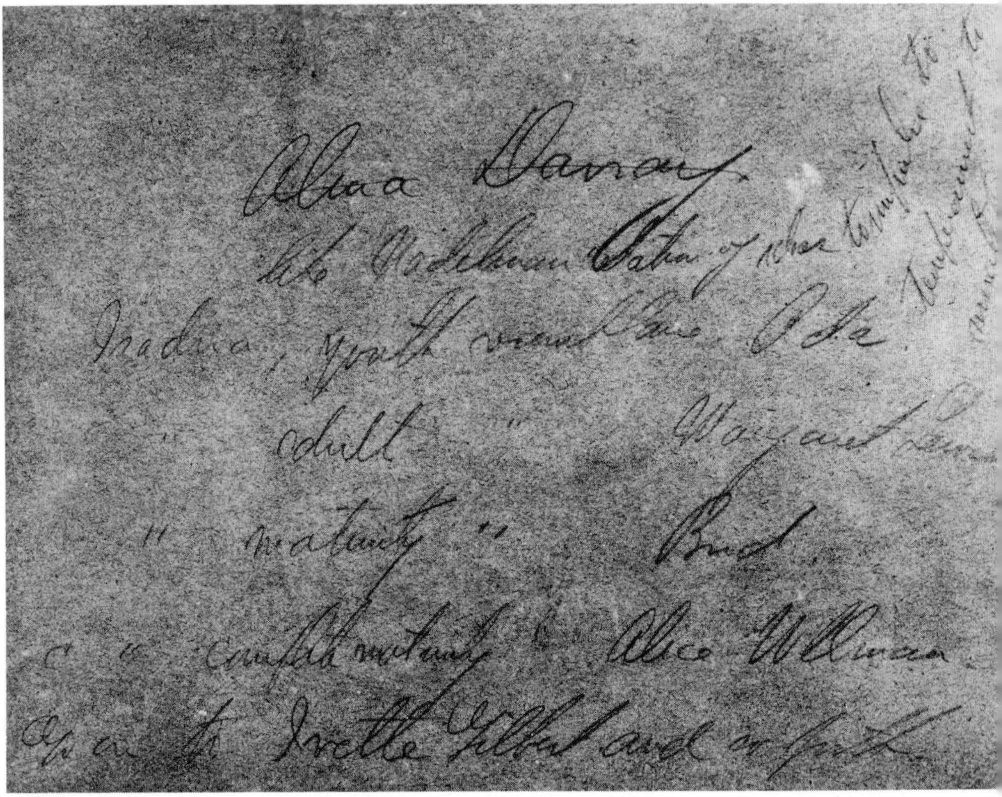

Figure 1. Schematization of Isadora Duncan's resemblance to other women.

The motivation for such classifying is explicitly stated by Stein: "I see a very certain thing in my way of seeing kinds in men and women, that I am really understanding the meaning of the being in them" (p. 230). To understand "the meaning of the being" in a person, his essence or identity, then, it is necessary to see him in terms of his relations to others, in terms of his type. A person's character is his difference from other *comparable* people.

An interesting illustration of Stein's concern with systems of classification of this sort may be seen in her attitude toward a book published in 1909 called *Sex & Character*.[8] Marian Walker Williams wrote to Stein in that year that she too had read this book, "which you said exactly embodied your views."[9] The book, rather astonishingly, turns out to be a quasi-scientific 'proof' of the inferiority of women and Jews, and since Stein was both, it seems incredible that the hashed logic of the book should have appealed to her.

However, an examination of *Sex & Character* reveals remarkable methodological and theoretical similarities to Stein's typologizing. The book discusses sex as an all-determining characteristic in human (and animal) nature, there being two sexual types, the male and the female. "We may suppose the existence of an ideal man, M, and of an ideal woman, W, as sexual types, although these types do not actually exist" (p. 7). Just as with Stein, here we find two abstract types, and the mode in which these types function in the individual is a typically Steinian tension. For everyone, regardless of sex, has components of both maleness and femaleness within him, with the result that individuals can be grouped along a range from the very strongly female or male to the sexually ambivalent. Within this range, moreover, differences are, by definition, of degree and not of kind, so that again we have a system that is based on comparison and contrast and on differences in the configuration of components rather than in the components themselves.

The author of *Sex & Character*, Weininger, sought to enhance the scientific quality of his typology by expressing his ideas algebraically, with the hope that the relations among people could be calculated and accurately predicted. He expressed sexual affinity, for example, as follows: "$M\mu$ (the truly male part in the 'male') + $M\omega$ (the truly male part in the 'female') will equal a constant quantity, M, the ideal male . . ." and likewise with the female components of the 'male'

8. Otto Weininger, *Sex & Character* (New York and London, 1909).
9. *The Flowers of Friendship: Letters Written to Gertrude Stein*, ed. Donald Gallup (New York, 1953), p. 45; letter dated June 11, 1909.

and 'female' involved. Attraction takes place when both the male and
female components of the two add up to 100 percent. The naiveté of
this schematism must again remind us of Stein's attempts to describe
every person and every possible interrelation among people on the
basis of her types.

A final similarity between Weininger and Stein is in their notion of
identity. Whether Weininger knew James's work or the idea was simply in the air, his definition of identity involves most of the factors
of the one in the *Principles*: "the continuous memory is the psychological expression of the logical proposition of identity" (p. 148).
And further, "I assert that the judgment of identity depends on conceptions, never on mere perceptions and complexes of perceptions
. . ." (p. 147). Identity is thus a product of memory involving an ab-
stractive process of likening.

Weininger uses this definition of identity to prove that women,
defective in memory, are wanting as well in identity: "Unlike man,
her experiences float past without being referred, so to speak, to a
definite, permanent centre; she does not feel herself, past and present, to be one and the same throughout all her life" (p. 146). Because the instances of 'self' in perception are so indistinct, sameness
cannot be recognized, and woman is bereft of identity and, in fact,
of genius, the ultimate state of male clarity of thought. Since we
know that Gertrude Stein had a very high opinion of herself (she
later declared that the three geniuses of the twentieth century were
Picasso, Whitehead, and herself),[10] it would seem that her embracing
of *Sex & Character* was based on a purely methodological affinity
and a simultaneous disregard of virtually every substantive claim
made by the book. Again, this is typical of the intensely theoretical,
'scientific' approach to phenomena which characterizes all of her
work.

Stein describes this earliest phase of her notion of identity as follows:

> This being resembling, this seeing resemblances between those
> one is knowing is interesting, defining, confusing, uncertain and
> certain. You see one, the way of looking at any one in that one
> that is like some one, the way of listening, a sudden expression,
> a way of walking, a sound in laughing, a number of expressions
> that are passing over the face of that one, it is confusing, too

10. Gertrude Stein, *The Autobiography of Alice B. Toklas* (New York, 1933), p. 5.

many people have pieces in them like pieces in this one, it began
as a clear resemblance to some one, it goes on to be a confusing
number of resemblances to many then, some resemblance that
is very clear one is not remembering then it is baffling, more and
more resemblances come out in that one, perhaps that one is not
independent dependent and yet that was so clear in the beginning,
more and more then with knowing resemblances are multiplying
and being baffling and confusing and always each one of all these
resemblances one who sometimes wants to have this one as a
whole one, wants to really know kinds in men and women must
completely feel, admit, remember and consider and realise as
having meaning. This is then a beginning of learning to make kinds
of men and women. Slowly then all the resemblances between
one and all the others that have something, different things in
common with that one, all these fall into an ordered system
sometime then that one is a whole one, sometimes that one is
very different to what was in the beginning the important resemblance in that one but always everything, all resemblances in
that one must be counted in, nothing must ever be thrown out,
everything in each one must be included to know that one and
then sometime that one is to some one a whole one and that is
then very satisfying. [*The Making of Americans*, pp. 226–27]

The difference in tone between this statement and Pope's discussion of portraiture in the "Epistle to Cobham" is instructive. Pope's
argument is predominantly polemical, insisting on the ruling passion
as the only key to character by showing the weaknesses of the various forms of evidence available to the portraitist. But when Stein
speaks of the difficulties of character judgment, what comes through
most forcefully is the struggle of the portraitist in her desire to come
to know people, and to know them as a scientist (albeit a very humanistic one), thoroughly and passionately pursuing her work. "I
was sure that in a kind of a way the enigma of the universe could in
this way be solved" ("The Gradual Making of The Making of Americans," p. 142). This profound desire to know people perhaps explains Stein's openness to new approaches to characterization. As
obsessive as it may appear, as naive as it surely was, this desire nevertheless led to valuable artistic discoveries in her conceptualizing of
the human being and in the expression of that conceptualization.
   Gertrude Stein wrote *The Making of Americans* over a seven-year
period ending in 1912, and most of her ideas which we have so far

outlined are to be found in this book. Toward the middle of writing it (1908), she began to produce portraits, and soon afterward (1909–1912) two longer works—*Many Many Women* and *A Long Gay Book*.[11] All of these were supposed to fulfill the program she had developed for describing the essential being of people and their relations to other people.

In *Many Many Women* (1910) Stein set out to describe all the possible types of women. She conceived of them in terms of the Jamesian notion of identity dependent on memory: "Each one is one. Each one has been one. Each one being one, each one having been one is remembering something of that thing" (p. 119). In addition to the notion of identity based on remembrance, the opposition of type and individual found in *The Making of Americans* is present here in the constantly repeated "Every one is like every one. Each one is one" (p. 129). But as well, one can perhaps see here the beginnings of an interest in individuality and uniqueness as special considerations possible to discuss separately from the various types: "This one is not a kind of a one. This one is one. She is that one. She is that one and being one being creative she is creating being one who is not a kind of a one" (p. 159). The possibility of an individual independent of any type is not pursued in *Many Many Women* other than in the mentioning of this particular woman. Nevertheless, it is a case outside the system which Stein had so laboriously invented and elaborated, and her interest in it as a possibility is evident.

A Long Gay Book (1909–1912) also began with the program projected in *The Making of Americans*. It was to be a list of all possible types, individuals, and relations among groupings of types or individuals: "In this book there will be discussion of pairs of people and their relation, short sketches of innumerable ones, Ollie, Paul; Paul, Fernande; Larr and me . . . everybody I know . . . Sadie and Julia, everybody I can think of ever, narrative after narrative of pairs of people" (p. 17). The book begins with the by now familiar concepts of the "fundamental nature . . . with a kind of way of thinking that goes with this nature . . . in all the many millions made of that kind of them" (p. 16). The type, the basic nature, the Jamesian definition of the human being as thinker are all here, along with the activity of describing types and individuals, the "mixing and mingling and contrasting" (p. 18).

11. Both works are printed in *Matisse Picasso and Gertrude Stein with Two Shorter Stories* (also known as *G.M.P.*) (West Glover, Vt., 1972).

With this orthodox Steinian beginning, with the stated intention of producing lists and diagrams and ever-swelling typologies, the crack which had begun to appear in *Many Many Women* suddenly opens, and something truly extraordinary happens. The descriptions begin to omit any mention of "independent dependent" and the concomitant categories, become more and more word-oriented and playful, and finally give way to a great burst of what might be called concrete poetry (p. 115). The book ends with the punning line, "Etching. Etching a chief, none plush" (p. 116), where "etching" might be taken as 'description,' "a chief" as 'achieve' or alternately as the subject of a description, and "non plush" as 'nonplussed.' 'The achievement of description—nonplussed.' And that, as it turns out, is the end of the period of character typologizing according to resemblance and memory, and the announcement of a new discovery.

I would claim, as Stein herself does in the passage which follows, that this change was related to her new understanding of the nature of knowledge, particularly of what she had learned from William James:

> When I was working with William James I completely learned one thing, that science is continuously busy with the complete description of something, with ultimately the complete description of anything with ultimately the complete description of everything. If this can really be done the complete description of everything then what else is there to do. We may well say nothing, but and this is the thing that makes everything continue to be anything, that after all what does happen is that as relatively few people spend all their time describing anything and they stop and so in the meantime as everything goes on somebody else can always commence and go on. And so description is really unending. When I began The Making of Americans I knew I really did know that a complete description was a possible thing, and certainly a complete description is a possible thing. But as it is a possible thing one can stop continuing to describe this everything. That is where philosophy comes in, it begins when one stops continuing describing everything. ["The Gradual Making of The Making of Americans," pp. 156–57]

It is interesting that Stein understood this change as a departure from the direction set by James, since, in fact, it can readily be understood as a shift from James's notions of identity to the other possibility within his theory of knowledge. For if a portraitist is no longer to describe his subject, to provide "knowledge about" him, then there is only one other kind of knowledge that he can create, according to James. And whether Stein knew it or not, the concept which she used to replace identity was a version of Jamesian "acquaintance." We can understand Stein's shift to "philosophy" in the passage above as a focusing on a realm of knowledge concerned not with descriptive definition but with the immediate evocation of essence.

Stein saw her new conception, "entity" ('being'), as a mode in opposition to identity. Again we have two 'types,' but this time they are discontinuous, disjunctive modes possible in the same person. This conception developed out of another discovery of hers: "The thing one gradually comes to find out is that one has no identity that is when one is in the act of doing anything. Identity is recognition, you know who you are because you and others remember anything about yourself but essentially you are not that when you are doing anything." "At any moment when you are you you are you without the memory of yourself because if you remember yourself while you are you you are not for purposes of creating you" ("What Are Master-Pieces," p. 84). This departure from a mode in which memory functions is, in fact, a more extreme position even than James outlined in connection with acquaintance. For the distinction between the two forms of knowledge for him was a relative one. Acquaintance was a relatively less "fringed" knowledge of a subject than knowledge-about.

Stein's development of the idea of memory-free consciousness led to some very interesting implications for portraiture. Eventually it posed the question:

If they [the subjects of portraits] are themselves inside them what are they and what has it to do with what they do.

And does it make any difference what they do or how they do it, does it make any difference what they say or how they say it. Must they be in relation with any one or with anything in order to be one of whom one can make a portrait. I began to think a great deal about all these things. ["Portraits and Repetition," pp. 171-72]

To tell what someone is doing is to give his action a name, thus to compare it to other actions and to reify its process-quality. To tell *how* a person is acting also inevitably involves comparison and memory. And finally, to treat a person in terms of his relations to others is the old error of the typologizing stage of Stein's thinking. She is thus rejecting conventional modes of conceiving action, and insisting upon the state of being in action, the movement of the moment without concern for past or future. The answer Stein gave to this question then was that a person's actions are irrelevant from the point of view of portraiture: "And so what does it really matter what anybody does. The newspapers are full of what anybody does ... but the thing that is important is the intensity of anybody's existence" (p. 182). And this intensity was to be seen in terms of "movement":

> I had to find out inside every one what was in them that was intrinsically exciting and I had to find out not by what they said not by what they did not by how much or how little they resembled any other one but I had to find it out by the intensity of movement that there was inside in any one of them [p. 183]

In its most mature form, the portrait was to present the individual as an entity, as a degree, a mode, of movement. Stein saw this movement, and existence as a variety of it, as a way of dealing with the particularly American, and as something with which any modern American must come to terms. She pointed out in "Portraits and Repetition" that

> the strange thing about the realization of existence is that like a train moving there is no real realization of it moving if it does not move against something and so that is what a generation does it shows that moving is existing. So then there are generations and in a way that too is not important because, and this thing is a thing to know, if and we in America have tried to make this thing a real thing, if the movement, that is any movement, is lively enough, perhaps it is possible to know that it is moving even if it is not moving against anything. [p. 165]

Thus, the portrayal of the individual as a nonrelational movement was an expression of the fact that the generation in America had ceased to operate as the stable basis of comparison it once was. Stein thought of America as discontinuous from its past, as caught up in a frantic movement which was constantly changing and recreating it. And as an American, she claimed to see people this way, to see herself this way, as a dynamic force of movement without remembrance and relation. In her most mature portraits, all conventional traits of the subject are missing; the subject is simply a dynamic, immediate movement of language:

> It really does not make any difference who George Hugnet was or what he did or what I said, all that was necessary was that there was something completely contained within itself and being contained within itself was moving, not moving in relation to anything not moving in relation to itself but just moving. . . . [p. 202]

Stein often described the state of living as an entity as talking and listening at the same time: "Nothing makes any difference as long as someone is listening while they are [i.e., he—the same one—is] talking" (p. 170). Though this statement seems to imply a relation of the self talking to the self listening, the fact that the two activities are absolutely simultaneous removes the possibility of memory and even relationality. The movement is a simultaneous transmission-reception existing only in the moment and constantly in flux. Moreover it is completely self-contained. One thinks of someone talking into a microphone connected to ear phones which he is himself wearing. Stein associated entity with being a genius, that state of self-creativity in which the identity no longer exists, but in which movement, perhaps the super-sensitized movement of more than one faculty, goes on. Knowledge of a person on these terms is Jamesian "acquaintance" of the rock-bottom phenomenon of the person, but bereft even of the feelings of warmth normally surrounding instances of sames in thought. This is a program for a pure individuation of the subject, and an isolation of him in the immediacy of the moment.

If we were to characterize the development in Stein's conception of the individual, then, we might say that it is a shift from a highly elaborated typologizing in which characteristic or repeated acts— thinking, loving, resisting—define an individual by placing him in relation to others comparably defined, to a position in which character implicates simply do not function. In this latter phase anything that functions as 'evidence' of character is disregarded, because it is mediate. That is, it evokes a mental process beyond perception[12] and thus opens the way to comparison, remembrance, relations. Instead,

---

12. I am aware of the objections to this usage of "perception" by Gestaltists (see, e.g., R. Arnheim, *Visual Thinking* [Berkeley, 1969]). The notion of perception as free of conceptualization will be criticized later in the chapter.

the immediate experience with the 'moving' subject is all that Stein
is interested in, for this does not lead to any conclusions. Like identity, the notion of entity defines the individual in terms of process—
movement—but this process is no longer to be thought of in terms
of 'acts' which have their own conventionalized system of character
implications. Instead, the individual is seen as a completely unique,
non-relational movement.

It should be clear that the portrait subject conceived of as entity
requires indexical mimesis rather than description, for the simple
reason that there is no other way to represent something conceived
of as unique in all respects without bringing in the factors of type
and classification. The portrait must have the autonomy of the living subject; it must have the status of an independent datum of
perception. What we now have, in effect, is a program for a text-
object—a piece of writing that is to have the very degree and intensity
of movement that its subject has, that becomes independent and
unique in order to render with immediacy the independence and
uniqueness, the essence, of its subject. Stein had created a conception of the individual which both necessitated and for the first time
permitted imitative literary portraiture, demonstrating a necessary
connection between mimetic representation and the individuality of
the portrait subject. This connection had been implied by the persistence of the "imitation of an individual" definition of portraiture,
but had never been understood in any consistent way. We can see
Stein's development in conceiving the individual then as tied to her
recognition of the *exigencies of the portrait genre as classically defined.*

The opposition of identity and entity, as we have seen, is directly
related to the individual's time sense. The time sense of identity is
one in which memory operates, so that there is a carry-over of various past moments into the present. Entity cannot function in such
confusion, and as a result artistic creativity is also inhibited. "Time
is very important in connection with master-pieces, of course it
makes identity time does make identity and identity does stop the
creation of master-pieces" ("What Are Master-Pieces," p. 92). The
problem for Stein, then, was to elaborate a time sense suited to the
perception of the individual as entity.

The ideas about time which she inherited from James were particularly important, for he not only held that the essence of the human
being is his thinking, but that thought is most fundamentally a temporal operation—it "goes on" (p. 225). Its mode of going on is as

follows: thought is always part of a personal consciousness, it is always changing, it is continuous, it deals with objects independent of itself, and it selects the objects of its interest. The second and third characteristics—constant change and continuity—imply a notion of thought as a succession of 'now's linked by contiguity and similarity, that is, by their context and the 'sameness' of their objects, respectively. This was James's "stream of consciousness," and later on, with certain modifications, Stein's "continuous present."

However, though James claimed that thought really did progress as a continuous succession of now-points, he argued that no one perceives his own thought or his own temporality in this way. For one moment cannot be held onto separately from others; the present is constantly eluding us, forcing us backward into the past and forward into the future. Because of this, "The unit of our perception of time is a *duration*. . . . It is only as parts of this *duration-block* that the relation of *succession* of one end to the other is perceived" (pp. 609–10). "We are constantly conscious of a certain duration—the specious present—varying in length from a few seconds to probably not more than a minute, and . . . this duration (with its content perceived as having one part earlier and the other part later) is the original intuition of time" (p. 642). Now in speaking of the normal time sense as "specious" James is claiming an accuracy or 'truth' for the stream of consciousness concept which is supposedly lacking in the other. In fact, according to James, normal time perception is a misconception, an illusion. And when we consider that he connected it with memory and resemblance and a beginning-middle-end structure, it is not surprising that Stein discarded it as a sham from the point of view of creativity and entity.

Despite this connection between entity and now-perception, however, Stein claimed that she began using the continuous present (or the "prolonged present" as she calls it here) in her earliest writings, in which identity and its concomitant, memory, were so important.

In beginning writing I wrote a book called *Three Lives* this was written in 1905. I wrote a negro story called *Melanctha*. In that there was a constant recurring and beginning there was a marked direction in the direction of being in the present although naturally I had been accustomed to past present and future, and why, because the composition forming around me was a prolonged present. A composition of a prolonged present is a natural composition in the world as it has been these thirty years it was more and more a prolonged present.[13]

Thus, Stein's thinking about the time sense of the individual appears to have been out of step with the development of her overall concept of individuality, for if she really was using the continuous present in *Three Lives* and *The Making of Americans*, she was at the same time at the very height of her "mixing and mingling and contrasting" of her subjects.

The discrepancy was due, most likely, to the early awareness of time created in Stein by her experiments in psychology. One of Solomons' and Stein's important observations about what sort of material to use to divert the subject's attention from the experiment itself was that "when the idea [in the piece of writing read to the subject] cannot be grasped without a conscious effort to keep past facts in mind to compare with present, the attention is kept in a general condition of alertness, unfavorable to the complete neglect of any class of sensations" ("Normal Motor Automatism," p. 23). Thus, Stein was in a position to observe that the interference of the past with the present in a temporal sequence would inhibit the secondary personality. Now the secondary personality was understood by the two experimenters as engaged in a perfectly spontaneous activity "without any express desire or volition" (p. 24), and as such—as a part of the personality that was normally hidden and that was capable of expression—it might well have seemed connected with artistic creativity. Because it could be totally inhibited by memory, and because Stein was familiar with James's theories about time, she might well have been led to think about the relation between spontaneous creativity and memory. This is not to say that the secondary personality is an equivalent for the much later concept of entity—for one thing, the secondary personality was capable of memory (p. 22) even though inhibited by the operation of memory in the mind as a whole—but rather that Stein's concern with time might easily have developed earlier than the corresponding notion of entity because of her association of the secondary personality with creativity and spontaneity.

Stein's psychological experiments probably stimulated not only

13. "Composition as Explanation" (London, 1926), reprinted in *Gertrude Stein: Writings and Lectures 1909–1945*, p. 25.

her ideas about time but also her ideas about the possibilities of expressing entity through repetition, the best known feature of her
writing. She and Solomons discovered that one of the characteristics
of automatic writing was "*A marked tendency to repetition.—A
phrase would seem to get into the head and keep repeating itself at
every opportunity, and hang over from day to day even*" (p. 21).
Solomons cites some examples of this: "When he could not be the
longest and thus to be, and thus to be, the strongest." "This long
time when he did this best time, and he could thus have been bound,
and in this long time, when he could be this to first use of this long
time" (pp. 21–22). Thus, Stein must have been aware that an aspect
of the personality that seemed spontaneous and 'creative' expressed
itself in repetitions. (For an even earlier stimulus to repetition, see
"Portraits and Repetition," pp. 168–69).

The fact that repetitions occur in both automatic writing and
Stein's work has led a number of critics to believe that Stein's prose
was in fact automatic writing. This idea appeared to be supported by
Solomons' statement that he and Stein "had now gained so much
control over our habits of attention that distraction by reading was
almost unnecessary. Miss Stein found it sufficient distraction often
to simply read what her arm wrote, but following three or four
words behind her pencil" (p. 21). Because of this statement, B. F.
Skinner, in his rather sensationally entitled article, "Has Gertrude
Stein a Secret?"[14] suggests that not only did Stein employ in her
creative writing many of the 'slips' she had observed in automatic
writing, but she also *practised* automatic writing in order to create
her texts. He even hypothesizes the release of a secondary personality through automatic writing, but claims that the one Stein released
in *Tender Buttons* would have been better left undisturbed.

Skinner's hypothesis has been echoed by more serious students of
literature. It is a bit hard to understand why these critics have been
so offended at the idea of using techniques from or even the technique of automatic writing. Yet, whenever the issue is discussed, the
suggestion that this technique of writing is involved in Stein's work
is treated either as an accusation or as an elevated, spiritualized ex-
cuse—"meditation."[15] I have tried to show that Stein was an extraordinarily conscious writer, and what is still to be said will illustrate
this even more fully. However, anything that Stein observed in her

14. *Atlantic Monthly* 153 (Jan. 1934).
15. See Allegra Stewart, *Gertrude Stein and the Present* (Cambridge, Mass., 1967), pp.
52–53.

experiments that fit into her scheme was certainly fair game stylistically. And repetition, the double nature of personality, and the interference of memory with the spontaneous element of this double nature clearly were vital to both her psychological and literary experiments.

Stein at first thought of repetition, or 'insistence' as she preferred to call it, as the prime means by which people expressed their inner being: "Repeating is a wonderful thing in being, everything, every one is repeating then always the whole of them . . ." (*The Making of Americans,* p. 207). This observation led her to postulate an individual rhythm of personality in everyone:

> I began to get enormously interested in hearing how everybody said the same thing over and over again with infinite variations but over and over again until finally if you listened with great intensity you could hear it rise and fall and tell all that that there was inside them, not so much by the actual words they said or the thoughts they had but the movement of their thoughts and words endlessly the same and endlessly different. ["The Gradual Making," p. 138]

This notion of the personality as a regular succession of 'sames' with constant variations is similar to James's conception of the knowledge of sameness in perception and of its special case—identity. It involves a time sense in which memory and duration play an important role.

Gradually Stein became aware of the problem in using such a notion in portraiture:

> When I was up against the difficulty of putting down the complete conception that I had of an individual, the complete rhythm of a personality that I had gradually acquired by listening seeing feeling and experience, I was faced by the trouble that I had acquired all this knowledge gradually but when I had it I had it completely at one time. . . . And a great deal of The Making of Americans was a struggle to do this thing, to make a whole present of something that it had taken a great deal of time to find out, but it was a whole there then within me and as such it had to be said. [p. 147]

The problem, then, was an inconsistency in Stein's treatment of time. A rhythm is a kind of repetition and automatically implies perception over a period of time, comparison, and memory. Yet for Stein, the individual had become "a whole there then within me," a unity, which was later expressed as the concept of entity. Thus, though she was aiming at a prolonged or continuous present, her conception of the essential mode of the individual—repetition—made this impossible to realize. The contradiction is fully expressed in "Portraits and Repetition":

> I conceived what I at that time called the rhythm of anybody's personality. If listening was talking and talking was listening [the two simultaneous and essential activities of the mode of 'entity'] then and at the same time any little movement any little expression was a resemblance, and a resemblance was something that presupposed remembering.
>
> Listening and talking did not presuppose resemblance and as they do not presuppose resemblance, they do not necessitate remembering. Already then as you see there was a complication which was a bother to me in my conception of the rhythm of a personality. I have for so many years tried to get the better of that the better of this bother. The bother was simply that and one may say it is the bother that has always been a bother to anybody for anybody conceiving anything. [pp. 174-75]

The solution to this problem was the *continuous present*. It arose, Stein claims, while she was working on *The Making of Americans* and the early portraits. Hence it seems to anticipate the conception of the portrait subject as entity. The sense of time in thought as a rhythm of relations becomes in the continuous present a series of self-contained nows. The earlier 'misconception' is often distinguished from the later continuous present by the term "prolonged present," although we have seen that Stein herself did not distinguish between these terms with any precision. Donald Sutherland describes the difference between the two as follows:

> a prolonged present asserts a theme and then proceeds to complicate and elaborate it, in the manner of a fugal theme in Bach, so that the presence of the original theme, no matter how elaborately overlaid with variations, is maintained or prolonged as a going existence in each present passage or moment. It is as if one counted one two three four five six and so on, where the original unit of one is prolonged and present in the other figures

> in which it remains a component. But a continuous present . . .
> would be one in which each unit, even if identical or nearly
> with the previous one, is still, in its present, a completely self-
> contained thing, as when you say one and one, the second one
> is a completely present existence in itself, and does not depend,
> as two or three does, on a preceding one or two. . . . [It] arrives
> in a continuous present, that is, the present is so continuous it
> does not allow any retrospect or expectation . . .[16]

Here the older perception based on remembrance has given way to
a notion of perception in nows, in moments unconnected or irrelevant of connection, and "insistence" as a term has begun to designate
the force of each individual sentence rather than the contextual difference from one sentence to the next. As Stein says in the final section of *The Making of Americans*, a section different in kind from
the typologizing of the earlier portions, "All that some one knows
about some one is what is true of that one as being one doing what
that one is doing when something is happening" (*The Making of
Americans*, p. 395).[17]

Stein tried to make the continuous present understandable by using her famous movie metaphor. Through it she hoped to illustrate
the distinction between repetition and insistence, as well as the fact
that her seeminly repetitious sentences did not work by means of
memory or rhythm, but by their enclosed, discontinuous nature.

> I was doing what the cinema was doing, I was making a continu-
> ous succession of the statement of what that person was until I
> had not many things but one thing. . . .
>   You see then what I was doing in my beginning portrait writ-
> ing and you also understand what I mean when I say there was
> no repetition. In a cinema picture no two pictures are exactly
> alike each one is just that much different from the one before.
>   . . . Each time that I said the somebody whose portrait I was
> writing was something that something was just that much dif-
> ferent from what I had just said that somebody was and a little

16. "Gertrude Stein and the Twentieth Century," *A Primer for the Gradual Understanding
of Gertrude Stein*, ed., Robert Bartlett Haas (Los Angeles, 1971), pp. 146–47.

17. In this early statement, Stein was still including the actions of the subject and the configuration of events around him (the "something [else] happening") within her perception
of the subject; her mature notion of the time sense of entity had emerged before entity itself
was a fully developed working concept.

by little in this way a whole portrait came into being, a portrait
that was not description and that was made by each time, and I
did a great many times, say it, that somebody was something,
each time there was a difference just a difference enough so that
it could go on and be a present something. ["Portraits and Repetition," pp. 176–77]

The basic idea, then, is of a series of similar but not identical statements each perceived as a now. The fact that the sentences are similar but not identical, of course, is not to be perceived in the act of
reading, but is an imitation of now-perception where everything is
in constant flux. In Stein's entity writing, these repetitions were
eliminated altogether, since they are irrelevant to now-perception
and indeed may interfere with it. But in either case, now-ness or
immediacy was to be a part of the perception of each portrait sentence, so that there is a continuity of perception in the present, a
unity in this perception. Apparently, by virtue of the continuity of
the present in perception, the subject himself is perceived as a unity,
but not a unity dependent on remembrance. The unity and immediacy of the subject are based on unity and immediacy in perception
per se.

The movie metaphor thus implies that the subject is whole not because one perceives *him* as a whole, but primarily because one *perceives* in a uniform mode. Though characteristics of subjects can be
found in many of Stein's portraits, there are many with very little
particularity; the metaphor warns us that the felt correspondence
between the mode of the subject and the perception of the portraitist is heavily weighted on the side of perception, that unity of perception is almost a precondition for the unity of the subject, and
consequently that perception can become a virtual subject in itself
with the human subject secondary, if not absent.

The moment has come (perhaps long overdue) for a discussion of
the soundness and consistency of these ideas of Stein's about time.
First, it is clear that perception in terms of totally disconnected con-
text-free nows never occurs, or at least we can never know that it
occurs, for this would mean that we were perceiving as if we had no
accumulated experience and no language. Objects would be disorganized sets of blotches undifferentiated from their background if one
came to each moment of perception as a *tabula rasa*. Second, the continuity of now-perception which we have inferred from the movie
metaphor is impossible to know unless we are able to remember this

quality of perception in other past moments. To be perfectly consistent, we would never realize the unity of the portrait subject, which is dependent on perceptual unity, while reading a portrait, since we would not be capable of making such generalizations. We would never know what we supposedly were 'knowing' at every moment. And even if one argued that such enclosed islands of *ur*-perception are exactly what Stein intended, and further, that they can be achieved by means of linguistic (conceptualizing, generalizing) signs, then there is still the problem of the extent of the nows involved. For the present is 'fast-fleeting'; it vanishes as soon as one tries to hold onto it, as Stein well knew. In order to catch it, she was forced to give it the dimensions of the sentence, a "specious present" all her own.

It would seem then that as a philosopher Stein is found wanting in many respects. But as a practising writer and a theoretician of her own art, perhaps her performance should not be judged so harshly. For though her claims are at times questionable, nevertheless they indicate a fascinating attempt to create a new mode of perception through language. How far can a reader with the whole conceptual framework of rationalism, referential language, and relational thought be made to perceive with complete immediacy? What factors can at least come close to producing perceptions free of memory and resemblance? Though such questions show an extraordinary awareness of the problems of the medium of language and the portrait genre, Stein's solutions carry inconsistencies and even absurdities along with them. However, as constantly reworked hypotheses questioning the conventional restrictions of literature, they generated a lifetime of artistic productions which were new, influential, and, as Stein called them, "exciting."

Indeed, this quality of newness, modernity, was one of the most frequent of Stein's claims, and of her supporters' as well. For instance, she thought that her development of the continuous present, a technique that could be described in terms of the newest, fastest-rising art of the early twentieth century, the cinema, was a sign of her modernity. She claimed never to have seen a film when she began writing in the continuous present (p. 177), but explained the correspondence as a kind of osmosis. If a person was really tuned to the modern world as an artist, he would be aware of the mechanisms and structures of the new, even if he had never encountered the facts of the modern world. This is another instance of the concentration on methodology and disregard for substance apparent in Stein's interest in *Sex & Character*. It is also consistent with her trans-media comparisons linking painting, drama, poetry, prose, and film on the basis of factors so technical or abstract that one is reminded of the generalizations of Marshall McLuhan, the self-proclaimed genius of the modern. When we consider that Stein's ideas about language, her bracketing-off of various factors in order to concentrate on only one, and her intricate analysis of time have led several critics to wonder if she might not have been well acquainted with the writings of the phenomenologists,[18] one begins to feel that she may indeed have grasped some essential structure of the modern which was capable of generating any of the phenomena of the twentieth century.

The second fundamental issue in portraiture, as described in chapter 1, is the semiotic relation between portrait and subject. We come then to the question of iconicity, which I suggested earlier is the most revolutionary aspect of Stein's portraiture. She attempted an uncompromising mimesis, a direct equivalence between her words and her subjects' thought or speech, or more frequently, between her words and her own thought in perceiving her subjects.

The basis for such programmatic iconicity can be found, along with so many other starting-points for Stein, in the work of William James. Indeed, one of the most striking features of James's theories is the easy correspondence that he sees between thought and language. So natural does this transition seem to him that he does not try to justify it in a theory about language; he simply treats language as if it were a direct reflection of thought. For example, in discussing the difference between "knowledge-about" and "acquaintance" James says, "The grammatical sentence expresses this. Its 'subject' stands for an object of acquaintance which, by the addition of the predicate, is to get something known about it" (p. 222). Grammatical relations involve or represent knowledge relations, and the building of a sentence mirrors the building of knowledge from acquaintance

---

18. B. L. Reid, *Art by Subtraction: A Dissenting Opinion of Gertrude Stein* (University of Oklahoma, 1958), p. 66.: "'Exact reproduction' . . . is something very close to the so-called 'reduction' process of the Phenomenologists, and one cannot help wondering whether Miss Stein had encountered Husserl or his followers." And Allegra Stewart notes that Stein's concern with language *qua* language is a sign of modern "technological alienation" as discussed in Hegel's *Phenomenology of Mind*.

The influence of William James is probably the significant factor in any relation between Stein and the Phenomenologists, since he is in part their precursor; see Johannes Linschoten, *On the Way toward a Phenomenological Psychology* (Pittsburgh, 1968) and Bruce Wilshire, *William James and Phenomenology* (Bloomington, Indiana, 1968).

to knowledge-about. It is thus a thought unit in the conventional sense, that is, one related to identity.

For James, thought is translated not only by functional units, such as subject and object, but also by the parts of speech. He explains these in a very famous passage describing the rate of change in the objects of our thought in terms of the 'pace' of the sentence:

> When the rate is slow we are aware of the object of our thought in a comparatively restful and stable way. When rapid, we are aware of a passage, a relation, a transition *from* it, or *between* it and something else. As we take, in fact, a general view of the wonderful stream of our consciousness, what strikes us first is this different pace of its parts. Like a bird's life it seems to be made of an alternation of flights and perchings. The rhythm of language expresses this, where every thought is expressed in a sentence, and every sentence closed by a period. The resting-places are usually occupied by sensorial imaginations of some sort, whose peculiarity is that they can be held before the mind for an indefinite time, and contemplated without changing; the places of flight are filled with thoughts of relations, static or dynamic, that for the most part obtain between the matters con-templated in the periods of comparative rest.
>
> *Let us call the resting-places the 'substantive parts,' and the places of flight the 'transitive parts,' of the stream of thought.* [19]

Here, even in the naming of the parts of thought, James uses terms which apply to language—"substantive" and "transitive."

He goes on to say that the aim of the transitive states is to have us arrive at substantive ones: "It then appears that the main end of our thinking is at all times the attainment of some other substantive part than the one from which we have just been dislodged. And we may say that the main use of the transitive parts is to lead us from one substantive conclusion to another" (p. 243). Here, most explicitly, James makes the parallel with language: "The truth is that large tracts of human speech are nothing but *signs of direction* in thought. . . . These bare images of logical movement . . . are psychic transi-tions, always on the wing, so to speak, and not to be glimpsed except

19. *Ibid.,* p. 243. This passage is also quoted in connection with Stein by Ronald Bartlett Levinson in "Gertrude Stein, William James, and Grammar," *American Journal of Psychol-ogy,* 54 (January 1941), p. 126.

in flight. Their function is to lead from one set of images to another"
(p. 252).

James explains that the transitive states of thought cannot be
'trapped' or held onto: *"for a state of mind to survive in memory it
must have endured for a certain length of time.* In other words, it
must be what I call a substantive state. Prepositional and conjunctival
states of mind [along with verb states] are not remembered as independent facts" (pp. 643–44). Thus the substantive, or the substantive
state, is the currency of memory. It has temporal dimension and is
concerned with lasting visual images, "sensorial imaginings" (p. 243),
while transitive states or verbs, prepositions, conjunctions, and so on,
are not available to memory.

The implications of this classification for Stein should be obvious.
If "entity" is the individual in a state of perception in which memory
does not operate, then substantive states of mind will of necessity be
absent and substantives themselves will be eliminated for the purposes of representation. Transitive words, on the other hand, will be
favored since they express pure flux, the state of motion itself without regard to the beginnings or endpoints of the process.

It is interesting that James himself seemed to favor these transitive
words, not in his own writing, of course, but in theory. For they
have an additional quality which struck him as particularly mimetic
of thought. We recall that one of James's primary notions about
thought was that it was in constant flux and that no two thoughts
were ever precisely the same. Since many of the transitive words
have the ability to appear in different shapes, or to have the same
shape and refer to different phenomena—to be "shifters," as the
modern linguistic term stresses—they reflect materially the changes
of thought. English nouns, on the other hand, are invariable except
for the plural and the possessive, and thus present a problem which
James discusses as follows: "What, after all, is so natural as to assume
that one object, called by one name, should be known by one affection of the mind? But if language must thus influence us, the agglu-
tinative languages, and even Greek and Latin with their declensions,
would be the better guides. Names did not appear in them inalter-
able, but changed their shape to suit the context in which they lay.
It must have been easier then than now to conceive of the same
object as being thought of at different times in non-identical conscious states" (pp. 236–37). Because of this Ronald Bartlett Levinson
concludes from Stein's enthusiasm for verbs and shifters that "among
the virtues attributed to them is the truly Jamesian excellence that

they move and change, thus manifesting their relative adequacy to the changeful 'stream of consciousness'" (p. 127). "Most if not all of Miss Stein's writing which resembles in form and content the early automatic writing, is the attempt to put into practice some notions of the ideal function of language, notions which were in all probability derived from . . . William James" (p. 125).

It might well be true to say that Stein's fascination with language was the most abiding of all her literary interests. It entered her work not only insofar as writing technique was concerned, but also as subject matter. She clearly felt that "being existing," thinking, the human essence, were tied up with language: "I like the feeling the everlasting feeling of sentences as they diagram themselves. In that way one is completely possessing something and incidentally one's self" ("Poetry and Grammar," p. 211).

This diagramming of sentences is, of course, the old-style parsing into sentence elements, and Stein, as already stated, had very particular views about the different parts of speech. She criticized the noun, for example, for being less changeable than its referent:

> A noun is a name of anything, why after a thing is named write about it. A name is adequate or it is not. If it is adequate then why go on calling it, if it is not then calling it by its name does no good.
> . . . things once they are named the name does not go on doing anything to them and so why write in nouns. [pp. 209–10]

> As I say a noun is a name of a thing, and therefore slowly if you feel what is inside that thing you do not call it by the name by which it is known. Everybody knows that by the way they do when they are in love and a writer should always have that intensity of emotion about whatever is the object about which he writes. [p. 210]

Stein also objects to the noun because it refers to classes and hence involves memory:

> The Georges whom I have known have been pleasant not uninteresting and finally one and finally more often very well estimated as succeeding intelligibly and not more than is necessary as presidents are useful. They are useful in extremes. So can there be doubt of Pauls Christians Virgils and Williams and

> even Franks and Michaels and James and pleasures. [*How To Write*, p. 289]

As it happens, most of the names Stein uses here were of particular friends or acquaintances of hers—Christian Bérard, Virgil Thomson, Paul Draper, etc.—some of whom she had used as the subjects of her portraits. Yet in the passage just quoted these individuals, or any individuals for that matter, are lost from sight; the names refer to general categories, as general as the word "pleasures" which is used in parallel with them. (The singular "James," is a counter-case—an individual that seems, paradoxically, to be a class.) Categories involve comparison, resemblance, and memory, and are hence unsuitable for portrait immediacy. As Stein puts it, "A noun should always be replaced by now" (p. 180).

However, just as the class quality of the noun (and even the name in the above quotation) presents a problem for the writer, the particularity of the name—its indexicality—can be an equal difficulty. "If there is a name in a sentence a name which is familiar makes a data [sic] and therefor [sic] there is no equilibrium" (p. 167). That is, a familiar name has a peculiarly marked referential value—it "makes a data." Because of this, the balance of the rest of the sentence, created by considerations of sound, syntax, and some play of sense, is disrupted, for the attention of the perceiver is drawn from the structure of the sentence to some datum of reality and the mode of the sentence shifts from the aesthetic to the referential. Stein managed to overcome this difficulty at first by limiting her use of names to the titles of portraits,[20] where they performed their necessary indexical function without disturbing the balance of the text.

Nouns were not alone in receiving Stein's scrutiny. In "Poetry and Grammar" she discussed all the other parts of speech as well, except for adjectives—"after all adjectives effect [sic] nouns and as nouns are not really interesting the thing that effects a not too interesting thing is of necessity not interesting" (p. 211)—and interjections, which "have nothing to do with anything not even with themselves" (p. 214). However, verbs, adverbs, conjunctions, prepositions, pronouns, and articles were Stein's delight because of their ability to be "mistaken":

---

20. See the interesting exception to this in "If I Told Him—A Completed Portrait of Picasso" (1923) in which the name "Napoleon" appears over and over.

Nouns and adjectives never can make mistakes can never be mistaken but verbs can be so endlessly, both as to what they do and how they agree or disagree with whatever they do. [pp. 211-12]

Besides being able to be mistaken and to make mistakes verbs can change to look like themselves or to look like something else, they are, so to speak on the move and adverbs move with them and each of them find themselves not at all annoying but very often very much mistaken. . . . Then comes the thing that can of all things be most mistaken and they are prepositions. Prepositions can live one long life being really being nothing but absolutely nothing but mistaken and that makes them irritating if you feel that way about mistakes but certainly something that you can be continuously using and everlastingly enjoying. . . .

Then there are articles. . . . They are interesting because they do what a noun might do if a noun was not so unfortunately so completely unfortunately the name of something. Articles please, a and an and the please as the name that follows cannot please . . . an article remains as a delicate and a varied something and any one who wants to write with articles and knows how to use them will always have the pleasure that using something that is varied and alive can give. That is what articles are.

Beside that there are conjunctions, and a conjunction is not varied but it has a force that need not make any one feel that they are dull. Conjunctions have made themselves live by their work. . . .

Of course then there are pronouns. Pronouns are not as bad as nouns because in the first place practically they cannot have adjectives go with them. . . .

Then . . . they of course are not really the name of anything. They represent some one but they are not its or his name. In not being his or its or her name they already have a greater possibility of being something than if they were as a noun. . . . [pp. 212-14]

"Being something" for a part of speech is thus its ability to be changeable, to create referential or grammatical mistakes. Rather than being a transparent sign of some object in reality, such words, especially as used by Stein, become objects in themselves and enter concrete relations of balance or disequilibrium with other words in the sentence. Throughout *How To Write*, which is much more a

demonstration than an explication of its title, Stein delights in saying "I made a mistake" (p. 21), for "A word which is in any sentence
is made to be confused with elegant and with inadvertence. But not
with speed nor with mainly. . . . It all comes back to partly and what
they do. It all comes back to known and negligence" (p. 199). The
multiple word plays—"partly"/"parts," "known"/"noun"—and the
constant 'misuse' of parts of speech create a tangible word texture,
as well as suggesting many associations for each word.

Stein carries even further this insistence on the tangibility of the
word, its existence as a self-enclosed entity, and on the sentence as
a special balance or "equilibrium" of these objects: "A sentence
should not refer make it a reference to hyacinths or bulls or their
kind or equivalent it should refer to beauty and decision it should
also have contentment it should never think a sentence should never
think of letting well enough alone" (p. 186). This denial of direct
reference is a reflection of Stein's switch from conventional or symbolic reference to mimesis. The distinction between the two was a
great discovery for her: "I became more and more excited about how
words which were the words that made whatever I looked at look
like itself were not the words that had in them any quality of description . . . words that to me very exactly related themselves to
that thing the thing at which I was looking . . . as often as not had
as I say nothing whatever to do with what any words would do that
described that thing" ("Portraits and Repetition," pp. 191–92).

What Stein intended to achieve by the reification of her words and
sentences was not to do away with a referential subject, to obliterate
the sign-function of language, but to create a text which would be
mimetically adequate to her subject. Each of her sentences was to be
a self-contained unit with a particularly intense internal make-up,
just as each perceptual 'now' was to be isolated and intense. If each
moment of perception was linked to the next only through the continuity of the *quality* of the perception, each sentence was likewise linked
to the next not by a continuity of sense or reference but by the con-
stancy of *aesthetic perception* created by the very structure of the sentence itself. The unit of perception or thought is parallel to the sentence,
and the intensity of now-perception is produced by the intricate, enclosed balance or equilibrium which Stein planned in her sentences.

This notion of sentence balance refers properly to the portraiture
of entity and the continuous present. Before this, Stein created
rhythmic sentences and paragraphs as a complement to her "rhythm
of personality." Not only did these sentences largely repeat one another, but so did their elements—words, sounds, and syntactic

configurations. The regularity of these recurrences produced a rhythm rather than a balance.

The need for "balance" rather than "rhythm" in the entity phase of Stein's writing caused the 'transitive' wording of the earlier period to give way to a use of all the parts of speech. For Stein had made several discoveries with regard to the noun that enabled her to use it in portraiture. First, she began to see that nouns could be made to make 'mistakes' too. An example of this occurs in the following paragraph of *How To Write*:

Name names familiar famish a trump he is a triumph of the James is an even invented cordially a loosen loosening a grown growing give obstinate with her with an appointing it is about time cousin decent deceive deserve district displace deserve does and delight. . . . [p. 375]

This passage not only demonstrates how nouns can be mistaken—by sound similarity ("trump"/"triumph"), by acting as other parts of speech ("name"/"names"), and by having other parts of speech act like them ("a grown")—but also describes this process, although admittedly in a rather obscure way. Names or nouns become a Jamesian "triumph" in the phrases, "a loosen loosening" and "a grown growing," which at once demonstrate the process of extending an established category and describe it—as "loosening" and "growing." Further, to "deceive" the "decent" (with Stein's spelling this could as easily be "descent," the history of the name) and to "displace" the "district" (the field of meaning in which the word operates) "deserves" to be done—"does"—because it will "delight." If this reading-in of meaning is unconvincing, it is at least true to observe that Stein did use nouns and that they apparently served a vital need. When we remember that James singled out the subject of a sentence as creating acquaintance, we can understand the renewed importance of the noun, especially in its 'mistaken' forms, in a portraiture of entity.

Furthermore, at the same time that Stein was concerned with entity, as she explains in "Portraits and Repetition," she conceived a new interest in visuality, which had presented itself first as a problem within her system of ideas. "The trouble with including looking . . . was that in regard to human beings looking inevitably carried in its train realizing movements and expression and as such forced me into recognizing resemblances, and so forced remembering and in forcing remembering caused confusion of present with past and future time" (p. 188). "In writing the thing that is the difficulty is the question of confusing time" (p. 189).

The addition of looking to the other faculties of now-perception—listening and talking—was an expansion of Stein's concept of perception. Where before she had systematically excluded certain questions in order to be as precise as possible in exploring her notion of entity and creativity, now she was forced to consider the factor of visuality, of separate, independent objects. But visuality seemed to involve the stasis of nouns, substantive expanses of thought, memory and resemblance, and a conflicting (non-mimetic)[21] time sense—in short, identity. Problematic as this was, she had now come to the point where she "needed to completely face the difficulty of how to include what is seen with hearing and listening . . ." ("Portraits and Repetition," p. 189).

In order to do this, she distinguished two kinds of visual perception parallel to the two modes of thought: the visuality of concept, category, and resemblance, and that of immediate perception. She saw the first as created by description, and the second by the discovery of a direct correspondence between the sense aspect of the word—its sound—and the visuality of the object: "I began to wonder at at about this time just what one saw when one looked at anything really looked at anything. Did one see sound, and what was the relation between color and sound, did it make itself by description by a word that meant it or did it make itself by a word in itself" (p. 191). The answer, of course, was that "it made itself by a word in itself," a concrete object open to the senses. This eventually led Stein into experiments with synesthesia, where the moving force of her portraiture was a sometimes rollicking, sometimes rapturous sound play.

The problem with this second stage of portraiture was that Stein finally became so interested in the purely musical properties of

21. The importance of exact correspondence between the time sense of the reader and of the work caused Stein to characterize both the novel and drama as non-mimetic from a temporal standpoint, and hence as flawed art forms. For "the business of Art . . . is to live in the actual present, that is the complete actual present, and to completely express that complete actual present" ("Plays," *Lectures in America*, pp. 104–05). The fact that the "complete actual present" refers both to the contemporary world and the actual time sense of the present is not an accident for Stein. She believed that the sense of time in the modern world is what we have been terming 'now-perception,' a high-pitched, intense creativity of the self, so that the modern mode for art is a mode mimetic of this special time sense, a mode that eliminates any confusion or conflict of time in perception.

words that she began to ignore her subjects, and hence the portrait situation, as she herself admits in "Portraits and Repetition" (pp. 197–98). Her reaction to this error was to impose a severe discipline upon herself. As a result, in the final phase of portraiture, in such works as "George Hugnet," "All the looking was there the talking and listening was there but instead of giving what I was realizing at any and every moment of them and of me until I was empty of them I made them contained within the thing I wrote that was them" (pp. 199–200). This is the final stage of an indexical-iconic program, for the intention here is to produce a portrait sign that does not work mediately, but instead, immediately, so that a perception of the sign functions as a perception of the subject himself. Though such a claim about a literary work begins to sound a bit mystical, it is the pushing toward this impossible state that is significant in Stein's ideas, as we saw before with her ideas about time. She herself felt that she had achieved both a conception of the individual and a technique for rendering him that were logically consistent and 'true' to her perception. As an intellectual exercise, this development represented a very complex quasi-scientific process of fitting theory and technique to precise observation. Seldom has any author examined and experimented with the possibilities of a genre so consciously, and no one but Stein has ever done so with the literary portrait.

3

The Portraits: Three Phases

> She has written portraits of practically everybody she has known, and
> written them in all manners and in all styles.
>
> *The Autobiography of Alice B. Toklas*

Stein's elaborate theories of portraiture take on added significance
when compared to her portrait texts. For the technical means by
which she put these ideas into practice were of necessity startlingly
original, a brilliant implementation of abstract requirements.

Unfortunately, it is sometimes difficult to tell precisely which of
her works are in fact portraits, partly because of her capricious use
of genre designations, as in the title, "A Play Without Roses—Portrait
of Eugene Jolas," and partly because of her periodic merging of
genres. The early novels, for example, may be seen as extended portraits; one would be hard put to discover a generic difference between *G.M.P.* and the 150 page portrait, "Two."[1] Stein even calls
the descriptions of *Tender Buttons* "portraits of rooms and food and
everything" ("Portraits and Repetition," p. 188). Though these extensions of the portrait designation are troublesome, they reveal the
central position of portraiture in Stein's thinking, an issue to be discussed at length in chapter 5.

For the purpose of the present chapter, however, it is desirable to
eliminate as many figurative uses of the term 'portrait' as possible.
Tender Buttons, then, is not a group of portraits because it has no
human subjects. The early works, *Things As They Are, Three Lives,*
and *The Making of Americans,* are not portraits but novels (or nov-
ellas), in that they are narratives and their subjects are fictionalized,
that is, their names are changed and they operate in an imaginary,
though 'realistic,' space. *G.M.P.*, which calls its subjects by their real

1. The assumption that "Two" is a portrait and *G.M.P.* is not is based more or less on
critical tradition and Stein's feeling that "Two" was a portrait. In "The Gradual Making of
The Making of Americans," however, the two works are treated in parallel: "I began several
shorter books which were to illustrate the Long Gay Book, one called Many Many Women
another Five, another Two and another G.M.P, Matisse Picasso and Gertrude Stein . . ."
(p. 148).

names, is certainly a borderline case, but its length and Stein's description of it as a separate "book" lead us to place it with the early novels.

There are then approximately 132 portraits[2] within Stein's oeuvre, written with varying frequency from 1908 to her death in 1946. They may be divided into three distinct periods based upon the scheme set forth in the last chapter: the typologizing portraits, written from 1908–1911 (with some works appearing as late as 1913), the visually-oriented period, beginning in earnest in 1913 and lasting until approximately 1925 (with a few works as early as 1911), and the last period, 1926–46, in which the portrait of "self-contained movement" appeared along with works of other styles. This outline differs only slightly from Stein's chronology in "Portraits and Repetition," and will be justified as we proceed.

I

Within the early period there are thirty-six portraits, of which seventeen are group portraits and nineteen are portraits of individuals. (See appendix 2, below.) It is the group portraits that are the most problematic from the point of view of definitional or generic concerns. In only two cases do the titles of these works name their subjects: once in the sub-title of "Two. Gertrude Stein and Her Brother"[3] and again in "Jenny, Helen, Hannah, Paul, and Peter" where, however, the names are fictitious (see appendix) and no attempt is made to indicate which sentences in the text pertain to which subject. Five group portraits[4] are named for places which presumably unite the people in them into a coherent group; but at least one of these, "Rue de Rennes," appears to have so little discernible connection between its title and body that rather desperate biographical attempts have

2. I am eliminating a number of works which are either generically indeterminate or which have been called portraits for no discernible reason. It is hard to see, for example, why "Look At Us," "Universe or Hand-Reading," and several other pieces should have been included in the chapter of *Painted Lace* called "Portraits."

3. The manuscripts suggest that it was not Gertrude but Sarah Stein that was the subject of this portrait, along with Leo. However the content of the portrait seems directly autobiographical.

4. "Rue de Rennes," *Two: Gertrude Stein and Her Brother and Other Early Portraits (1908–1912)* (New Haven, 1951), p. 349; "Bon Marché Weather," *ibid.*, p. 351; "Flirting at the Bon Marché," *ibid.*, p. 353; "Galeries Lafayettes," *Portraits and Prayers* (New York, 1934), p. 169; "Mi-Careme," *ibid.*, p. 173.

been made to explain it.[5] Though such extra-textual explanations
have on occasion revealed very plausible models for some of the
group portraits,[6] they are not, of course, available to the reader.
Thus, "Men" or "Five or Six Men" can hardly be perceived as portraits proper, even though it seems obvious from the texts that specific people and events are involved. With "Italians," any assumption
of specificity must be abandoned.

These difficulties can be partially explained by Stein's early typologizing of character, positing a person's essence in his shared "bottom nature." Donald Gallup suggests further that Stein was forced to
mask her subjects' identity because of the frequently scandalous or
insulting nature of her portraits, while the opacity of the later style
obviated this necessity.

The early portraits of individuals, on the other hand, are more consistent with genre norms, though two of them—"Ada" and "Orta or
One Dancing"—use fictitious names for their subjects.[7] Here external
information is necessary to confirm the most basic premise for portrait perception—the fact that the subject is a real person.

But even when the title of the portrait is actually the subject's
name, one feels a need for extra-textual information. Who are the
Russell, Chalfin, Hessel, Pach of the early portraits? One critic voices
such a complaint even about Stein's "Picasso" (1909): "We would
not even know from the portrait that Picasso was a painter."[8] This
sort of dissatisfaction stems from the expectations created by

5. Janet Flanner, Introduction to *Two*, p. xiii. Stein herself seemed dissatisfied with this
portrait and the one following it, "Bon Marché Weather." After "Rue de Rennes" in the
manuscript version she wrote, presumably to Alice Toklas: "Dearest, This is a trial, I have
no idea what its like and very much doubt if it tells the story. If not I will try it again. . . ."
Toklas's response must have been quite negative, for Stein wrote at the end of the 'second
try,' "Bon Marché Weather": "Dearest, I wish I had been good and not written this, first
place because I would have liked to obey you, second place because its *rotten*."

6. E.g., the discussion of "Men" by James R. Mellow in *The Charmed Circle* (New York,
1974), p. 136.

7. *The Autobiography of Alice B. Toklas* (hereafter, *Toklas*), p. 114, informs us that Ada
is Alice, although any biographical knowledge of Stein at all would make this a likely assumption: "It was the portrait called Ada, the first in Geography and Plays. I began [to
read] it and I thought she was making fun of me and I protested, she says I protest now
about my autobiography. Finally I read it all and was terribly pleased with it." As for
"Orta," Stein tried out the following titles for the portrait in her manuscript: "Alma Davray" (crossed out), "Orta Davray," and "Isadora Dora Do. Ra." These titles and the fact
that the portrait is about a dancer have suggested that the text is about Isadora Duncan
(Bridgman, p. 96*n*).

8. Michael J. Hoffman, *The Development of Abstractionism in the Writings of Gertrude
Stein* (Philadelphia, 1965), p. 165.

traditional literary portraits which proceed by supplying "knowledge-about." The indexical portrait by definition never identifies its subject in this way.

A further obstacle to portrait perception for several critics has been the seemingly uniform effect created by the "film technique" of the continuous present. Bridgman, for example, says: "The rest of the early portraits, like 'Roche,' 'Julia Marlowe,' and 'Russell' are of minimal interest, because in them Gertrude Stein tried to eliminate as many specifics as possible in order to create a uniform prose surface" (p. 96). This cart-before-the-horse picture, with stylistics dominating reference, or perhaps with stylistics as a kind of thematics, constitutes a serious criticism of the early portraits, for the works mentioned are among the most typical of the period. If the representational function is inoperative here, the status of all the early portraits is in question, for we have claimed that portraiture is definitionally a blend of aesthetic and referential norms. I shall try to show that both are in play in the early portraits in the discussion that follows.

First of all, the manuscripts reveal that Stein conceived of her portrait subjects under a series of *thematic* headings. This fact is apparent in breaks in the manuscript where she stopped writing for the day and jotted down instructions to herself for the next day's continuation of the portrait.[9] A typical example occurs in the first volume of the manuscript of "Five or Six Men," between what became the first and second paragraphs of p. 262 of *Two*: "Go on to his love adventures and his intellect and his loyalties and his sentimentalities and ideas and conventions. . . ." The frequency with which such instructions can be found in the early portrait phase indicates rather conclusively that Stein propelled her texts by thematic shifts rather than by a simple stylistic intention.

These thematic headings appear in the manuscript of the very first portrait, "A Man," which takes a very conventional 'evidential' stance in describing its subject in terms of what he does. The typicality of this procedure can be seen in the subtitle of the portrait of Isadora Duncan, "Orta Or One Dancing," where the activity and the name are simply alternatives for identifying the subject.

"A Man" begins:

He was interested in eating. He was a very fat one. He had been

---

9. I am grateful to Mr. Donald Gallup for pointing out these manuscript notations.

> When he had been a thin one he was not trying being a fat one. He was not then trying the being a thin one, he was not then trying being a fat one or a very thin one, he was then coming to be an enormously fat one. When he was a very thin one he was pretty nearly completely trying that thing trying being a very thin one. He was completely trying being a very thin one when he was being a very thin one. He went on with this thing he went on being a thin one. . . . [p. 236]

Does "then" mean 'at that time,' 'after that,' or 'as a result of that'? When we hear that "he was not then trying being a fat one or a very thin one" are we to think that he was trying to be a slightly thin one, or that he was not trying to be anything? And what is the relation between "trying" and "being a thin one"? Syntactically they are co-temporal—"When he was a very thin one he was . . . trying being a thin one." But "trying" implies temporal-causal priority: first you try and then the result is achieved. If this is not the situation described, and the "trying" and "being" are semantically as well as syntactically co-temporal, then the "trying" is aimed at some other future "being," though it is accompanied by a related present "being." The ambiguity and complexity of this simple pair of verbs is another illustration of Stein's disruption of relationality in normal language use.

However, unconventional as its treatment of time may be, this portrait has narrative traits. Statements such as "He was then completing having been living" (p. 252) imply that the temporal scope of the portrait is a lifetime. Furthermore, the dominance of different verbs in various portions of the portrait suggests phases of activity which have beginnings and ends.

Another conventional feature is the presence of value-laden adjectives. We find the sequence: "He was then one two were supporting in being one completely having been living. He was enormously fat then. He was exciting" (p. 252). Being "living" obviously has a special meaning in Stein's work, and "exciting" is found throughout the early portraits as a positively charged word. It describes the interaction between the subject and those who perceive him at a 'power' above the ordinary; a person who is able to produce this effect is a suitable portrait subject. As we shall see later, Stein develops a large number of such special words which function similarly from portrait to portrait.

Furthermore, the traits of character which Stein was considering at "coming after" or "operating in a succession." The two meanings work together to insist on "succeeding" as a process rather than the reaching of an end point. Thus, to have been "succeeding" but not to be "going on being living" suggests that one has had a 'success' rather than that one's life is characterized by "succeeding." This double implication of the word operates throughout the first-phase portraits.

The next paragraph of "Five or Six Men," in contrast, exhaustively lists all the similarities among the men: "They were all ones naturally succeeding in living" (p. 253), "Very many could believe in them. . . . They were honest ones" (p. 254). Their likeness is stated here in terms of acts, characteristics, and the attitudes of others toward them.

Following these statements of group similarity come others which emphasize the uniqueness of each in sharing these qualities: "Each one of them was a sad one. . . . Each one of them was one feeling something" (p. 254). Such constructions, used in most of the early works, are epitomized in the statement, "Some are wonderful ones" (p. 342) in "Chalfin," another early portrait. Here, the major categorizing term of the piece, "wonderful," contains "one" phonologically as its first syllable. Being wonderful is being unique, but paradoxically "some" have this quality.

The development up to this point in "Five or Six Men" is from statements of difference, to similarities, to uniqueness in similarity through the construction, "each one of them." This dialectical solution to the relation between individual and type is refined and elaborated in the following paragraph:

> They are each one of them very solidly doing that thing that is being one. They are, each one of them, solidly doing that thing doing being one. They each one of them solidly do do that thing, do do being one. Each one of them is one, they are solidly doing that thing, each one, they are solidly being one. [p. 256]

Not only are the individual and his group related through such grammatical forms as the constantly repeated "each one of them," but they are shown to be fundamentally linked through their activity. This activity—what they do—is "being one," and the whole construction of the paragraph creates a special bridge between "doing" and "being."

The first sentence of the paragraph has each of them "doing that thing that is being one." The activity is a "thing" equivalent to "being one." In the second sentence, the "thing" is "doing being one" where the activity and the state are ungrammatically combined. This is next varied as "do do being one," equally ungrammatically though more emphatically stated. The core sentence gradually developed by these first three sentences is equivalent to 'Each does being each' where the subject and object are virtually identical and the "does" and the "being" are equivalent. It is a rather nice chiasmus where the actor is also the acted upon, and the act and the result of the act are simultaneous.

Much of this effect, of course, depends upon the presence of the gerund "being" with its combinations of verbal and substantive qualities. The whole force of the first three sentences is to make "being" an engaged activity, rather than a state, resulting in the unique self. The self is in process as well, constantly in the process of self-creation. The seeming contradiction here in the time-status of the self— a being becoming—is a demonstration of the conflict between the noun as a kind of identification-judgment dependent on fixed time categories and the verbal, indicating incompletion and process and not associated with fixed points of time.

The final sentence of the paragraph is the resolution of the elements of the problem into conventional grammar: "Each one of them is one"—identity and reflexiveness; "they are solidly doing that thing, each one"—activity; "they are solidly being one"—activity as state of being. But this dissolution of the non-grammatical core sentence loses the important semantic complexity of the formulation, substituting finally a progressive present "is . . . being" for the gerund in "does being."

Critics have discussed the importance of the gerund in Stein's work at great length. Bridgman, for example, writes:

> Gertrude Stein had early utilized the progressive form of the verb to extend the action. 'As I said' became 'As I was saying.' But subject and verb were still separated.
>
> Gertrude Stein's escape from this was the gerund, which at once represents an entity and a continuous action. Unity and movement were fused in what for a time became her favorite word-form. Her shift from narratives to portraits has its equivalent in her replacement of a noun and verb with a gerund. [p. 97]

The importance of this observation to the paragraph which we have been considering should be obvious. Stein was clearly experimenting here with the possibilities of the gerund, locating the minimal conditions for transforming a present progressive into a 'gerund act'—the replacement of the copular auxiliary in "is being" by the most colorless verb of action "do." By this simple syntactic divergence, Stein was able to describe the state of shared uniqueness which she had posited in "Five or Six Men" as existing among individuals. Their similarity is their shared activity of self-creation and individuation.

The relation between this essential human activity and the specific activities of individuals was defined in a special way in Stein's early portraiture. We might remember first of all the importance of the verb and of transitive states of thought in her ideas about rendering the subject as thinker. Very often she seems to have chosen one verb as particularly characteristic of her subject and to have repeated it throughout his portrait. This repetition has led to criticisms of her abstraction and uninformativeness (Bridgman, p. 96). Yet the evidence provided by those who knew the subject often stresses the accuracy of such verb-oriented portraiture. Kahnweiler writes of "Picasso" (1909), for example: "The *Leitmotiv* of the 'Picasso' . . . the 'This one was working'—strikes truly at the crux of the problem of the man and the painter Picasso, who lives only in order to work and is unhappy when he is not working."[13] Yet even with such true life testimony, a portraiture based upon the association of one man and one verb does not seem very promising. However, this is not an accurate description of the use of verbs and acts and their relation to self-creation in Stein's work. We should look more closely at what occurs in "Picasso."

An extremely unhesitant portrait, "Picasso" is composed largely of declarative sentences, "completely"s, and "certainly"s, and is relatively unbothered by qualifications, contradictions, or negations. The 'facts' of the portrait are as follows: Picasso had a following, he was charming (to a variety of degrees), the following knew he was working and bringing something out of himself, the "something" was "heavy," "solid," "complete," and meaningful, Picasso needed to work for the sake of working rather than for the thing produced, and he never worked "completely." The leitmotiv, then, is not simply that Picasso was working, but a whole set of modifications of this activity. Moreover, "working" is equated with Picasso's very reason for living, with his basic self-creation: "This one was one who was

---

13. Daniel-Henry Kahnweiler, Introduction to *Painted Lace* (New Haven, 1955), p. xi.

working and he was one needing this thing needing to be working so
as to be one having some way of being one having some way of working" (*Portraits and Prayers,* p. 17). He worked because he had to
work and he had to work in order to be one working.

The nature of this working was his "bringing something out of himself." Even lacking knowledge of Picasso's painting one would recognize this as some form of creative activity.[14] The product of this
activity is "a heavy thing" (p. 17; a precursor of the modern slang
"heavy"?) as well as "a solid thing, a charming thing, a lovely thing,
a perplexing thing, a disconcerting thing, a simple thing, a clear thing,
a complicated thing, an interesting thing, a disturbing thing, a repel-
lant thing, a very pretty thing."[15] Most of these adjectives, especially
the participial ones, reflect the interaction between the work and its
audience; they are in fact both judgmental of the work and descriptive of this interaction. But especially noteworthy is the fact that the
adjective "charming" is applied both to the work and to its creator,
and, as we learn, to the meaning of the work: "it had meaning, a
charming meaning. . . ." Were it not for this correspondence, the depiction of Picasso in the first paragraph as "a charming one" would
be a sort of throw-away, not appearing anywhere else in this portrait
so full of repetitions. Now logically, if a person creates both things
and himself, then both products of the same creator would naturally
be alike, in this case "charming." And we might note a similar equation in the portrait "Hessel" where the subject is described as "solid,"
his manner of "telling" as "solidly," and the satisfaction he thus
created in others as a "solid thing" (*Two*, p. 348).

The equivalence of "working" and "being," of the created identity
and the created artefact, has important implications throughout the
early portraits. For almost half of the early portraits are certainly of
artists, and several unidentified subjects might easily have been artists
as well. If a creator and his creation are alike, then an assessment of
his work can stand for an assessment of him; artistic judgment and
character appraisal seem to go hand in hand. And because artistic
judgment usually implies comparison among works of art, new

14. Bridgman points out a passage of *Tender Buttons* in which there is a punning association of "creation" and "excretion," p. 131.

15. *Ibid.,* p. 18. The contradictions in this catalogue are consistent with Stein's notion of
great art—that it is beautiful because it shows the struggle of its making and because it dis-
turbs the viewer. Stein explains this in *Picasso* (1938), in "Pictures" (*Lectures in America*),
and elsewhere.

standards of character judgment are implied as well.[16] For this reason, it is possible to read many of these portraits inter-textually, understanding their subjects in relation to each other, and deriving meaning for common descriptive words from their uses in several contexts. In this way, the original "working" which struck Kahnweiler as such a good way to depict Picasso is the link between the human act and the human state, between the group and the creative individual—the epitome of the latter for Stein being Picasso.

Though in "Picasso" the association of creative "working" and self-creative "being" leads to a very clear-cut depiction of Picasso, this cannot be said of many other portraits. For example, in "Matisse," written in the same year and style, the difficulty of arriving at a judgment is very apparent on the part of the outside world, the subject himself, and the portraitist:

> Some said that he did not clearly express anything. Some were certain that he expressed something very clearly. . . . [*Portraits and Prayers*, p. 12]

> One [Matisse] was quite certain that for a long part of his being one being living he had been trying to be certain that he was wrong in doing what he was doing. . . . [p. 12]

> This one was one, some were quite certain, one greatly expressing something being struggling. This one was one, some were quite certain, one not greatly expressing something being struggling. [p. 16]

The portrait ends with this contradiction, the author offering no resolution but the stated irresolution. This problematics of character—and art—judgment was an unstated theme throughout the early

16. The importance of the element of appraisal in describing both people and works of art can be seen in Stein's notion of the artist as one who has "made something that is to be measured." Her notes indicate that she was in fact thinking of Picasso in comparison to others when she wrote his portrait (Mellow, p. 157): "Do one about Pablo his emotional leap and courage as opposed to the lack of courage in Cezanne and me. His laziness and his lack of continuity and his facility too quick for the content which ought to be so complete to do what he wants to do. Too lazy to do sculpture. His work is not because it is too strong for him to resist but because his resistance is not great. Cezanne's resistance great but dragged along. Pablo is never dragged, he walks in the light and a little ahead of himself like Raphael, therefore his things often lack a base. Do him."

portraits, particulary in portraits of artists. And in fact Stein's concern with this question can be dated from the very earliest of the portraits, "A Man," where her manuscript jottings read: "A man of genius is what. is it David. Is he an artist, is he not" (ms. 3, vol. 1, *YCAL*). Such stress on the process of arriving at a character judgment, as we noted in chapter 1, is a common strategy in portraiture, where the portrait is sometimes an imitation of the thoughts in the portraitist's progress toward judgment.

Stein approached the problem of judgment in a variety of ways. For example, in the group portrait "Four Protégés" the very word "protégé" is chosen to imply the relation between assessment and prediction: "Four are ones some one has been selecting to be ones succeeding in living" (*Two*, p. 305). Throughout the portrait, Stein tries to test the prediction against her own contrary judgment that "Four certainly are not going to be succeeding in living, not really succeeding in living." The problem of the protégés is that of all people with a goal, that is, people trying to "succeed." For we have seen that to be an artist is, for Stein, not a generalization about one's activity but a value-laden state. To depict a young "artist" one is inevitably involved in predictions about the promise of his art.

Presented with this difficulty, Stein began to use her portraits to analyze the problem itself. In "Pach," for example, she demonstrates the inadequacy of logic in proceeding from empirical evidence in the present to a judgmental prediction of the future. The portrait begins by considering the possibility of Pach's "succeeding," stated as two identical conclusions dependent on contradictory conditions:

> If he is a young one now he will perhaps be succeeding very well in living. If he is not a young one now he will perhaps be succeeding well in living. [*Two*, p. 338]

Then come the empirical fact, "He is a young one now," and the logical conclusion, "Perhaps he will be succeeding well in living." Apparently youth simply opens the possibility for success, present at any age, and we are no closer to a definite prediction.

Next, Stein tries to make an inventory of what is "certain" about Pach, but even here little is definite: "Certainly he is believing in being a lonesome one. Certainly he is not believing in being a lonesome one." In the third paragraph, Stein contrasts the status of the prediction with that of the empirical observation. She states twice with slight variations that Pach may be going to succeed in living—the tentative prediction—and then contrasts this with the facts: "He certainly is now still a young one. It would be very easy to be certain that he is now not a young one." The statement of fact is certain and open to verification; the judgmental prediction is not.

Then Stein tries to decide whether her subject is "persevering."

> When something has happened and he has been hurt by that thing and he does not at all then know it inside him that he has been hurt by that thing he is not persevering. When something has been happening that has hurt him and he knows that he has been hurt by that thing he is completely persevering.

"Persevering" is related to knowledge and self-awareness, and if it is necessary to persevere in order to succeed then knowledge is also a prerequisite of success. Therefore, Stein turns to the possibility of Pach's knowing. She considers his wisdom, what he thinks of as beautiful or desirable. She is certain that he is one "feeding on needing it that he would be a wise one" (p. 339). Thus, at least as far as Pach's intent is concerned, he will seek out knowledge and succeed. But mere intent is not a guarantee either, for Stein proceeds to restate the previous generalities that perseverence is dependent upon self-knowledge. Such knowledge, then, remains merely a possibility.

Next, Stein recreates the tangle of conditions and predictions, but this time with physical variables:

> He was sometimes pretty nearly a white thin one. He was sometimes a quite white one, he was not ever quite a thin one. He certainly could come to be not at all a thin one, he certainly would always be quite a white one. He could have been not a white one not at all a white one. He could not ever be not more or less a white one.

Here we have concomitant factors, "thin" and "white," which float in a realm of possible relations where predictions are impossible to make. Stein is providing a physical analogue with most of the tenses and verbal modes of the psychological situation in order to illustrate the disjunction between empirical certainties and judgmental predictions.

She retreats from this impasse finally, by ignoring the future altogether:

> It was certainly an important thing that he was one being living.

> Certainly very many were knowing something that they would
> not have been knowing if he had not been one being living. . . .
> He was one completing living being existing. . . . He was one
> completing anything and recording that thing. [pp. 339–40]

This is high praise from Stein, for she is saying in effect that Pach
fulfills the conditions for being called an artist. Yet as a final resolution of the dilemma of this portrait, it seems to imply that only present facts are open to judgment, and that a judgment in the present
need not imply anything about the future.

A similar and even more graphic presentation of this dilemma occurs in "Roche," but whereas in "Pach" it seems that at least judgmental statements about the present based on empirical observations
are possible, here even this is placed in doubt. "Roche" begins with
two questions: "was this one a complete one" and did he have it in
him to do something well" (*Geography and Plays,* p. 141); the first
calls for a present judgment, the second for a predictive one. As soon
as Stein tries to answer the first question, however, difficulties arise.
She says that Roche is a complete one, at least "certainly he was one
completely listening." But immediately his being "completely listening" is restated as a question, since it depends upon a judgment about
completeness. And on this judgment depends the further judgment as
to whether "it is a pleasant thing."

The portrait proceeds, supplying factual certainties and exploring
possibilities and logical dependencies. It is remarkable in containing
one of the very few question marks in all of Stein's work, in "Was
this one a complete one?" of the second paragraph. But after covering the inventory of knowledge and relations, the portrait ends:

> Certainly if this one is one really completely listening and cer-
> tainly perhaps this one is one completely listening then that is
> a completely pleasant thing. [p. 143]

The only certainty is the interdependence of these factors, and it is
the particular set of factors and relations, of facts and conditions,
that apparently characterizes Roche. This extremely dynamic notion of the individual and of the nature of knowledge of him shows
the complexity of Stein's character depiction in the early portraits.

A variant of this dilemma of judgment is the problem of knowing
whether an activity or trait of a subject is the one that is characteristic of him. In one of the earliest individual portraits, for example,

there is a disagreement over whether "laughing" is a sufficient criterion to place Elise Surville within a kind of people:

> Some said of this one yes she is of such a kind of them and then later some of them said of this one, any one could be doing this thing and not be of such a kind of them, perhaps this one is not of such a kind of them. . . . [*Two*, p. 317].

Similarly, a much later portrait, "Mi-Careme" (1912), begins with

> a man who said one could recognize him when one saw him again by the scar on the end of his nose and under his eye but these scars were very little ones almost not anything and one would remember him because he was one who had been saying that he was a man tired of working. . . . [*Portraits and Prayers*, p. 173]

Even the basis of a person's self-identity is not always his identifying feature.

The ultimate fate of the problems of description, judgment and prediction seems to be spelled out in a portrait written in 1911 and entitled "Four Dishonest Ones. Told by a description of what they do." Several critics have been puzzled by this piece, for though it is highly organized in a way typical of the early portraits, it contains contradictions. Bridgman, for example, states: "Mechanical as the basic form of these group portraits was, they still contained some mysteries. Just as there is no evidence of flirting in 'Flirting at the Bon Marché,' so there is no indication of dishonesty in 'Four Dishonest Ones.'" [p. 93]

The solution to "Flirting" is relatively simple. The portrait states that there are many sad, bored people who go shopping because it is "an interesting thing" (*Two*, p. 354). But shopping does not really change the sadness of their lives because "changing is not in being one buying, changing is in being one having some one be one selling something and not selling that thing . . ." (p. 355). Change is really an interaction, some form of influence, rather than the interchange of things—buying. Thus, the shoppers are "flirting" with life, with real experience and change, by confusing the activity of shopping with its end—the goods acquired.[17] Interestingly, Stein was a

17. Stein left some instructions (presumably for Toklas) in the manuscript of this portrait that reinforce its bitter-sweet tone: "Read it fast so as not to be sad in it. To make it sound gay. Flirting at the Bon Marché."

passionate window-shopper, an activity which apparently provoked
several of these "portraits of places" (Flanner, *Two*, p. xiii), and led
to her awareness of the distinction between buying and window-
shopping, end-directed act versus pure activity.

"Flirting" establishes for us the key-word "changing," which has
great importance in "Four Dishonest Ones." Obviously it is a positively charged word, like "exciting" or "succeeding." Yet in "Four
Dishonest Ones" it occurs as follows:

> They are what they are. They have not been changing. They are
> what they are.
>
> What is she doing. She is working. She is not needing to be
> changing. She is working very well, she is not needing to be
> changing. [*Portraits and Prayers,* p. 57]

Though all the subjects are not changing and are not needing to be
changing, they are also "working," and their work is done "delicate-
ly," "solidly." Thus, there seems to be a mixture of positive and
negative elements here, until we hear that the four produce things
by their work and receive money for selling these things. This makes
them, perhaps, pseudo-artists, unlike Picasso who worked solely for
the sake of working.[18]

But the "dishonesty" in the portrait is probably even more involved than this. Stein used "Four Dishonest Ones" in her lecture,
"Portraits and Repetition," to illustrate the function of time in the
continuous present:

> Every time I said what they were I said it so that they were this
> thing, and each time I said what they were as they were, as I was,
> naturally more or less but never the same thing each time that I
> said what they were I said what they were, not that they were
> different nor that I was different but as it was not the same mo-
> ment which I said I said it with a difference. [p. 185]

18. One of the most persistent concerns for Stein was the effect of success on the creative
personality. She constantly warned her friends against being turned from their proper
artistic pursuits by fame and wealth, and since she herself achieved recognition very late in
her career her warnings were often treated as sour grapes. Her fears proved both sincere and
well-founded in the thirties, when the attentions of the reading public toward her led to
writing blocks and "audience-directed" work.

Now it is strange that immediately after this statement in the lecture Stein reads a portrait about four people who are not changing; for the style described is based upon the assumption that the mind is constantly in flux and that this very sense of change is the proper mode for the literary depiction of a subject.

The key to this contradiction, I believe, lies in the subtitle of the portrait, "Told by a description of what they do." Not only does the subtitle epitomize the basic evidential premise of the early portraits —description according to characteristic acts—but its very form— "what they do" rather than 'what they are doing'—contradicts the intentions of the continuous present. For description through a generalized act, no matter how 'presently' presented, creates knowledge-about. This is the major factor in the theoretical contradiction within the early portraits which we described in the last chapter—the attempt to create a stylistic immediacy while at the same time using descriptive categories that involve memory. One wonders then whether this very characteristic Steinian portrait, framing each individual's description by a comparison to "some" and carefully marking differences and similarities among the "four," is not the rejection of the entire enterprise of these early portraits, and whether a "dishonest one" is not simply a person depicted through a perceptual and conceptual contradiction. When we consider that this portrait was written in 1911, the year in which Stein wrote the revolutionary *Tender Buttons*, the possibility of her suggesting such a rejection through the term "dishonest" seems quite strong.

However, despite the new developments in Stein's thought, she continued to write portraits in the early style well into 1913. As with the last chapter of *The Making of Americans*, the late first-phase portraits seem to condense all the characteristics of that style into a schematic, highly organized and simplified form. For this reason, I have chosen to analyze a late portrait, "One. Harry Phelan Gibb,"[19] as a description of the early portraiture as a whole. The inevitable distortion involved in using a late work as a model for all the works of a period is perhaps offset by the great clarity and conciseness with which this work unites the vital elements of the early style.

19. This portrait is entitled both 'One. Harry Phelan Gibb' in the index and "A Portrait of One. Harry Phelan Gibb" on the page of the portrait in *Geography and Plays* (p. 201); but its first appearance in print carried only the title, "II," as the second of "Two Cubist Poems" in the *Oxford Magazine*, May 7, 1920.

This analysis may strike some as being overly technical and unnecessarily prolonged. After all, "Gibb" is certainly not an opaque portrait. But I must warn the reader that this discussion is not to be taken as a paraphrase. It is an analysis of the technical conditions in the text that give rise to the remarkable process quality of the portrait, and an attempt to show how closely these reflect the theoretical program of the early phase of Stein's writing.

The text of "Gibb" is short enough to be presented here in its entirety:

One

Harry Phelan Gibb

Some one in knowing everything is knowing that some one is something. Some one is something and is succeeding is succeeding in hoping that thing. He is suffering.

He is succeeding in hoping and he is succeeding in saying that that is something. He is suffering, he is suffering and succeeding in hoping that in succeeding in saying that he is succeeding in hoping is something.

He is suffering, he is hoping, he is succeeding in saying that anything is something. He is suffering, he is hoping, he is succeeding in saying that something is something. He is hoping that he is succeeding in hoping that something is something. He is hoping that he is succeeding in saying that he is succeeding in hoping that something is something. He is hoping that he is succeeding in saying that something is something.

The single most striking feature of this portrait is its extreme redundancy. Of its 141 words there are only 18 different words, and 15 of these are introduced in the first paragraph. The other three, moreover, are preceded by similar words—the pronoun "that" by the conjunction and the demonstrative adjective of the same form; "anything" by "something" and "thing"; and "saying" by other gerunds and by present participles with the same suffix.

Redundancy can be seen not only in the large word-frequencies, but also in the phonological and syntactic levels of the portrait. Of the first 100 words, 27 are present participles or gerunds and 10 are words ending in "-thing." Thus, more than one third (37 percent) of the words in the passage end in /iŋ/. The word "he" occurs 13 times in

the first 100 words, and "succeeding" 9 times, adding /i/ to the
ubiquitous /iŋ/. Further, the finite verb count of 22 percent—very
high—accounting in all cases for the verb "is," results in the presence
of 'short' i, /I/, in 22 percent of the words of the passage. And "in,"
appearing only in combination with gerunds, occurs 10 times in the
first 100 words. This produces the really amazing occurrence of the
related elements and grouping /I/, /In/, /iŋ/, and /i/ in 85.5 percent
of all the words of the passage!

The phoneme /ə/ appears in "suffering," "some," "one," "something," and "succeeding," that is, in 25 percent of the words. Initial
/s/ is present in "suffering," "succeeding," "saying," "some," and
"something," that is 28 percent of the words, and initial /h/ and /I/
in 19 percent and 31 percent respectively ("hoping" and "he," and
"is" and "in").

The only verb constructions are "is" plus present participle, and
"is" as an equational copular followed invariably by "something."
Gerunds occur only after "in." There are no nouns. There are no
adjectives, except for one occurrence of the demonstrative "that."
There are no adverbs. The only personal pronoun is "he." The only
preposition is "in." The only coordinating conjunction is "and"
(three times), and the only subordinating conjunction is "that"
(twelve times), forming noun clauses after the verbals "hoping,"
"saying," and "knowing." On the other hand, indefinite and universal pronouns—"thing," "something," "some one," "everything" and
"anything"—are present in abundance, and contribute to the extreme
lack of concreteness of the portrait. This is the writing of relational,
"transitive" language which we described in the last chapter.

The lack of nouns, adjectives, and adverbs, and the reduction of
verbs, personal pronouns, prepositions, and conjunctions to one
often-recurring form—"is," "he," "in," "that," "and"—tends to create a very bland background. Against this, the polysyllabic, phonologically unified verbals and indefinite or universal pronouns emerge
in high relief. They occur at fairly regular intervals in sentences,
usually separated from each other by one or two 'background' words,
and create significant units or sentence places—usually six per sentence. The first two sentences have six; the third has only one and
thus makes the introduction of "suffering" very striking. The second
paragraph is "irregular," with sentences of five and nine units, while
the third paragraph has two sentences of six units, one with seven,
and two with five. The result is rhythmic prose, an expression of
the "rhythm of personality." Vexed as the issue of rhythm in prose

may be, it is not unreasonable to see these more or less regularly repeating units as coming very close to the effect of poetic or even
musical rhythm. It should be noted, too, that the articulation of
sentences into similar units acts anti-syntactically, for the structural
unity of clauses and sentences is largely destroyed as our attention is
focused on one individual word or phrase at a time.

Increasing this isolation of sentence elements is the special status
of "succeeding" and "suffering," the only romance words of the portrait. They are the two most semantically charged words, "suffering"
being introduced very dramatically by a sentence in which it is the
only 'significant' word, and dropping out of use only after the second
sentence in the last paragraph. "Succeeding" enters early and is used
in every sentence from the second paragraph on, sometimes twice,
and in the last five sentences always in the same construction. "Suffering" appears quite starkly, usually ending a natural sentence, while
"succeeding" almost always leads to some other activity through a
construction with "in" plus gerund. The two are thus syntactically as
well as semantically opposed, though united phonologically through
their common initial /sə/, the number of their syllables, and of
course their /iŋ/-ending. At the same time, they stand out from the
other verbals, which, in contrast, are cognitive and introduce noun
clauses. Through these means, "suffering" and "succeeding" are established as the most important features of Gibb.

Typically, the only deviation from the pattern described above
comes in the title, which contains a noun (a proper name) providing
the referent for all the personal pronouns which follow. The title
contains one of the most compact epitomes of a genre that we are
likely to find through its first element "One." It identifies its subject
both as "one" in the sense of a unique individual—this man and no
other—and at the same time it makes him a "one," a unit of a group
or sequence. His identity is both crucial and incidental, as the portrait in which he is depicted is both representational and aesthetic.
And this double sense of "One" is completely consistent with the
early notion of identity as the essential trait linking an individual to
his type.

The thematic content of the portrait is the familiar problem of
deciding whether the subject will succeed, although the elaborate
associations between "working," "being," and "succeeding" are
implicit rather than stated here. The one indication that a creative
activity is involved is that Gibb is "saying" a number of things, expressing his condition. This condition seems to be great insecurity,

with Gibb hoping that he is "something," but, unlike the author,[20] not knowing it. Because of this he is "suffering," and the course of the portrait charts his struggles.

The initial question, then, is whether "some one is something." Though throughout her work Stein separated "someone" into two words while leaving "something" as one, the spelling is particularly effective here, for the word "one" is thereby stressed in the double sense mentioned above—as a unique individual and as one of a type. Furthermore, "some one is something," like "a rose is a rose . . ." is the type of semi-tautological equation that Stein felt to be especially powerful. It is an example of "insistence," the seeming repetition of a word to catch its referent at each separate moment of its existing. And since "something" ends in "-ing" along with all the gerunds and present participles around it, it begins to sound like a participle itself, so that "some one" seems to be engaged in the act of having identity—'some-ing.' By analogy with such common phrases as "That's really something," the content of the identity is apparently highly significant. Its indefiniteness only contributes to its aura of importance.

We learn further that Gibb is "succeeding in hoping that thing," that is, that "some one is something." By now, the importance in Stein's character assessment of "succeeding"—twice mentioned in the second sentence—should be obvious, and we have mentioned its phonological, syntactic, and semantic importance in this particular portrait. Though Gibb is only "hoping" to be "something," still his "succeeding in hoping" is a very positive sign.

Our optimism increases throughout the second and third paragraphs, and especially in the third, where in strikingly powerful parallel sentences Gibb is presented as "saying," "hoping," etc., that "something" rather than "some one" is "something." This shift from self-concern to concern about expressing and understanding the significance of things outside himself seems to be a further strength in his development.

If we return to the first paragraph, we notice that the second sentence begins by presenting "some one is something" as an independent statement, but ends by making it subordinate to "hoping," which is, in turn, subordinated to "succeeding." In fact, every verb seems capable of being subordinated to every other verb, and clauses

20. Bridgman states that "some one" seems to have been used in a number of early portraits to refer to Stein herself (p. 94).

are nested one inside the other like interchangeable parts in a design. Thus, the introduction of "saying" in the second paragraph not only brings in the factor of Gibb's self-expression, but also provides another verb which can subordinate or be subordinated to any of the previously used verbs. As a result, sentences of considerable complication appear, for example, "He is suffering, he is suffering and succeeding in hoping that in succeeding in saying that he is succeeding in hoping is something." Though every clause here adds new information, and though the whole sentence clearly imitates the tortuousness, the "suffering," of Gibb's struggle for expression, still the extremely complicated nesting of subordinate clauses militates against transparent referentiality. It is almost impossible to integrate such a sentence without multiple readings or even analyses of the clausal relations. Otherwise, the sentence dissolves into a welter of constituent elements.

The mechanism used here is the transformation of a declarative main clause into a subordinate noun clause. This is described in language philosophy as the difference between the statement of a fact and the naming of that fact.[21] We have seen the importance of the distinction between the reception of a statement and the reception of a name in James's and Stein's thinking. A statement predicates knowledge about its subject while a name provides acquaintance, an immediate experience with the referent itself with no implied relations or associations present. Thus, when Stein constantly transforms her data into the names of those data she is causing us to respond to the facts with this immediacy of perception so important to mimetic portraiture. The intricate complexity of this fact-naming—the nesting of large numbers of noun clauses—comes closer to simulating perception in a continuous present than any other technique in Stein's early portraiture. When it enters into combination with the repetition of severely limited numbers of words and constructions, with elaborate dislocations of time and reference, with the complex phonological

21. "This very important difference between naming a fact and stating a fact is further explained by Husserl in the following manner. The same fact is objectified in two different ways. In the one case when the fact is *named*, the entire fact with all its inner complexity is grasped all at once, in one ray of consciousness as it were. When the same fact is *stated* or *judged*, there is a many-rayed awareness, a synthetic awareness in which many constituent representations are brought into a unity. The mode of consciousness is in each case different. The one-rayed apprehension of the fact that S is P no doubt presupposes the many-rayed awareness which makes possible the statement 'S is P'; nevertheless the name is phenomenologically different from the statement out of which it 'arises.' Naming and stating are therefore not merely grammatically different, but essentially different (*wesensverschieden*)" (J. N. Mohanty, *Edmund Husserl's Theory of Meaning* [The Hague, 1964], pp. 99–100).

relations established among "key-words" and syncategorematic words, and with the periodization of sentences into isolated units, the early portrait style goes a long way toward making "present perception" a reality. Nevertheless, as we have seen, Stein's use of activities, states, and physical and personality traits to characterize her subjects creates a contradiction which could not be resolved within the givens of the first phase of her portraiture.

II

It would be hard to imagine a greater contrast to the redundancy and schematism of the early portraits than the style developed in the period that followed. Moving from a limited vocabulary, syntax, and phonology, we suddenly encounter a veritable cornucopia of words, constantly novel and surprising. And yet, as we shall see, there are striking similarities between the two portrait styles.

I have limited the second period to the years 1911 to 1925. The first date marks the appearance of "Portrait of Mabel Dodge at the Villa Curonia," a departure from any previous portraiture, which was hailed by Stein and her contemporaries as a literary innovation. The second date, 1925, is somewhat more problematic, and will be discussed in part III of this chapter. The unifying feature of the period was the discovery of visuality and the partial elimination by Stein of the contradiction inherent in the first period. Nevertheless the work of this phase was certainly not homogeneous in the way that the early portraiture was. It began with a set of experiments which produced a totally revolutionary kind of writing, and then explored some of the implications of this style.

There are two works that mark the experimental transition between the two styles: "Mabel Dodge," and "Portrait of Constance Fletcher." They were written in 1911 during a visit by Stein at Mabel Dodge's villa in Florence. However, despite the fame of "Dodge," Constance Fletcher's portrait is the more interesting for our purposes. The first two pages of it are written in the early style: they describe the subject as one who has had "family living," and who still has it and who knows that she has it. Then suddenly in a switch parallel to that in *A Long Gay Book,* the following paragraph occurs:

If they move in the shoe there is everything to do. They do not move in the shoe. [*Geography and Plays*, p. 159]

And the rest of the portrait is similarly disjoint from the "living" and "loving" of the first pages.

Bridgman (p. 122) has suggested that the line is an echo of the Mother Goose rhyme of the old woman who lived in a shoe; thus it would be a recasting of the "family living" of the first section of the portrait. But the problem comes when we begin to use the allusion as an interpretive device. It might mean that Fletcher's "family living" was over, that the children "do not move in the shoe." But it is rather difficult to see what this has to do with the rest of the portrait.

It would seem, instead, that the significance of the two sentences lies in the fact that they are a reference to nonsense language *per se*, and that their form resembles that of a logical structure. For these two sentences at first glance look like the major and minor premises of a syllogism. One would thus expect some conclusion to follow. However, the second sentence denies the conditions governed by the initial proposition, and therefore the predictive possibilities of the major premise do not apply here. That is, if "they do not move in the shoe," then what? There is either everything to do, something to do, or nothing to do; in other words, the entire range of possibilities is open, unlimited by the existence of a logical contingency. We might recognize here the same failure of logic as in "Pach" and "Roche," although in this case the use of nonsense terms makes this a "pure" demonstration of the inadequacy of logic rather than the locating of this failure is a specific context.

The short puzzle is followed by the paragraph,

> The language of education is not replacing the special position that is the expression of the emanation of evil. There is an expression when contemplation is not connecting the object that is in position with the forehead that is returning looking. It is not overpowering. That is a cruel description. The memory is the same and surely the one who is not older is not dead yet although if he has been blind he is seeing. This has not any meaning.

Just as in the pseudo-syllogism where nonsense and logic were opposed, two types of expression are being contrasted in this paragraph: the "language of education" and "the special position that is the expression of the emanation of evil." We assume that "the language of education" is associated with logic or science, and that "the expression of the emanation of evil" is a kind of Blakean depiction of imaginative expression. Since the language of science or logic does not "replace" the other, we may assume that it "is not overpowering," so that the "language of education" is synonymous with "an expression when contemplation is not connecting the object that is in position with the forehead that is returning looking," that is, expression not based on the visual perception of an object. Thus, the "language of education" is devoid of visuality and is associated with logic or science, the inadequacy of which was demonstrated by the 'moving in the shoe' paragraph. Such language is "a cruel description," and by association, a cruel deception as well. Surely all this is a condemnation of the early style which programmatically ruled out "looking," which was a quasi-scientific description (a "language of education"), and which involved a distortion of the immediacy of thought and perception. This interpretation seems to be confirmed in the mention of memory and the denial of meaning in the last sentences of the paragraph.

Nevertheless, Stein goes on to describe the "triumph" of the early style "where the light is bright and the beauty was not losing having that possession." But, "that was not what was tenderly." "Tenderly" is perhaps a reference to *Tender Buttons*, the beginning of her visually-oriented writing. Stein even imitates the early style in discussing it: "There was the writing and the preparation that was pleasing and succeeding and being enterprising." This writing took place "when there was the room that was not a dream," that is, in Stein's study between approximately midnight and dawn when it was her custom to work.

The next paragraph is one sentence:

> This is all to prepare the way that is not the way to like anything that in speaking is telling what has come that like a swelling is inside when there is yellowing. [p. 160]

We are being prepared to like something that does not speak of its subject as having been "ripened" in the writer's mind. The "swelling" is the fullness of awareness of the subject's being. The "yellowing" can be taken in two ways. Either it is the state of ripeness of an autumnal fruit such as a squash or pumpkin, in which case we are not to like writing in which the subject is presented as the fruit of a long process of perception on the writer's part; or else it is the sere, death-like quality caused by the discrepancy between the time of the conception and the period of immediate perception of the living subject

leading up to it. The latter interpretation corresponds to the statement in "The Gradual Making of The Making of Americans":

> When I was up against the difficulty of putting down the com-
> plete conception that I had of an individual, the complete
> rhythm of a personality that I had gradually acquired by listen-
> ing seeing feeling and experience, I was faced by the trouble that
> I had acquired all this knowledge gradually but when I had it I
> had it completely at one time. [p. 147]

To paraphrase the paragraph from "Fletcher" then, "this," the
development of ideas up to this point, has been a preparation for
the reader to like a form of writing which does not involve the time
discrepancy described above.

The next paragraph continues with this idea:

> There is that liking. That does not shape the way to say that
> there is not anywhere anything that is resembling. Perfection is
> not adulteration. There is the substance that has not any defect.
> [p. 160]

The "liking" is the taste in readers for the early contradictory style,
and it is also the 'likening' of that style to the "swelling" that "is
inside when there is yellowing." This taste or the style toward which
it is directed cannot eliminate "resembling," for the style is not consistent, but instead 'adulterated' with heterogeneous elements. However, there is an essential writing, a "substance," which is without
this "defect." And as we learn in the next paragraph, "If the program is not despondent and it has that substance then certainly the
beginning is the tender blessing [blossoming] that unfolding is not
subduing." The new writing, again described through the organic
metaphor, is vital throughout, rather than defeated through the time
of its sequential flow or any temporal inconsistency between its
presentation of the subject and the subject himself. And "tender"
here is probably again a direct reference to the use of the word in
Tender Buttons.

The culmination of this argument occurs in the next paragraph:

> Come in and that expression is not that one of waiting. To use
> a name is not the time that seeing has not been. This is discussion.
> This is obligation. This is the composition.

The reader is being invited to enter into the writing, to participate in it, without any time discrepancies—"waiting." The use of "a name" ushers in a new time of "seeing," the visual revolution in Stein's writing, and the name or noun, seeing, and temporal immediacy are the defining conceptual elements of the new style.

The portrait continues, recapitulating its argument through a series of headings and illustrative paragraphs. It goes back to the subject, "She," to her relations to others, "They," to the revolutionary shift in conception, "The change," and finally to the new approach to writing and character depiction, "To face that way." The portrait is thus much more a literary metastatement than a depiction of its subject. This is another sense in which it is transitional, being so conscious of its own revolutionariness that the stylistic shift itself becomes the subject. Stein is not yet using her break from memory categories to depict a human subject, and the only link which we can see between this metaliterary riddle and the purported subject, Constance Fletcher, is perhaps that Stein had been discussing the ideas in question with her.

Nevertheless, it is obvious that the thematics which I have uncovered here is neither easily available nor the central fact of the portrait. I have simply reconstructed the links among mental data that Stein took such great pains to omit, and I have done this not only for the purpose of illustrating the transitional status of "Fletcher," but also to counter the usual claim that such writing is absolutely meaningless. Perhaps, however, it would be more to the point to describe the ways in which Stein obscures the relations among the mental data presented rather than to rush in and fill the gaps. For the invention of the means whereby the transparent signifying of language can be almost totally disrupted is no mean feat. In order to catch her perceptions of the subject with complete immediacy, rather than to depict her as an "identity" developed in the mind over a period of time, Stein was forced to use words in such a way that they could not involve the reader in memory. Thus she invented various techniques to translate 'raw perceptual data' into language which, like those data, could be transformed upon reflection into concepts.

The devices Stein gathered to achieve this non-referential surface would gladden the heart of a Freudian, for they are as various a group of displacements and condensations as one could wish. For example, in the Mother Goose syllogism-manqué, the actual sentence structure and configuration of sentences is substituted for the idea "logic" and the Mother Goose allusion takes the place of "nonsense" or "illogical expression." Stein constantly replaces words by rather tenuously related expressions, such as "the language of education" for the scientifically oriented description of the early typologizing. The motivation for the opposed "expression of the emanation of evil" is even more difficult to see. Further, the punning substitution of "description" in the cliché, "a cruel deception," is based on sound associations, one of the most frequently used techniques in Stein's work at this time.

Circumlocution and its opposite, condensation, are also present here. For example, "an expression when contemplation is not connecting the object that is in position with the forehead that is returning looking" is a dissection of the situation of 'non-visually-oriented writing' into its constituent parts in an elaborate circumlocution. The process of condensation is revealed in another portrait: "Handing a lizard to any one is a green thing receiving a curtain" ("Portrait of Prince B. D.," *Geography and Plays,* p. 151). The lizard is reduced to its color and the hand to its effect, and the act of handing on the part of one person to another person is switched to the effect produced on the object handed—"receiving a curtain." This reduction and change of perspective effectively mask the subject at hand and its connection to its context, especially when Stein does not supply the original stimulus for the transformation.

Often, Stein substitutes very general words for more specific ones, for example "the passing out of what is not about when it is there where there is no care to say that anything is better" ("Fletcher," p. 161). The constant rhyming here is a further hindrance to reconstituting the "meaning" of the words since it links words which are either semantically unrelated or which refer specifically to other words. Our attention is thus diverted into nonsensical paths and connections, and shifters such as "it" in this example, with their total lack of reference, only increase this difficulty.

The negative is used very frequently to mask reference. Such sequences as "the way that is not the way" with its internal identical rhyme tends to confound the reader, even though the contradiction is resolved as the sentence proceeds. Compound negatives are even more confusing, as in the example, "That does not shape the way to say that there is not anywhere anything that is resembling." It is almost impossible to understand this sentence in a single reading. It is only when one passes from the immediate experience with the text to an analytic reflection upon it that one can sort out what is logically positive and negative. Here is another example of Stein's shifting of referentiality to a level of cognition beyond the immediate experience with the writing. The multiple negatives and the emphatic character of the positives—"anywhere anything that is"—make the qualities of negativity and positivity stand out from the text as separate elements, in contrast to their usual function as semantic modifiers.

As a result of this camouflaging, when the more or less conventional organic metaphor—"garden," "swelling," "yellowing," "unfolding" —appears, it is so indefinitely related to its context that it becomes ambiguous. It might refer to the growth of the portrait subject through the course of the portrait, or to the work as it proceeds, or to the general stylistic development in question. In fact there is always a broad choice of metaphoric referents, sometimes contradicting each other, in this phase of portraiture. In this way the substitutions and circumlocutions of "Fletcher" not only work together against thought connection and reference, but enlist conventional literary devices such as the metaphor in their obfuscations. The result is a totally opaque surface with all connections to its subject or theme obscured.

However, whereas in "Fletcher" these techniques are used to mask a metaliterary subject matter, the later portraits used these techniques on human subjects, the proper subjects for portraiture. The first portrait after "Mabel Dodge" and "Constance Fletcher" was "Monsieur Vollard et Cézanne" (1912). It was apparently stimulated by a visit paid to Stein by the art dealer, Vollard, just after he had finished writing a book on Cézanne,[22] and as Bridgman notes,[23] this is the first piece of Stein's writing with sentences and phrases placed

---

22. Mellow (p. 194) finds a reference to the writing of this work in Stein's correspondence: "When Ambroise Vollard's book on Cézanne was published in Paris, she wrote McBride about the book and the author: 'It's about Vollard. He has just finished a book about Cézanne and it's really extremely good. . . . He is delightful he comes in in great haste in a cab, you remember how big he is, with original paintings and drawings and reproductions and a page of texts and asks to be admired and you do and he says he esteems your advice and he litters the floor with papers and then cab and all goes off and he comes with a new supply. I have done rather a nice sketch of him.'"

23. Bridgman, p. 139; he goes on to suggest that "Vollard" resembles a lovers' quarrel, which may perhaps have been part of the associational framework of this piece. The manuscript jotting to the text might support this view: "M. Vollard et Cezanne/Histoires des bonnes/M. Vollard et Cezanne/Histoires des femmes."

in a vertical column. It is also the first work written as a thought conversation. Like so many of the portraits which follow, it is a would-be dialogue which is virtually taken over by mental associations. The switch in and out from thought to conversation is not marked by any of the usual signals, in an attempt to imitate the shifting modes of the objects of our attention.

The portrait begins with a snippet of conversation—"Oh you could" (*Portraits and Prayers*, p. 37), then a thought about the encounter—"I was pleased by a smile, " then perhaps a comment on some picture of Cézanne's—"Loud tones are smiling," and another about the book—"Plain letters." The next line, however, "Plain in letters," is a pure thought variation on the preceding line, as "I was not occidental" is a recasting, no doubt, of a spoken 'It was not accidental,' which, unlike "Plain letters," does not occur in the text. The 'conversation' continues, with associations based on syntactic and phonological similarities, conversational fragments, and observations about the encounter.

Then come the rites of leaving. First the guest is urged to stay longer: "Please me./By staying" (p. 39). More talk follows: "It's pretty, it's nice./I asked a question./No I'll never think of it again." Finally come the last politenesses: "Please do be seated./A watch." The "watch" is probably the visitor's looking at his watch to indicate that it is time to go. This is a typical condensation of the situation, like the lizard-in-the-hand example above.

The portrait ends with the realization of the new technical discovery Stein has made and a prayer for it to work and be appreciated:

> Yes I have gotten a new form. That isn't the word. Yes I have gotten a new form. That isn't the word.
> Please Please
> Please be good.
> That's the end of that.

This little *envoi* suggests that "Monsieur Vollard et Cezanne" is also somewhat transitional. Like its two predecessors it is self-conscious of its technical devices and places them before the reader as part of the thematics of the piece.

This is not the case, however, with "Guillaume Apollinaire," a portrait written in 1913 and used by critics as an example of Stein's most opaque prose:[24]

Guillaume Apollinaire

Give known or pin ware.
Fancy teeth, gas strips.
Elbow elect, sour stout pore, pore caesar, pour state at.
Leave eye lessons I. Leave I. Lessons. I. Leave I lessons, I.

One would not dispute the opacity of this work if it were not for the last paragraph. It is obviously a set of variations on the sentence 'I leave eye lessons.' And this immediately refers us to the subject, Apollinaire, whose diagrammatic poems could easily be termed "eye lessons," lessons for the eye. Since "I" and "eye" are homonyms, and since the sentence order is permuted so variously, the lessons might also be taken as being lessons about the "I," that is, that Apollinaire's poems are expressions of himself. This would take us back to the "being" through "working" of the first phase of portraits. But, since "I" is a shifter, and since the context does not limit it, the "I" could be Stein as well, whose portraits are records of her perceptions as well as of the objects of those perceptions. She even used her famous phrase, "When this you see remember me"[25] as the factor distinguishing portrait perception from that of narratives. When we remember, too, that "lessons" is virtually homonymous with the French "laissons"—'we leave'—the possibility of the inclusion of both writer and subject seems great.

The correspondence of "lessons" and "laissons" is probably not an

24. Hoffman uses "Guillaume Apollinaire" as an example of his fourth category of portraits: "Poems using *non sequiturs* and depending predominantly on word play and poetic effects" (p. 163). ". . . even though Apollinaire is a well-known figure, as poet, art critic, and pornographer, there is little that we recognize as relating to the subject even by the suggestion of a fragment. . . . the entire unit bears no relation to the supposed subject, creates no continuity of subject of its own, juxtaposes totally unrelated words such as 'gas' and 'strip,' and depends for whatever effect it may have on the textural elements of language itself" (pp. 173–74).

Mellow (p. 132) comes perhaps closer to the truth when he describes the portrait as language "purged of most of its associational values . . . like a Cubist painting, with only hints and guesses of the subject that lay behind her disjunctive style."

25. *How to Write*, p. 228: "There is this difference between narrative and portrait a narrative makes anybody be at home and a portrait makes anybody remember me."

accident. For though Stein insisted on her 'loyalty' to the English
language (*Toklas*, pp. 70, 75–76, 119 and elsewhere), precedents for
English-French puns can be found in several pieces of this period. In
"Americans," for example, the portrait listed immediately prior to
"Guillaume Apollinaire" in the *Yale Catalogue,* the following para-
graph appears:

> B r, brute says. A hole, a hole is a true, a true, a true. [*Geo-
> graphy and Plays,* p. 43]

"Hole" in French is "trou," quite close in sound to "true." The two
are presented here as a lexical equation, and it would be inconceiv-
able that the French were not being included. Further, the letters
of "true" are contained in "brute," the separation of "B" and
"r" giving added stimulus to this observation, and "brut" in French
means 'in a raw or natural state.' Since English "hole" is homonymous with "whole," a new set of interlinguistic connections has
come into being by means of sound coincidence. The American brute
—the title, we remember, is "Americans"—is associated with natural-
ness, wholeness, and truth through a mingling of the French and
American idioms, a very Steinian sentiment indeed. Going back to
"Guillaume Apollinaire," we see that the subject of the portrait
in which the "lessons"/'laissons' play occurs is a French writer, so
that the motivation for such interlinguistic play is obvious.

Thus, far from being an abstract play of words, "Guillaume Apollinaire" makes metonymic reference to its subject through his work
and associates the work of the author, Stein, with this work. We do
not find such transparent reference, however, in the first three lines
of this portrait, which appear on first sight to be nonsense, and not
very entertaining nonsense at that. Still, the example of the last
paragraph suggests that there must be some significance to the other
lines. And indeed, on reading over the first line-paragraph, "Give
known or pin ware," we realize that it is a phonological echoing of
the title, "Guillaume Apollinaire." Although the coincidence in
sound is too great for accident, one does not note it immediately because of the associative discontinuity between French and English as
well as the very puzzling semantic character of the line. Nevertheless,
the portrait begins as an association based on the sound of the subject's name—again it is referential.

As to the motivation for the specific words used, we enter more
shaky ground. "Give known" may refer again to the "lessons" of

the final paragraph. But "pin ware" does not seem to suggest anything. However, judging from the disruption of word order in the
last line, it seems likely that the actual ordering of words may not
be significant. If we divide the first two lines into their constituent
halves, the first halves of the two lines give us the grouping "Give
known" "Fancy teeth." The word "teeth" appears in "Monsieur
Vollard et Cezanne" as "teetch" (*Portraits and Prayers*, p. 37), an
amalgam with "teach," perhaps a teaching by means of speech, the
mouth. If we take "Fancy" as the imaginative faculty, then 'giving-
knowledge-teaching-fancy' emerges, a highly appropriate collocation
for an experimental-didactic poet whose name is Apollinaire (Apollo).

The other two half-lines, "pin ware" and "gas strips," can be
crossed and slightly modified to produce "pinstripes" and "glassware," the first a reference to the fashionable clothing which Stein
thought of in connection with the poet.[26] The second is intelligible
if we assume that these two half-lines refer to the "Guillaume" side
of the title, since the other half-lines referred to "Apollinaire". In
that case, "glassware" and "wear glass" suggest the monocle of Kaiser
Wilhelm, called Guillaume by the French and also associated with
Apollinaire in Stein's memory.[27] Apollinaire himself was christened
Wilhelm—Wilhelm Apollinaris Albertus de Kostrowicki. It is true that
these interpretations of the first two lines are much less plausible,
and certainly less available, than that of the last paragraph, but the
two lines are undoubtedly full of such suggestive associations about
the subject.

In the third line-paragraph we find a set of phonologically repeti-
tive phrases, which have little semantic relation other than the political suggestion in "elect," "caesar," and "state." The last two words,
however—"state at"—seem inconsistent with the rest of the line, almost demanding the translation, 'l'état.' As soon as this is carried
out, the last phrase becomes 'pour l'état,' the French 'pour' suggested
by the English spelling of what had appeared twice before as "pore."

26. *Toklas*, p. 59: "He had a brother whom one heard about but never saw. He worked in
a bank and therefore he was reasonably well dressed. When anybody in Montmartre had to
go anywhere they had to be conventionally clothed, either to see a relation or attend to a
business matter, they always wore a piece of a suit that belonged to the brother of Guillaume."

27. *Ibid.*, pp. 59–60: "the crowd passing were shouting, à bas Guillaume, down with William and as every one always called Guillaume Apollinaire Guillaume, even in his death
agony it troubled him." This event of course occurs after the portrait had been written, but
it seems quite possible that the association between the Kaiser and Apollinaire was made
much earlier by Stein.

But if one English spelling of /por/ is French 'pour,' then the others can be too, and we have "Elbow elect, sour stout *pour, pour césar, pour l'état.*" Working backward again, we shift the phrase "sour stout *pour*" to '*source tout pour*' or '*source pour tout.*' If we interpret "Elbow elect" as 'below elect,' that is, elections from below, popular elections, we have 'Popular elections, *source pour tout, pour césar, pour l'état.*' Though I believe that something could be done in French with "Elbow elect" (perhaps, 'coude élect,' 'cou d'électorat'), the English component of the sentence is consistent with the American-French interaction of Stein and Apollinaire, as well as the Franco-American institution of republican democracy, where the source of all power supposedly resides in the people. When we remember that "Guillaume" is associated by Stein with *Kaiser* Wilhelm and that Stein specifically states that Apollinaire "had a head like one of the late Roman emperors" (*Toklas*, p. 59), a comparison frequently made •
of Stein as well, the political reference again can be seen as motivated by the portrait subject.[28]

If any doubt remains as to the referentiality of the early second-phase portraits, the manuscripts provide more or less conclusive proof. In "Braque" (1913) between what were to become the first (incomplete) and second paragraphs on p. 145 of *Geography and Plays*, Stein jots down the same kind of reminder to herself of where to continue at the next sitting as in the first period of portraiture: "Braque's neuresthenia and talk with Marvel with crowd." The text takes off from there with the words, "Brack and neuresthenia and lean talk with a marvel," a sequence directly related to the thematic cue. In the same portrait, Stein breaks the text to write "Difference between his commonplace womanishness and Delaunay's nasty." This note would suggest not only that Stein was considering her subject under conventional thematic headings, but that she was even comparing him to others who shared some trait of character with him. This anachronistic feature does not appear in the text; indeed it is rather difficult to see the relation between the comment and the text that follows it. However the pervasiveness of the old ideas in Stein's thinking at this time is apparent. She clearly began her second phase believing that the same kind of information could be conveyed in the styles of the first and second phases. For in *GMP* (1911–1912)

---

28. The further presence in "Elbow elect, sour stout pore" of 'erect elbow, pours sour stout' should also be noted. Perhaps this is a reference to apollinaris water, a bitter mineral water. In any case, such a possibility illustrates the enormous semantic suggestiveness of the portrait.

she notes to herself in the manuscript: "Not Pablo yet. Do all Matisse's life in the new manner, then Pablo in the old." Obviously, the sharp division between the character depiction of the first two phases, as outlined in "Portraits and Repetition," was not worked out when the experimentation began in 1911–1913. The same traits were merely being masked under a riddling new style.

What I have tried to show is first that the early second-phase portraits are intelligible, second, that they make direct reference to their subjects, and finally, that they call attention to this reference by fairly obvious clues. The other important fact about them is that they have an unintelligible surface which, we might say, is militantly unintelligible through striking disruptions of syntax, time-space reference, and sense, through the rhyming of words devoid of semantic relation, the multiplication of negatives, and the use of circumlocutions so disjointed as seldom to suggest their real meaning. These two groups of facts must be kept in mind in dealing with such portraits, for they explain the most important characteristic of the early second-phase portraits. This might be termed their 'allegorical' quality, for like an allegory they have both a surface level and one or several interpretive levels. The allegory does not work unless the surface level is taken seriously, and the value of the reading of the 'higher' levels depends on an understanding of both the surface and the norms of the other levels in question.

The surface texture of the early second-phase portraits, read and perceived as such, provides no knowledge-about. It is meant to recreate the flow of immediate perceptions of the subject—and the second "of" here is deliberately ambiguous—without the reader's being able to understand the motivations for these 'thoughts.' He is to experience Jamesian 'acquaintance' of the subject. And then afterward, the clues we have mentioned are to lead him to a different level of cognition—memory—where he can reconstitute the meaning of the portrait, where, in effect, he discovers 'knowledge about' the subject. The norms involved in this second level are the norms of portraiture itself. For if we were not accustomed to the representation of people in terms of their work, their clothes, their resemblance to the great, their nationality, and so on, the interpretation of these portraits would be impossible. Thus these portraits are doubly representational—imitatively so on the surface, and conventionally so on the interpretive level.

That these difficult portraits could be entertaining as well as bewildering for the reader can be seen in "Susie Asado" (1913), which appears three items ahead of "Guillaume Apollinaire" in the *Yale Catalogue.*

Susie Asado

Sweet sweet sweet sweet sweet tea.
    Susie Asado.
Sweet sweet sweet sweet sweet tea.
    Susie Asado.
Susie Asado which is a told tray sure.
A lean on the shoe this means slips slips hers.
When the ancient light grey is clean it is yellow, it is a silver seller.
This is a please this is a please there are the saids to jelly. These are the wets these say the sets to leave a crown to Incy.
Incy is short for incubus.
A pot. A pot is a beginning of a rare bit of trees. Trees tremble, the old vats are in bobbles, bobbles which shade and shove and render clean, render clean must.
    Drink pups.
Drink pups drink pups lease a sash hold, see it shine and a bobolink has pins. It shows a nail.
What is a nail. A nail is unison.
Sweet sweet sweet sweet sweet tea.

                [*Geography and Plays,* p. 13]

The subject, Susie Asado, supposedly based on a Spanish dancer whom Stein and Toklas saw on a trip to Spain,[29] is depicted in connection with a tea party, as the first four lines equating "Susie Asado" with "Sweet sweet sweet sweet sweet *tea*" or 'sweetie' suggest. The "told tray sure" seems to be a triple condensation of 'an old/gold/ bold treasure,' 'a told tale sure,' and of course 'a cold [tea] tray.' There are comfortable "slips hers" or slippers, and a "silver seller" or cellar, perhaps for salt.

A pseudo-teatime conversation goes on as a recasting of a nursery rhyme in "This is a please this is a please there are the saids to jelly," with the ladies very politely asking each other to pass items on the

---

29. Bridgman, p. 138, reports that Carl Van Vechten claimed both "Preciosilla" and "Susie Asado" were depictions of Argentina, a flamenco dancer seen by Stein in Spain in the summer of 1912.

table. The teapot is there: "A pot. A pot is a beginning of a rare bit of trees [tea]." The "trees"/teas "tremble, and the old vats are in bobbles" or bubbles. Everyone is urged to "Drink pups" or 'Drink up' and as they do so the babbling/bubbling/"bobolink" hastens/ "has pins." This is by no means a complete unravelling of all the puns of the portrait, but it does indicate the playfulness, charm and euphony of several of the early second-phase works, despite their difficulty. Here, the unintelligible surface with its rhythmic repetitions and nursery rhyme evocations creates an impression that one might be willing to accept as equivalent to the person referred to as Susie Asado. Such a portrait is like an implicit simile: the experience of these words, suggesting a cozy tea-party, is as pleasant as an experience with Susie Asado.

There were fourteen portraits written in 1913, compared with seventeen in all the time from 1914 to 1920 inclusive. Thus, 1913 saw a concentration on portrait writing unprecedented in Stein's career, growing out of the possibilities outlined in "Mabel Dodge," "Constance Fletcher," and "Vollard." However, with 1914 came World War I. Stein and Toklas were temporarily stranded in England with the Whiteheads, and their old style of life was drastically disrupted. The upset is reflected in Stein's portraiture as well, for the disciplined opacity of the 1913 portraits gives way slightly and the number of portraits written decreases sharply. That extreme difficulty still operated in these works can be seen from the rather desperate commentary of an editor about one of them, "Tillie" (1914): "'Tillie' (the title suggests) may be a portrait."[30] But the innovative quality seems to have gone out of the portraits of the war years and Stein's decreasing interest in her "new form" is obvious. The already well-explored techniques were being used over and over to gain the same effects, or were being greatly simplified in such portraits as "Mr. Miranda and William" (1916). Here there is little left of the complex two-level portrait; we have only the indirect speech of an old man, presented as typical, and thus revealing, of him.

The portraits of the war years can be distinguished from the earlier second-phase ones, in general, by Stein's frequent use of conversation as the mode of encounter between the portraitist and the subject. "Gentle Julia," for example ("probably written in England a few days before the outbreak of war, because the person it describes was

30. *Bee Time Vine and Other Pieces (1913-1927)* (New Haven, 1953), ed. Virgil Thomson, p. 173.

a guest of the Whiteheads just at that time" [*Bee Time Vine*, p. 178])
is a kind of dialogue between two people who are planning an outing.
One of them is anxious to go; the other seems to be busy with different thoughts, but does not want to be left out of the plans. The
obvious impatience of the first purposeful character with the delay-
ing tactics of the second, Julia, is brought out clearly in the portrait,
and the title itself, "Gentle Julia," is a sarcastic stab.

Here and in many of the dialogue portraits of this period, as in
their prototype, "Monsieur Vollard et Cezanne," there is little correspondence between paragraphing and changes of speaker. Often a
single speech is spaced into several paragraphs, e.g., "All./The./Time."
("Johnny Grey," *Geography and Plays*, p. 169), or different speeches
are fused into a single paragraph, as in the indirect speech of "Mr.
Miranda and William": "Did he like invitations. He did not. Did he
accept them. Not unless he had decided not to go. . ." (*Painted Lace*,
p. 274). The implication seems to be that the extent and unity of an
utterance in a dialogue are mental constructs, a point that will be
discussed more fully in chapter 5.

Another example of a portrait as a confrontation of characters,
this time of three, is "Henry and I" (1916). Here "Henry" accuses
"I" of not liking his wife. "I" denies this, ending with rather humor-
ous exasperation and, as in "Gentle Julia," sarcasm:

> I said I liked your first wife. I said I liked all your wives. How-
> ever you can do as you please. I am a dog lover. [p. 274]

Then a second section of the portrait begins, entitled "Writing Letters." Here "I" indignantly defends "Henry" against someone who has
written: "I do not mean to say that his work is not important I mean
to explain that it is doubtful if he is reasoning." The answer to this
criticism is brusque and absolutely loyal: "What difference does it
make whether he was reasonable or not. I liked him. . . . Thank you
for writing. I don't care to hear your opinion." "Henry" is thus depicted through both his conversation with "I" and through "I"'s
defence of him before others. More precisely the relation between
the two characters is depicted in this way.

That both "Henry and I" and "Gentle Julia" involve more than
imitations of conversations should be obvious. The situations they
depict are essentially dramatic in nature, and the fact that the first
section of "Henry and I" actually has "Henry" and "I" prefaced to
each speech, as if stage directions, makes the resemblance of these

dialogue-portraits to drama even more blatant. We even find the stage direction, "This is the scene" (p. 272), in "Captain William Edwards" (1916), although this is not a dialogue between two people.

Such examples raise the problem of what difference, if any, exists between a play and a portrait in this period of Stein's writing. The association of the two in her thinking is obvious in the following statements from "Plays," one of the *Lectures in America*:

> I had before I began writing plays written many portraits. I had been enormously interested all my life in finding out what made each one that one and so I had written a great many portraits.
>
> I came to think that since each one is that one and that there are a number of them each one being that one, the only way to express this thing each one being that one and there being a number of them knowing each other was in a play. ["Plays," *Lectures in America*, p. 119]

The main difference between portraits and plays as explained here, then, is the number of people involved in each—one in a portrait, more than one in a play. However, this distinction ignores one of the essential features of the second-phase portraits: the presence of the portraitist-perceiver within the portrait itself. The literary portrait implies a special, privileged position for the author as a perceiver of, rather than a fellow actor with, the subject.

Though in "Gentle Julia" the title seems to imply a portrait format rather than that of a play, "Henry and I" seems closer to a play, even though it appears in the section of *Painted Lace* entitled by its editors "Portraits." And when we consider that in the period from 1913 to 1923 Stein launched into playwriting with the same energy as in her portrait-writing, we might even consider the dialogue portraits as exercises for this playwriting, and thus as a kind of hybrid form arising from her sudden interest in the possibilities of drama. Though their origin can be traced back to "Monsieur Vollard et Cezanne," and though the early second-phase techniques of rhyming, punning, illogical connection, are all present in these works, their focus is different from the earlier portraits. They are concerned with character relations rather than with the direct perception of individuals, and thus they are somewhat anomalous in the development of the second phase of portraiture.

From 1914 to 1917, then, Stein wrote portraits in the 1913 style as well as ones inspired by her interest in drama. However, by the end of this time, her attention was drawn exclusively to drama and other forms, and no portraits were written between 1918 and 1920, inclusive. It was not until 1921 that she again began writing portraits, slowly at first and then in considerable numbers in 1923 and 1924.

We might consider the period from 1921 to 1925 as a kind of revival of the early second-phase portraits, for the stylistic features are largely the same and even a few of the subjects are recast from previous portraits. "Finish Constance" (1921) is a second treatment of Constance Fletcher and implies an intention to 'finish the job.' "Van or Twenty Years After—A Second Portrait of Carl Van Vechten" (1923) and "If I Told Him—A Completed Portrait of Picasso" (1923) also follow this pattern, although the prior "Picasso" was written during the first portrait period.

There are, however, differences between the twenties portraits and those of the early teens. The syntax is much less convoluted, the semantics is less opaque though still puzzling, and there is a much greater emphasis on phonological repetition, rhyme, and rhythm. All of this produces a relaxation of the discipline that allowed only direct perception within the portrait, and non-immediate reference to the subject is often to be found. This relaxation can be seen, for example, in "Mildred's Thoughts" (1922), where a rather lyrical progression of direct thought is interrupted by reference to the meta-situation of the portraitist recording these thoughts:

> Mildred's thoughts are where. There with pear, with the pears and the stairs Mildred's thoughts are there with the pear and the stairs and the pears.[31]

A certain sympathy with Futurism is evident here too. As Stein later said of herself: "She was much influenced by the sound of the streets and the movement of the automobiles. She also liked then to set a sentence for herself as a sort of tuning fork and metronome and then write to that time and tune. Mildred's Thoughts . . . was one of these experiments she thought most successful" (*Toklas*, pp. 206–207).

Stein characterized this period as a time of intoxication with the sound of words:

31. *Reflections on the Atomic Bomb*, ed. Robert Bartlett Haas (Los Angeles, 1973), p. 84.

this strictness [of the early second-phase program] perhaps
weakened a little weakened a little because and that in a way
was an astonishment to me, I found that I was for a little while
very much taken with the beauty of the sounds as they came
from me as I made them. ["Portraits and Repetition," p. 196]

This emphasis on pure sound in language is a possibility latent in the
1913 style, for as soon as a word surface is meant to be perceived as
such its aesthetic aspects move to the foreground and the patterning
of sounds itself becomes the central point of the work. The beginnings of such a tendency can be seen, for example, in "Susie Asado."
This part of "A Valentine to Sherwood Anderson" is typical.

A VERY VALENTINE

Very fine is my valentine.
Very fine and very mine.
Very mine is my valentine very mine and very fine.
Very fine is my valentine and mine, very fine very mine and
mine is my valentine. [*Portraits and Prayers,* p. 152]

Originally every instance of "mine" in these lines read "Stein" instead. Though appealing, this version was altered, most likely to al-
low both meanings of "valentine"—the person as well as the poem—
to apply. The word "valentine" thus establishes an identity between
the representation and the person represented, which is the ideal of
the portrait genre.
  Along with a pleasing sound composition, many portraits of this
period provide the mental stimulus of a difficult but discoverable
reference to the portrait subject, the two cooperating to form a single level of portrait perception involving comparison and memory.
For example, the second "Picasso" begins:

If I told him would he like it. Would he like it if I told him.
Would he like it would Napoleon would Napoleon would
would he like it. [*Portraits and Prayers,* p. 21]

The rhythmic repetition of groupings of elements, which continues
for another paragraph, the amusing rhyming of "I told him" and
"Napoleon," the variations in word order through the repetition of

parts of the groupings ("would Napoleon would Napoleon would would he like it"), and the comparison of Picasso with Napoleon (both dynamic but diminutive leaders) all contribute to the pleasure of reading this portrait. Indeed, several portraits of this period are among the most appreciated of Stein's works precisely because of their easily perceptible wit and the charm of their phonological composition.

But we should not forget how similar the techniques enumerated here, with the exception of the Napoleon metaphor, are to those of the first portrait phase. Compare this passage from "Mi-Careme":

> Perhaps each one is one needing to be living each one of all of them, very many being together then. If each one of all of them is one needing being living then certainly each one of all of them, very many being together then are ones needing being living. Each one being ones needing being living is then one in a way showing this thing showing being one needing being living. [pp. 176–77]

Instead of the playful music of "If I Told Him," the repetitions and variations of "Mi-Careme" create an effect of density, even ponderousness. The same technique is obviously functioning differently in these two pieces. In "Mi-Careme" the variations—"if," "perhaps," etc.—indicate different degrees of possibility of knowledge. They are important in themselves in revealing what is known of the subject, and what the mode of this knowledge is. Furthermore, the predication in each repeated block of the initial sentence is significant as a piece of knowledge in the present. In "If I Told Him," on the other hand, the repetition and variation do little to modify the meaning of the initial question, nor do they relate to the epistemological status of our perception of the subject so as to create 'present perception.' They are, instead, ornamental. It is perhaps an indication of Stein's economy that a technical discovery was never lost or abandoned, but simply put to new use from one period to the next.

However, it would be wrong to think of "If I Told Him" as totally disjoint from Stein's developing theory of the genre. If anything, it demonstrates her concern with these theories as such, as themselves the data of thought. And it is natural that such thoughts should have been spurred by Picasso, the stimulus to so much of her aesthetic awareness. For example, she plays with the idea of temporal immediacy: "Now./Not now./And now./Now." (p. 21); with the idea

of mimesis: "Exact resemblance to exact resemblance the exact resemblance as exact as a resemblance . . ."; with repetition: "Now
atively repeat at all. . . ." Then the whole Picasso/Napoleon metaphor is examined:

> I judge judge.
> As a resemblance to him.
> Who comes first. Napoleon the first . . .
> Presently. Exactly do they do.
> First exactly.
>
> [p. 22]

Variations on this continue for some time, and then comes the laughing portrait pronouncement:

> He he he he and he and he and and he and he and he and and
> as and as he and as he and he. He is and as he is, and as he is and
> he is, he is and as he and he and as he is and he and he and and
> he and he.

The subject is invoked by the calling out of his pronoun name, his
existence is assured to us ("and he is"), he is like himself ("as he is
and he is, he is"), and the process of depicting him is playful and
joking—it amounts to a great burst of laughter.

This disintegration of grammatical continuity, here by means of
fragmental repetitions, is raised to the thematic level in the last line
of the portrait: "Let me recite what history teaches. History teaches"
(p. 24). Here the metaphoric and stylistic premises of "If I Told
Him" are laid bare. For if Picasso is like Napoleon, and if Napoleon
was eventually beaten, and if history teaches, then Picasso should
realize that he is in trouble. (By this time Picasso had turned away
from cubism to neoclassicism and Stein was growing less and less
enthusiastic about his work.) However, the content of the "teaching" of history is simply the assertion that history does teach. And
this fact is presented as an echo of the problem that it was meant to
elucidate. The only message of historical time is repetition or more
precisely "insistence," the fact of time itself. One does not learn
anything from history—Picasso will not learn anything from it; one
simply goes on making it. And as a general characteristic of this portrait period, words generate words rather than new meanings and the
answer to a question consists in an echo of the question itself.

What this portrait illustrates, as much as the elements of the late second-phase style, is Stein's consciousness of and familiarity with this style. This period is overripe[32] with its assumptions, to the point where portraiture becomes almost a thematic play with first principles rather than an earnest effort to see them functioning in character depiction.

The clearest example of this comes in "Fourteen Anonymous Portraits" (1923) in which several different techniques of portraiture are tried out in separate "portraits." The most revealing is the seventh, the first to be entitled "Anonymous Portrait." It reads in full: "I know I know I know you. You know you know that" (*Portraits and Prayers,* p. 229). This is the portrait situation in miniature: the mutual awareness of two people, and their awareness of that awareness. The 'anonymity' applies to both the portraitist and the subject, equal partners in portrait generation, and because it is the general situation of portraiture that becomes the substance of this portrait, it is fitting that both of the people involved should be unnamed. But since the portrait by definition is specific rather than general, a rather nice paradox is in play. The paradox is improved by the fact that the portrait subject is termed "you" rather than "him." Either the portrait is an address to its subject, in which case it is a kind of inside joke between the portraitist and a particular but unidentified subject; or else the "you" is the reader, in which case the interaction of reader and author, a teasingly tenuous knowledge, is at issue.

In either case, this portrait is about portraiture. It is a literary metastatement presented as the kind of literature it describes, and thus it is quite a clever and witty invention. More than this, however, it illustrates an important fact about Stein's notion of the portrait. For when it is claimed that her portraits are often nothing but elaborations of a particular style, it should be remembered that her ultimate reduction of the portrait situation, as presented in "Fourteen Anonymous Portraits," is the mutual knowledge between the portraitist and the subject, with stylistic features—repetition, the transformation of proposition into name—supporting rather than dominating this interrelation.

Another interesting stylistic feature of Stein's portraiture emerges at this time: the incorporation of accidental detail into the body of

---

32. The overlapping of statement and metastatement can be seen as well in Stein's frequent incorporation of headings, e.g., "Part II," in the body of a portrait, "A part of two" ("Jo Davidson," *Portraits and Prayers,* p. 195).

the portrait. Though she had certainly made use of idiosyncratic associations throughout the first and second phases (see, for example, the analysis of "Guillaume Apollinaire"), in "He And They, Hemingway" the fortuity of these inclusions reaches new heights. The portrait reads in full:

He And They, Hemingway

Among and then young.
Not ninety-three.
Not Lucretia Borgia.
Not in or on a building.
Not a crime not in the time.
Not by this time.
Not in the way.
On their way and to head away. A head any way. What is a head. A head is what every one not in the north of Australia returns for that. In English we know. And is it to their credit that they have nearly finished and claimed, is there any memorial of the failure of civilization to cope with extreme and extremely well begun, to cope with extreme savagedom.
There and we know.
Hemingway.
How do you do and good-bye. Good-bye and how do you do.
Well and how do you do. [p. 193]

Before dismissing this portrait as unintelligible, one must take a rather peculiar fact into consideration. Stein wrote the portrait in a French school-children's notebook with an illustrated cover (see figure 2). The cover belongs to a series depicting "Les Educateurs de la Jeunesse." Victor Hugo is the particular "éducateur" being honored on the "Hemingway" notebook, his oval portrait appearing near the top of the page surrounded by four vignettes from his works: cannoneers from *Quatre-vingt treize,* a woman pouring poison into the ear of a sleeping man from *Lucrèce Borgia,* soldiers from *Les Chatiments,* and a girl dancing before a crowd from *Notre-Dame de Paris.*

If one keeps this in mind, the opening sequence of vertically arranged lines in "Hemingway" takes on a totally new character. The "young" of the first line recalls "Jeunesse" in the title of the notebook series, and refers as well to Hemingway's age and to his place "among" the other young men of Stein's acquaintance. "He was an

Figure 2. Cover design of "He and They Hemingway" notebook.

extraordinarily good-looking young man, twenty-three years old. It was not long after that that everybody was twenty-six. It became the period of being twenty-six. During the next two or three years all the young men were twenty-six years old" (*Toklas*, p. 212). These young people, Hemingway in particular, frequented Stein's salon evenings and sought her opinion about their art. Thus, Stein, like Hugo, was an educator of youth. At the same time, Hemingway can be seen as a teacher of youth through his writings about adventure and courage, a modern counterpart to the great romantic moralist, Hugo. The portraitist and her subject are in competition for the central role, a phenomenon which we saw in the overlap between Stein and Guillaume Apollinaire in his portrait. This competition is really the central point of the portrait, and a considerable source of irony. For the notion of instruction takes on different meanings when applied to Stein and Hemingway and the student/teacher relation keeps shifting between them. The title, "He And They, Hemingway," implies, partly through its sound organization, that Hemingway sees himself in opposition to others, either to the other young men, to Stein and other teachers, or to 'society,' as we shall see in the course of the portrait.

In addition to the reference to youth in the first line, the second to fifth lines take up each of the four works of Hugo mentioned on the cover. "Ninety-three" and "Lucretia Borgia" are direct translations of the titles, *Quatre-vingt treize* and *Lucrèce Borgia*; the "building" is probably a hint at *Notre-Dame de Paris*; the "crime" perhaps refers to *Les Chatiments* or *Lucrèce Borgia*. "In the time" and "by this time" suggest *In Our Time*, Hemingway's first major work, written precisely at the time of the "educational" meetings with Stein that gave rise to this portrait. It is obvious that Stein knew that these correspondences would not be available to the reader, for without the notebook cover the vertically arranged lines are quite unintelligible; no critic that I know of has ever discussed them. This deliberate disregard for the reader and the incorporation of details so accidentally related to her subject indicate the kinship between Stein and the experimental schools of the day—surrealism, futurism, cubism.

However, even with the clues provided by the notebook cover, the relation between Stein, Hugo, and Hemingway is not immediately apparent. For Stein, though setting herself up as an educator of youth, seems to be denying Hugo's modes of education, and Hemingway's as well: "*Not* ninety-three./ . . . *Not* by this time." Her

motivation here becomes apparent only from the study of outside
sources: "you see he [Hemingway] is like Derain. You remember
Monsieur de Tuille said, when I did not understand why Derain was
having the success he was having that it was because he looks like a
modern and he smells of the museums. And that is Hemingway, he
looks like a modern and he smells of the museums" (*Toklas*, p. 216).
The contrast between the real modern and the fake, between the
real "savage" and the poseur, is one that underlies the whole portrait.

If the vertically arranged lines are the words of Stein, the long
paragraph following them seems to be Hemingway's contribution to
a conversation. It length and convoluted syntax contrast sharply with
the short ellipitical phrase-paragraphs preceding it, although a few
short transitional phrases do appear at the beginning of the paragraph. These are phonological/grammatical variations on the preceding lines, with "their" probably a reference either to Stein and Toklas
(presiding together at the evening 'lessons') or to Stein and Sherwood
Anderson, who together felt themselves the aesthetic shapers of
Hemingway (see *Toklas*, p. 216). In either case, 'they' are or "he" is
"on *their* way" "to head away" from the normal path (of writing,
presumably). The verb "head" next becomes the noun in "A head
any way"; apparently if one goes "their way," the way of the modern teachers, one is 'ahead anyway' or one has "a head," an intelli-
gence, in any case or for any pathway. But as soon as this is asserted,
the question arises as to what "a head" is: "What is a head. A head is
what every one not in the north of Australia returns for that." Presumably, the northern Australians do not return a head "for that,"
because they have their own uses for heads (are cannibals, head-
hunters, etc., peculiar to the *north* of Australia?). That is, a head, on
the literal level, is a head.

Figuratively, however, everyone but cannibals returns a head "for
that." Returning a head for something could be bowing in acknowledgment of it. Or if "A head" is taken as "Ahead" again, the phrase
could mean that everyone returns ahead "for that," because of that,
because of taking "their way." Figuratively then, a head is recognition or benefit. Everyone but a cannibal bows to the avant-garde
writers, Stein in particular, or everyone but a cannibal who takes
the path of these writers ends up ahead. Hemingway (or Stein) is
talking here about the usual relation that exists between the acknowledgment of influence and the benefits of it. "Cannibals," on
the other hand, neither acknowledge nor benefit from the influence
upon them of literary pioneers; they are too busy cannibalizing the

fame, the innovations of these writers. Hemingway here is criticizing those who do not admit their debt to the avant garde. But if we remember Stein's depictions of him as "a pupil who does it without understanding it, in other words he takes training" (*Toklas*, p. 216), Hemingway's criticism of others seems to backfire. Here, not only do we learn that he "smells of the museums" but Stein suggests that he does not understand the avant-garde techniques that he is able to assimilate. He himself is a cannibal.

Next, Hemingway (or Stein, sarcastically) says, "In English we know." Either Hemingway is expressing undue confidence in his solidarity with the English tradition or Stein is sarcastically expressing it for him. The self-righteousness of Hemingway's previous pronouncement against the others, the "cannibals," again becomes through this sarcastic presentation an unwitting self-indictment.

Hemingway then asks, "And is it to their credit that they have nearly finished and claimed." He seems to be questioning the creative possibilities of the "they," the avant garde, for they "have nearly finished" and have made claims—on the public and perhaps on young writers. He continues rather pompously, asking if there is "any memorial of the failure of society to cope with extreme and extremely well begun, to cope with extreme savagedom." The extremely good beginning is "their way," the avant-garde way, which is also "extreme savagedom" in that it is rough and seemingly uncontrolled. (Laura Riding, for example, called Stein's work a "new barbarism" and associated it with primitive African art and the 'savage' rhythms of jazz; and of course Matisse *et al.* were called 'Fauves,' wild beasts.)[33] According to the speaker, Stein's experimentation is only a beginning, the beginning of the descent into the unconscious, the wild, and yet "society" has failed to cope with it. Further there is no "memorial of this failure," since little of Stein's work had been published by this time. Hemingway, at the same time that he questions the value of this work, is apparently bemoaning the lack of a published form of it or of an even more substantial monument to gall the unresponsive public. And in fact at the time the portrait was written, he was arranging for the first publication of part of *The Making of Americans* in Ford Maddox Ford's *Transatlantic*.[34] Hemingway's tone in this paragraph is that of the eager disciple trying

33. "Hulme, the New Barbarism, and Gertrude Stein," *transition* 3 (June 1927).
34. See *Toklas*, p. 215 for Stein's grudging gratitude toward Hemingway for his help.

to show his enthusiasm for the masters' words, his disgust with the insensitive public, and implicitly, his belief in his own work as the culmination of the efforts only begun by his instructors. His distaste for those who cannot cope with "savagedom" implies that he is able to do so. Nevertheless, despite his avowed championing of Stein's work, she portrays him here as an enemy to her writing.

With "There and we know" we have a shift back to Stein (and Alice or Anderson), sarcastically comforting the young outraged aco-lyte—'There, there, we know.' Then the name "Hemingway" appears, either as part of the greeting "Hemingway./How do you do" or as a summation by the narrator to the effect, 'This is Hemingway.' The final formulae for arriving and parting which follow should have been the beginning and conclusion of the preceding 'conversation.' But since both the hellos and good-byes appear jumbled together at the end, with the very revealing body of the talk coming before, the artificiality and over-enthusiasm of the greetings stand out. It is as if Stein were saying, 'This is how it began and how it ended, but we know what was really behind it all.'

The progression of this portrait, then, is from the accidentally metaphorical connections between the cover of the notebook and the subject of the portrait, to a rendering of a somewhat hypocritical conversation with Hemingway, to the gushy greetings that framed it. It proceeds from a comment on the old art (and on Hemingway's) to a presentation of Hemingway's character through his speech. The strategy is absolutely conventional, but the switch in speakers, the play on sound and grammar, the elliptical nature of the language, the circumlocution of the "Australians," and, most importantly, the arbitrary associations arising from the notebook cover make it an extremely difficult portrait.

After the lyricism and melody of the first half of the twenties, Stein wrote only one portrait in 1925 ("Sitwell Edith Sitwell"). I am using this natural break to demarcate the boundary between the second and third periods of Stein's portraiture, although Stein specif-ically included portraits written later in the twenties among those dominated by the beauty of the sound of words. The reasons for this divergence from her scheme will be made clear in part III.

III

The various metaphors that Stein used in "Portraits and Repeti-tion" to depict her succession of portrait styles have been quite helpful so far in understanding these styles. The simultaneous "listening and talking" of the first style stressed both the immediacy of time perception in the continuous present and the duplication of the subject's perception in the mind of the portraitist, a kind of mutual self-creativity. The "looking" of the early second period implied a distancing of the subject as a pure object of perception. And the "melody" of the subject, which Stein used to describe the late second period, accounts for the rhythm and euphony of these works. But when we come to the last period (1926–1946), Stein has a more puzzling metaphor, "self-contained movement":

> All the looking was there the talking and listening was there but instead of giving what I was realizing at any and every moment of them and of me until I was empty of them I made them contained within the thing I wrote that was them. The thing in itself folded itself up inside itself like you might fold a thing up to be another thing which is that thing inside that thing. . . .
>
> If you think how you fold things or make a boat or anything else out of paper or getting anything to be inside anything, the hole in the doughnut or the apple in the dumpling perhaps you will see what I mean. ["Portraits and Repetition," pp. 199–200]
>
> I wanted . . . to do portraits where there was more movement inside in the portrait and yet it was to be the whole portrait completely held within that inside.
>
> I began to feel movement to be a different thing than I had felt it to be.
>
> It was to me beginning to be a less detailed thing and at the same time a thing that existed so completely inside in it and it was it was so completely inside that really looking and listening and talking were not a way any longer needed for me to know about this thing about movement being existing. [p. 203]

As I tried to show in chapter 2, such a development was logical within Stein's notions about portraiture, but it is not at all obvious what it means as a description of the actual portraits of this period.

This discrepancy becomes even more pronounced when we consider the extreme diversity of the third-phase portraits. Some are as 'difficult' as the 1913 portraits, although differently so, while others are as close to straight expository prose as anything in Stein's writing (they are certainly precursors of *The Autobiography of Alice B. Toklas*), and still others seem to be doing what the "melodic" pieces of the early twenties do with reference and euphony. If we are to understand Stein's depiction of this period we must sort out this diversity.

First of all, I shall exclude the straightforward prose portraits from the discussions, e.g., "Duchess de Rohan—A Writer," "The Life of Juan Gris," "Picabia," "Elie Lascaux," "Stieglitz," "To Pierre de Massot." Though portraits, these texts are not part of the main line of Stein's experimentation. They are "appreciations": their function is not to render their subjects with immediacy, but to show Stein's approval of them and hence to show them as worthy of public approval.

R. B. Haas introduced the term "appreciation" into Steinian criticism in his introduction to the second section of *Reflections on the Atomic Bomb*, called "Portraits and Appreciations": "The balance of pieces in this section may be seen not only as portraits but as encomia. . . .This rather sentimental support of her friends is quite consistent with Gertrude Stein's theory of criticism: 'Nobody needs criticism, only appreciation.' Gertrude Stein's portraits and reviews were appreciations" (p. 42). The implication of this statement, which is applied to portraits of virtually every phase, is that all of Stein's portraits may be seen as appreciations. But, as we have seen, these works are neither generally positive with regard to their subjects, nor particularly concerned with expressing Stein's affection for them. Even when Stein's feelings about her subject are apparent, they are as often as not disapproving as appreciative, as in "He and They, Hemingway," and moreover the disapproval is not the central point of this portrait.

The second category of texts—those seemingly indistinguishable from the lyrical ones of the early twenties—have a special status in Stein's development. For though there is no difference in the technical devices in play, nor in the general 'musical' effect, these works are a bridge between the late second period and the portraits of self-contained movement. The most important difference between them and the lyrical portraits of the twenties is their lack of conventional reference to their subjects.

In the first portrait of this kind, for example, "Jean Cocteau" (1926), one of the works Stein specifically mentions as showing her intoxication with sound, there is no reference to the subject at all. The first part of it reads:

> Needs be needs be needs be near.
> Needs be needs be needs be.

This is where they have their land astray.
Two say.
This is where they have their land astray.
Two say.
Needs be needs be needs be
Needs be needs be needs be near.
Second time.
It may be nearer than two say.
Near be near be near be
Needs be needs be needs be
Needs be needs be needs be near.
He was a little while away.
Needs be nearer than two say.
Needs be needs be needs be needs be.
Needs be needs be needs be near.
He was away a little while.
And two say.
He was away a little while.
He was away a little while
And two say.
[*Portraits and Prayers,* p. 80]

It is conceivable, of course, that the "two" here are Stein and Cocteau, and that "he" is a reference to the subject, Cocteau, as well.
We also know from *The Autobiography of Alice B. Toklas* that the
friendship between Stein and Cocteau was a mutual appreciation
from afar,[35] which might account for the opposition of "near" and
"away." However such interpretations seem rather strained in this
overwhelming context of repetition, rhyme, refrains, and even musical instructions (e.g., "Second time").

In addition to the phonological organization, we find incomplete
sentences and semantic irregularity ("This is where they have their
land astray"). The first sentence, "Needs be . . . ," is also ambiguous,
for it resembles an invocation in form, but suggests as well the condi-
tional formula "If need be," so that even the mood of the verb is
complicated here. And as the portrait continues in "Part two," it
puts many of the elements already introduced into new relations.

35. *Toklas,* p. 204: "They met once or twice and began a friendship that consists in their
writing to each other quite often and liking each other immensely and having many young
and old friends in common, but not in meeting."

For example, the "two" of "And two say" turns up in "Part two," which is used not only as a structural demarcation but also as part of the body of the portrait. We have seen this mixture of levels in the second-phase portraits, and here it occurs as "Part two and part one/Part two and part two . . ." (p. 81). But since "two" figured prominently in the previous section with a different meaning, in "Part two and two say," "part" begins to function as much like a verb as a noun. And in the integrations

> He was near to where they have their land astray.
> He was near to where they have two say.
> Part two and near one. Part one and near one.

we begin to oscillate as well between "two" and "to," and "near" as verb and as preposition. The whole portrait operates as a steadily increasing field of grammatical/semantic ambiguity.

The familiar device of non-referential shifters is used here as well in the sequence:

> their elevation their safety their share and there where. This is where they have the land astray. Two say.

"Their" has no antecedent (except for the unidentified "two"), and is transformed through its phonology into "there." But "there" leads us to a truncated and equally referent-less "where." By the next sentence we find the referent for "where," but this turns out to be the old nonsense sentence from the first part, "This is where they have their land astray." We are thus led through a series of signposts to the nowhere "land" of the first part. Such a progression occurs in extreme form in the repeated chant:

> Put it there in there there where they have it.
> Put it there in there there where they halve it.

Relieved of specific reference, the words in this portrait have nothing more than their pale dictionary meanings, and even these are made ambiguous through the variations in context. Words thus are almost pure phonological quanta which turn up at more or less regular intervals through the distributing faculty of syntax. We are very close indeed to a musical, and certainly to a rhythmical use of language.

The importance of syntax as the relational force among the

word-sounds was not accidental. For the development of the portrait of self-contained movement was accompanied by Stein's new
interest in grammar:

> I had begun again some time before [the writing of portraits
> of self-contained movement] in working at grammar and sen-
> tences and paragraphs and what they mean . . . And soon I was
> so completely concerned with these things that melody, beauty
> if you like was once more as it should always be a by-product.
> ["Portraits and Repetition," p. 201]

Thus, the late melodic portraits were being written when Stein's
meditations on grammar had already begun. We might suggest that
the "concentrating"[36] of melody at this time was directly related
to the "self-contained movement" which came later. For melody
appears here as a patterning of elements created by their phonological similarity and grammatical properties. It is a set of intricately
varied, internal relations, a phonology and syntax devoid of semantic
reference. And this is precisely the meaning of the metaphor of self-
contained movement. It aims at a mimetic rendering of the essence
of the subject—essential movement for essential movement, a purely
structural equivalence.

However, the melodic portraits were 'faulty' in that their sensuous
sound surface itself became the primary object of perception, rather
than the configuration which the sound helped to create, and all the
cultural associations with music and lyricism entered in as well. The
aesthetic thus dominated the representational, and these portraits
missed the generic impact that the third-phase solution finally made
possible. For by substituting "movement" for "melody" Stein was
able to overcome the 'failings' of the late musical portraits.

Interestingly, however, it was the configurational rather than the

---

36. *Ibid.*, p. 197: "I concentrated the internal melody of existence that I had learned in
relation to things seen into the feeling I then had there in Saint Remy [c. 1922] of light
and air and air moving and being still. I worked at these things then with a great deal of
concentration and as it was to me an entirely new way of doing it I had as a result a very
greatly increased melody. This melody for a little while after rather got the better of me
and it was at that time that I wrote these portraits of which I have just spoken, the second
Picasso, the second Carl Van Vechten, the Jean Cocteau, Lipschitz, the Sitwells, Edith
Sitwell, Joe Davidson, quantities of portraits. Portraits after my concentrated effort at
Saint Remy to really completely and exactly find the word for the air and sky and light
and existence down there was relatively a simple thing and I as you may say held these
portraits in my hand and they came easily and beautifully and truly."

sound properties of "Jean Cocteau" that Cocteau himself noticed in reading it. For he wrote to Stein, "J'ai reçu ce soir votre grand sourire grammatical" (Mellow, p. 251). As plays on grammar and relationality in language, many of the late musical portraits thus can be seen as deviations from the musical-referential portraits of the early twenties, and as precursors of the portraits of self-contained movement. For this reason, I have included them within the third period of Stein's portraiture.

We come now, at long last, to "George Hugnet" (1928), which Stein herself used as an example of a particularly successful portrait of self-contained movement. (Paragraphs have been numbered to facilitate reference.)

George Hugnet

[1] George and Genevieve.
[2] Geronimo with a with whether they thought they were with whether.
[3] Without their finding it out. Without. Their finding it out. With whether.
[4] George whether they were about. With their finding their whether it finding it out whether with their finding about it out.
[5] George with their finding it with out.
[6] George whether their with their it whether.
[7] Redoubt out with about.
[8] With out whether it their whether with out doubt.
[9] Azure can with out about.
[10] It is welcome welcome thing.
[11] George in are ring.
[12] Lain away awake.
[13] George in our ring.
[14] George Genevieve Geronimo straightened it out without their finding it out.
[15] Grammar makes George in our ring which Grammar make George in our ring.
[16] Grammar is as disappointed not is as grammar is as disappointed.
[17] Grammar is not as Grammar is as disappointed.

[18]   George is in our ring. Grammar is not is disappointed. In
       are ring.
[19]   George Genevieve in are ring.

[*Portraits and Prayers*, p. 66]

As with "Cocteau," this portrait refers neither to its subject nor to
anything else that one could imagine. But though it is a semantic
"decomposition," it is highly organized phonologically and syntactically. In fact, it is similar in many respects to "One. Harry Phelan
Gibb," in that it presents a strikingly homogeneous surface against
which a small number of contrasting words are repeated. But where
the contrasts before were embodied in present participles or gerunds,
here they occur usually as nouns, in fact, names—"George," "Genevieve," and "Geronimo," as well as "Grammar," the hero of the
piece, which appears personified and often capitalized (e.g., "which
Grammar make George . . . "). The isolation of these names can be
seen in the fact that the three proper names all begin (and "George"
ends as well) with the cluster /dž/, not found elsewhere in the portrait. All four begin with the grapheme G̲ which does not appear
initially in any other word. Further, /or/ in "George" and /v/ in
"Genevieve" are limited to these words, and "Geronimo" contains
elements from "George," "Genevieve," and "Grammar." The names
are thus linked phonologically, visually, and syntactically, and are
set off sharply from their context. However, in "George Hugnet,"
unlike "One," the patterning of these key words does not suggest
any kind of regularity or rhythm. There is little about this portrait,
in fact, that would prompt the music metaphor.

Aside from the key words, the only nouns in "Hugnet" occur in
the seven lines from "Redoubt" to "our ring." Except for "ring"
they each make only one appearance in the portrait, and are linked
through rhyme to other parts of speech.[37] Thus they acquire an interesting intermediate position in terms of prominence and significance. They are introduced one at a time in consecutive lines, and
because of their novelty, they seem to promise much. But they end
up as variations on basic sound configurations. Even the sentence,

37. "Redoubt" and "doubt" are linked to "out" (which, in contrast, occurs 11 times),
to "without" (3 times), and to "about" (4 times); "azure" to "were" (twice), "whether"
(10 times), and "grammar" (7 times); and "thing" and "ring" to "finding" (7 times).

"Azure can with out about," which suggests "I sure can without doubt," remains merely semantically titillating rather than meaningful within the portrait. The five nouns, with their simultaneous similarities and differences from what precedes them, seem to mark out a transitional region in the portrait.[38] As a result of such transitional words, of anomalous words, parts of speech, and phonemes, the portrait can be seen as divided into three parts—six homogeneous "paragraphs" in the beginning, seven transitional paragraphs in the middle, and six homogeneous ones at the end. This is the basic structural organization of "George Hugnet."

The two six-paragraph sections, however, differ radically from each other. The first is composed of a highly restricted phonological repertoire: $/w/$, $/ð/$, $/\theta/$, $/r/$, $/t/$, $/I/$, $/\varepsilon/$, $/\partial/$, $/aU/$.[39] The vowel sequence of the first line, $/o \partial \varepsilon \partial \varepsilon/$,[40] is generally typical of what follows, several lines beginning with "George" and thus with the vowel $/o/$, and continuing with a patterning of a limited number of other vowels. This regularity occurs among the consonants as well, which are all either front or semi-vocalic. In the 61 words of this section, $/w/$ occurs 20 times and always in initial position, $/\theta/$ 11 times, $/ð/$ 18, $/r/$ 22, and $/t/$ 17 times.

The striking similarities and repetitions of sound elements produce many unexpected rhymes. "Whether" sounds like "with their" in the second sentence of paragraph four. In paragraph two, the sequence "they were with whether" establishes "they were" and "whether" as chiasmic twins. "Without their finding it out" matches "without" with "it out," and—also in paragraph three—"With whether" seems a faint echo of "Without their." These multiplied correspondences

38. This transitional quality can be seen in several phonological features as well as in the anomalous nouns. For example, the vowel /e/ in "Lain away awake" occurs three times here, three times in the first section ("they), and once each in "straightened," "makes" and "make" in the last section. Thus, an interesting symmetry in the distribution of this vowel can be seen—3-3-3. Furthermore, "awake" is linked through rhyme with "make" (appearing in the final section) and its /w/ along with that of "away" echoes one of the most frequent phonemes of the first section. The /l/ in "welcome" occurs only in the middle section (in "Lain" and "welcome"). This purely intermediate element is combined in "welcome" with the /w/ of the first section and the /k/ found only in the last, producing a blend of distinctive elements from all three divisions of the portrait.

39. The only exceptions to this are in the proper names already mentioned, the vowels of "they" and "thought" which match the equally anomalous "makes" and "not" of the last six paragraphs, the /b/ in "about" (which blends through rhyme with "out" and "without"), and the word "finding." The latter is unrelated in sound or morphology to anything in the first section, although it is echoed later in "thing" and "ring."

40. I am assuming a rapid pronunciation of "and," and an English pronunciation of both these names, as their spelling suggests.

among semantically and syntactically heterogeneous elements function similarly to the rhymes of the second portrait phase, although
the scale and complication here are perhaps greater than was usual
in the earlier portraits. The effect is the decomposition of semantics
and the creation of an elaborate network of meaningless connections
among individuated words, or even syllables or phonemes.

This breakdown of semantics is also brought about by syntactic
irregularity, for there is not one complete sentence in the whole of
the first section. We have already noted that most of the words (47
out of 61) are syncategorematic—prepositions, conjunctions, pronouns, articles. These certainly militate against a descriptive or
referential sequence. But they are, moreover, combined without
relief in meaningless syntagms, such as "With whether." And even
when a sequence follows a normal grammatical order, as in "Their
finding it out," it is either an isolated fragment as here, or becomes
varied, as in "with their finding it with out," thus suffering a loosening of whatever syntactic or semantic unity it once possessed. Thus,
the first section of "Hugnet" is dominated not only by phonological
connections which disrupt the syntactic and semantic unity of sentences, but also by syntactic fragmentation. It is a writing of bits and
pieces held together by sound.

In the middle section as well, there are no well-formed sentences,
although there are some finite verbs with subjects—"is" and "can."
"Azure can with out about" (if "can" is a verb here) and "It is welcome welcome thing" come close to being complete sentences, so
that syntactically as well as phonologically there is some deviance
from the uniformity and fragmentation of the first section.

However, as soon as we come to the last section we are confronted
with a complete, well formed sentence: "George Genevieve Geronimo
straightened it out without their finding it out." (Stein seldom used
commas or "and"s to separate the members of a list, so that "George
Genevieve Geronimo" is well formed by her standards.) Since this
sentence gathers together the three names in their only occurrence in
one line, since something was apparently "straightened out," and
since this is the first complete sentence, we begin to wonder (perhaps
whimsically) whether a kind of thematics is involved here: that
through the integration of the names with a complete grammatical
structure some problem in the portrait has been resolved.

The means of this "straightening out" is "Grammar," which makes
its first appearance in the following sentence: "Grammar makes
George in our ring which Grammar make George in our ring." In

order for this sentence to approach grammaticality, the "which" joining the two almost identical clauses would have to be a modifier of the second "Grammar" in the Latinate construction of the sort: "The note arrived today; which note was interesting to John." In this example, the "which" stresses the subject of the second clause; but frequently a displaced object can be stressed by the same construction, as in "The note arrived today; which note I gave to John." In the sentence which we are discussing, either "Grammar" is the subject of its clause, in which case an inanimate noun performs a direct act on an animate one (albeit through a plural verb), or the word order is reversed from the normal, and "Grammar" is made by "George." The point is that the syntactic arrangement of this sentence is totally ambiguous. We are suspended between a normal syntactic order which produces an abnormal semantics, and a more or less normal semantics which involves a totally non-English word order. Furthermore, we are witnesses to a kind of contradiction of equality, for the two clauses of the sentence are identical in almost all respects,[41] but prove to be unequal when related by the word "which."

This ambiguity functions in all the rest of the sentences of the last section of "Hugnet." For example, in "Grammar is as disappointed not is as grammar is as disappointed," grammar both is and is not as disappointed as it is. There is thus a simultaneous affirmation and denial of the same proposition. With "Grammar is not as Grammar is as disappointed" and "Grammar is not is disappointed" this contradiction is obvious, and we are reminded of the 'moving in the shoe' example of "Constance Fletcher" where logical relations were placed in question. We should note, too, that the contradiction applies most often here to a comparison—"as disappointed as"—and hence to identity as well, for a thing is equal to itself in that it has the same relation to another factor as 'itself' has. The obliteration of the whole logical mechanism of identity through comparison is built into the grammatical constructions of the last section of "Hugnet," and this is certainly consistent with the goal of absolute self-enclosure and non-relationality.

There are other deliberate ambiguities as well. The pair, "George is in are ring" and "George is in our ring," is an alternation between an ungrammatical string of words and a perfectly well formed

---

41. The only difference is "make" instead of "makes" in the second clause, perhaps a slip on Stein's part.

sentence. The difference is created by a change in one element of
the sentence and involves no phonological shift at all in rapid speech.
The syntactic/semantic properties of "our" are sufficient to change
a fragmented list into a unified structure. Now, we have seen that
"Grammar makes George in our ring," rather than making him "in
are ring." Thus, Grammar would probably be "disappointed" in "are
ring," a non-grammatical string. This would help to explain the paragraph, "George is in our ring. Grammar is not is disappointed. In are
ring." When "George is in our ring" "Grammar is not disappointed,"
but "Grammar is disappointed" "In are ring." The sentence, "Grammar is not is disappointed," is thus a condensation of two sentences,
while "In are ring" is separated from the sentence to which it properly belongs. It thus suffers the fragmentation which its own elements
demonstrate. This opposition of fragmentation and wholeness in the
"our"/"are" alternation is resolved at the end in favor of "are." As
the marked member of the pair, it carries both possibilities in it.
We are left again with ambiguity.

The opposition between fragmentation and unity is supported by
the phonology of the third section as well. The names, nouns, and
the adjective, "disappointed," are all polysyllabic, while the syncategorematic words—"is," "as," "in," "are," "our," "not," "it,"
and "out"—are monosyllabic. "George," monosyllabic but phonologically and syntactically related to the polysyllabic words, is a kind
of cross between the category of the name/noun/adjective and that
of the grammatical linker, as its ambiguous relation to both grammatical fragmentation and unity in the "George is in are/our ring"
case shows.

Such an opposition of parts of speech is outlined in Stein's theorizing, where nouns are in a kind of functional war with the other parts
of speech in creating isolation or relationality. She produced a blend
of these two possibilities through "balance," here manifested in
elaborate ambiguity and logical contradiction of equal elements, in
the final section of the portrait. The multiplied relations among
words here tends to loosen the categories of noun and linker, so that
to a large degree they overlap. This 'noun-verb-ism,' simultaneous
isolation and flow, is another realization of "self-contained movement."

If we turn now to "George Hugnet" as a whole, we find different
ways in which fragmentation and flow are combined. In the first
section, the homogeneous phonology fuses elements which are
semantically and syntactically unconnected. Like the names in this

part, the words creating linkage become isolated units. In the middle section, the phonological unity is disrupted by the appearance of several anomalous nouns, and the syntactic discontinuity is slightly dispelled by the presence of larger syntactic structures. The tendencies begun in the transitional section are fully expressed in the final part of the portrait. Here, not only are there complete sentences, but whole bunchings of sentences are suggested by ambiguous elements in a single grammatical sentence. Thus, this section—in which "Grammar" occurs for the first time—is dominated by very large, complicated syntactic structures. The phonology, on the other hand, tends to isolate the often-repeated, polysyllabic words from the flow of the syntax, or, in the "are"/"our" pair, contributes to the ambiguity between isolation and flow. As a whole, the portrait seems to opt for the possibilities offered by large syntactic structures, if we can place any confidence in our interpretation of "straightened out." However, the final line, "George Genevieve in are ring," contains neither grammatical nor phonological continuity in itself, and it is only through the presence of its elements in the preceding context that it suggests the opposition of isolation and flow.

What "self-contained movement" means then, according to this analysis, is a disruption of external reference in a structure in which elements are simultaneously separated and bound together. This oscillation between fragmentation and flow prevents the portrait from recalling other flows, such as music, while the lack of reference keeps us tuned on the dynamics of the work itself.

Such an experience with the structure of a work is intended by Stein to simulate "acquaintance" with the subject of the portrait. But it should be clear by now that the equation of a literary structure with a personality essence produces an extremely opaque portrait. We are simply not accustomed to seeing similarity between the two, other than that both a person and a literary work are dynamically organized, unique, and whole. But such categories make no attempt to express the nature of the organization, uniqueness, or wholeness of either the work or the person, and one would be hard put to say why this portrait should not have Picasso, Alice Toklas, or in fact anyone as its subject. Such a work seems to function more like a pronoun than a name. It is a matter of faith on our part to think that the association between our experience with this portrait and the man, Georges Hugnet, has any meaning. And when we consider how little trust an author like Stein is likely to generate in her overtaxed reader, the effectiveness of this generically ideal solution seems rather doubtful.

Our faith becomes further shaken when we consider the other portrait which Stein used as a successful example of "self-contained movement." This is "Bernard Faÿ," a very playful discussion of articles, where "a," "an," and "the" function both normally and as the terms under discussion, without the usual clues distinguishing the two uses:

> The this that and an and end in deed indeed intend in end and lend and send and tend intended. [*Portraits and Prayers*, p. 41]

We are astonished, however, to find that Stein has transferred whole sections of "Faÿ" into *How To Write* where they fit quite smoothly into the general grammatical exposition. One wonders, then, whether there is any reason other than the title to consider "Faÿ" a portrait, and this is a problem with the portraits of self-contained movement which can never be resolved. The portrait format is the only factor holding the subject and the writing together, along with our faith that Stein was not engaged in an elaborate literary joke.

The evidence does suggest, though, that Stein considered these portraits a satisfactory way of rendering her subjects. She had encountered a group of neo-romantic painters whose work she was at a loss at first to evaluate,[42] and, as in the first portrait period, she wrote portraits of these young artists as exercises in judgment. "More Grammar Genia Berman," "Pavlik Tchelichef or Adrian Arthur," and "Christian Bérard" are among these, although their resemblance to the first-phase portraits stops at authorial motivation. Stein clearly thought of these works as consistent with her portraiture as a whole, and in fact as advances upon the earlier solutions.

However, having once achieved this balancing of the demands of the portrait genre, Stein's attention was permanently shifted from the path she had followed since 1908. As she said, "Then slowly I got a little tired, all that had been tremendously exciting, and one

---

42. *Toklas*, p. 228: "Virgil [Thomson] had in his room a great many pictures by Christian Bérard and Gertrude Stein used to look at them a great deal. She could not find out at all what she thought about them.

"She and Virgil Thomson used to talk about them endlessly. . . . At this time she had come back to portrait writing with renewed vigour and she, to clarify her mind, as she said, did portraits of the russian [Tchelitchef] and of the frenchman."

day then I began to write the Autobiography of Alice B. Toklas"
("Portraits and Repetition," p. 204). The portraits appearing in the
next years were generally "appreciations." There were no new experiments with portraiture, except perhaps the book *Four In America* (1933), in which Stein was "trying to write Grant, and Wilbur
Wright and Henry James and Washington do other things than they
did so as to try to find out just what it is that what happens has to
do with what is" (p. 206). The work is divided into four long sections, each of which is devoted to one of the four men listed above
who carries out the deeds or duties of a different person. It is an
experiment with the relation between act and identity and the effect
of the two on America, for Stein was very concerned at this time
with the nature of the American character. *Four In America* added
little to the progression of ideas about portraiture which we have so
far followed, and its length prevents me from discussing it in detail.

In summary, then, we have seen the path Stein travelled from typologizing to immediacy of perception to self-contained movement.
The theoretical development is matched by the adaptation of a basic
storehouse of devices—repetition, non-referential shifters, rhyme,
verb-oriented writing—to the needs of the changing theories, ending
in the intellectually perfect solution to the demands of the portrait
genre found in "George Hugnet" and "Bernard Faÿ." That this 'perfect' solution was also a dead end is reflected perhaps in a statement
made by Stein in the year of her death, 1946: "Nobody enters into
the mind of someone else, not even a husband and wife. You may
touch, but you do not enter into each other's mind" (Mellow, p.
122). And, in a sense, this statement of the limitations of human
knowledge shows the limitations of portraiture as well. For not only
is "acquaintance" a realm of cognition outside of normal depictions
of others, but no matter how close Stein can take us to the immediacy and the essence of a person there remains a disjunction between
the subject and the perceiver, and between the perceiver and the
reader, that cannot be overcome. The portrait must ultimately become a depiction of the author's thoughts in a manner not available
to her audience. And this final isolation seems always to lurk in the
background of portrait communication, despite the enormous advances made by Stein in satisfying the ideals of the genre.

4

Literary Cubism: The Limits of the Analogy

> Exact resemblance to exact resemblance the exact resemblance as exact
> as a resemblance, exactly as resembling, exactly resembling, exactly in
> resemblance exactly a resemblance, exactly and resemblance. For this is so.
> Because.
>
> "If I Told Him. A Completed Portrait of Picasso"

The paradox reached at the end of the last chapter is a rather perplexing one. For Stein had approached the problem of the literary portrait in a very conscious and rational manner, and yet had ended up with a logical contradiction—non-representational portraiture. The explanation for this paradox does not lie in some failing of Stein's logic or in her inability to realize its demands in prose. Rather, the problem arose from her overextension of her medium. For we should remember that the most significant force in generating the development of Steinian portraiture was the indexical-iconic definition of the portrait derived from painting, and that Stein's activity may be looked upon as an attempt to accommodate a set of visual norms to a set of literary ones.

Part of the stimulus for this interaction of painting and literature was the impression made on Stein by the revolutionary experiments of the painters of her day, particularly the cubists. The circumstantial evidence for a connection between Stein and these artists is, of course, abundant and well documented. Her friendship with most of the major figures of cubism, her patronage of their art well before it had reached the notice or appreciation of the public, and her own writings on art—"Pictures," *Picasso*, etc.—indicate her involvement in the movement. In addition, Stein draws explicit parallels between cubist painting and her own writing. She claims that *Three Lives* was written under the influence of a portrait by Cézanne,[1] she compares the "elemental abstraction" of her own and Picasso's art (*Toklas*, pp. 63–64), and in one much-disputed quotation she even speaks

---

1. *Toklas*, p. 34, "[Cézanne's portrait of a woman] was an important purchase because in looking and looking at this picture Gertrude Stein wrote Three Lives . . . she had this Cézanne and she looked at it and under its stimulus she wrote Three Lives."

of Picasso and herself as doing the same thing in their respective media. [2]

This interartistic connection has seemed so important to critics that the term "cubist writing" is now a commonplace of Steinian scholarship. Unfortunately, the tag is seldom explained, except in the most general terms, and is applied, moreover, to such disparate writers as Apollinaire and William Carlos Williams. [3] In fact, there are some remarkable similarities between Stein's and the cubists' work, both in their assessments of the general problems of their arts and in the specific technical devices they invented to deal with these problems. In this chapter I shall examine the relation between Steinian writing and cubist painting to see if it does not shed light on the dilemma we have encountered.

The term usually used to describe those works of Stein's which are nonrepresentational (along with many that are representational) is "abstraction," [4] which like "portrait" itself is borrowed from the critical vocabulary of painting. [5] In fact, it is the transference of this

2. Arnold Rönnebeck, "Gertrude Was Always Giggling," *Books Abroad* 18, no. 4 (October 1944), p. 3. "Well, Pablo is doing abstract portraits in painting. I am trying to do abstract portraits in *my* medium, *words.*" Because of Stein's later insistence in *Picasso* that Picasso did not create abstract art, several critics have disputed the accuracy of this report. A more reliable statement of the correspondence between the two comes from Stein herself in *Picasso*, p. 16: "I was alone at this time in understanding him, perhaps because I was expressing the same thing in literature. . . . "

3. See Bram Dijkstra, *The Hieroglyphics of a New Speech; Cubism, Stieglitz, and the Early Poetry of William Carlos Williams* (Princeton, 1969), Gerald Kamber, *Max Jacob and the Poetics of Cubism* (Baltimore, 1971) and Mortimer Guiney, *Cubisme et littérature* (Genève, 1972). Richard Bridgman (p. 142) points out several areas of similarity between Apollinaire and Stein during the period from 1912 to 1914, a topic that requires further detailed research.

4. See Michael J. Hoffman, *The Development of Abstractionism in the Writings of Gertrude Stein* (Philadelphia, 1965) and B. L. Reid, *Art by Subtraction* (Norman, Oklahoma, 1958). The frequent description of Stein's work as "musical" usually implies some notion of abstraction; see Leonard Bernstein, "Music and Miss Stein," *New York Book Review*, May 22, 1949, p. 4; Wyndham Lewis, *Time and Western Man* (New York, 1928), p. 114.

5. The relation of the words "portrait" and "abstract" extends to their etymology. "Abstract" is a Latinate word from *abs + tractus* (*trahere*) meaning 'drawn away from' while "portrait" is derived from 'portray' which enters Middle English from Old French and thus ultimately from Latin *portrahere—pro + trahere*, 'to draw forth' (OED, Compact Edition, vol. 1, pp. 41–42, vol. 2, pp. 1146–47). The first stresses the distance between the product and its stimulus; the second the bond between the two. This distinction is consistent with the usual understanding of the portrait as firmly rooted in its subject, as containing its subject's essence, while an abstraction in art is usually understood as a break in the relation between the work and its subject. However the etymological similarity and the fact that an essence is itself abstract perhaps helps to explain the tendency of these two words to fall together, even though the intent of portraiture and abstract art toward a subject matter could hardly be more opposed.

term to its new context that brings about so much confusion. For the term "abstraction" has at least two meanings in the visual arts of the twentieth century. It applies to works with abstract subjects, and to works "without" subjects. The first of these meanings has relevance (with important qualifications) to the first-phase portraits, that is, to the typologizing works which make direct reference to their subjects; the second meaning to portraits of the second and especially the third phases of Steinian portraiture, where there is no overt mention of the characterisitcs or attributes of the subject.

We shall begin, then, with the first meaning—a work with an abstract subject. Malevich's *Black Square on a White Ground,* for example, is called abstract art because its subject matter, a black square on a white background, does not occur within the sensible world. There is no doubt that the painting looks like a black square on a white background. Here it is simply the abstract mode of the subject matter that endows its mimetic representation with the term "abstraction." But the element of mimesis in such abstractions is quite problematic. For the question immediately arises as to whether we are looking at a representation of a black square on a white background or simply at a black square on a white background. That is, is the painting a sign of an object or an object? This ambiguity is a peculiarity of abstract paintings of the first type, since geometric compositions are not imitations of anything (there is no 'idea' of a black square on a white background), yet occur in paintings, which are semiotic structures.

It is interesting, too, that the most universally offered illustration of the iconic sign, the basis of mimetic representation, is the geometric diagram. Presumably, such a drawing is an icon of abstract relations. Yet it seems paradoxical that the similarity of *signans* and *signatum* is most clearly demonstrated in a visual representation of an abstraction. Perhaps this can be explained by the fact that the geometric figure—e.g., circle or square—is by definition two-dimensional, like the surface of a canvas or a piece of paper. As a result, there is little resistance between the medium and its subject matter, and we have the situation of "immediacy," or lack of intrusiveness of the medium in the sign relation, which was described in chapter 1 as the basis for mimesis. In paintings of geometrical figures, there seems to be so little intrusiveness, in fact, that the distinction between sign vehicle and referent is almost totally obscured, the sign and the thing becoming one.

In fact, the very ease of this mimesis has conditioned the use of

geometrical figures in the visual arts. The whole artistry of painting
was thought to lie in its illusionism, its ability to overcome its two-
dimensionality and to be perceived as three-dimensional. As a result,
the introduction of such subjects into painting was considered a
completely revolutionary development in the twentieth century.
Since 'anyone can paint lines and circles on a canvas,' this purely
abstract, geometric subject matter was taken as anti-artistic, or at
least non-artistic, in its effect.

In contrast, we should note how foreign this complex of considerations is to literary art. The first meaning of visual abstraction is never
transferred to literature. We do not speak of literary works as "abstractions" if they happen to deal with abstract subjects, whether
geometric or otherwise, and a writer has always been considered
equally artistic whether he discussed circles, beauty, or his favorite
dog.

However, paintings have also very frequently represented abstract
subjects without being called abstractions. Allegorical paintings, for
example, Dürer's engravings of death, represent abstractions but are
not called abstract art. The real significance of geometry for the first
type of abstraction, then, is that its elements and concepts are both
abstract and capable of mimetic representation on a two-dimensional
visual surface. "Death," "beauty," etc., are abstract but are depicted
in the visual arts by arbitrary, conventional signs, "symbols" in Morris's terminology (although these signs also depend on iconicity—
unless the painted scythe looks like a real scythe it cannot signify
death). In the same way language, the medium of literary art, is largely composed of conventional signs. The ontological status of a subject—its abstractness or concreteness—is thus irrelevant to both
painting and literature as long as the subject is being signified by
symbols. But as soon as iconicity, mimesis, becomes the mode of
representation, the ontological status of the subject becomes crucial.

Now, since the usual mode of painting until the twentieth century
was mimesis, and since paint is a visual medium, we would expect
painters to have chosen concrete, material subjects. However, we
must realize that mimesis, even under such conditions, is not a simple matter, because there is considerable resistance between flat
canvas and the depths and volumes of the visible world. The Renaissance invented a number of devices, in particular vanishing-point
perspective and *chiaroscuro,* to overcome this resistance. These conventions presumed a fixed viewer and a fixed light source. The frame,
like a window, delimited a plane, and the size of the objects "seen"

through this window was proportional to their distance from it. 'Scientific perspective' "is readily understood by the untrained spectator since it rests on the same cues that he responds to in dealing with his everyday visual world."[6] The assumption behind such a system is that the picture is a representation of the field of vision of a perceiver at a fixed moment in time. Other systems do not make these assumptions. For example, children's art or medieval icons order the size of objects according to their relative importance. Such art does not posit a correspondence between the picture and a visual field. It is a conceptual rather than a perceptual arrangement.

As soon as artists became interested in representing reality as something other than the orthodox visual field of post-medieval art, the accommodation of reality to medium which had enabled mimesis to exist between static, two-dimensional paintings and constantly changing, three-dimensional objects had to be upset. And this is precisely what happened in twentieth-century painting. The invention of the camera, the new concern with time and perception provoked by the ideas of Bergson and Husserl, and advances in color theory first incorporated by the Impressionists led to the discarding of Renaissance illusionism as a means of representing objects in the world. One result was cubism, an extraordinary exploration of the medium of painting and of the ways in which this medium could be made to represent.

With two-dimensionality restored as a vital fact of painting, the special status of the geometric figure became extremely important. For Cézanne's "sphere, cone, and cylinder"[7] can be seen as the means of relating solid objects to a plane surface. They were structural abstractions of real objects, capable of both looking like the object and of conforming to the two-dimensionality of the picture plane. Furthermore, the elements of these figures—curves, lines, angles, etc.—were the formative principles of both the picture plane and three-dimensional reality.

It was the very prominence of this geometrizing tendency, and the hostility of the public toward it, that gave cubism its name: "[Braque] constructs deformed metallic men, terribly simplified. He despises form, reduces everything, places and figures and houses, to geometrical

6. Meyer Schapiro, "On Some Problems in the Semiotics of Visual Art: Field and Vehicle in Image-Signs," *Semiotica* 1, 3 (1969), p. 237.

7. This is the famous formula derived from the writing of Cézanne, which Erle Loran discusses in some detail in his introduction to *Cézanne's Composition: Analysis of His Form with Diagrams and Photographs of His Motifs* (Berkeley and Los Angeles, 1963).

schemes, to cubes."[8] And in a somewhat later stage of cubism, the importance of geometry was consciously understood. Apollinaire states in *Les Peintres cubistes* (1913):

> The new artists have been violently attacked for their preoccupation with geometry. Yet geometrical figures are the essence of drawing. Geometry, the science of space, its dimensions and relations, has always determined the norms and rules of painting. . . .
>
> The new painters do not propose, any more than did their predecessors, to be geometers. But it may be said that geometry is to the plastic arts what grammar is to the art of the writer.[9]

Thus, fundamental to the cubist approach to painting was the exploration of the geometrical laws of space, the abstract principle underlying both the two-dimensional plane and the three-dimensional represented world.

Apollinaire's equation of geometry in painting with grammar in writing, casual as this reference may appear, is of primary importance in understanding the relation between Stein and the cubists, particularly in regard to what I have termed so far her first phase. Not only can we be sure that Stein knew of the equation (see *Toklas*, p. 62 for a reference to *Les Peintres Cubistes*), but it seems clear that she would have agreed with it and understood it as a point of contact between her own and the cubists' art.

For just as the cubists translated reality into geometric relations which were not only in harmony with the medium of their art but were also the principles governing that medium, Stein translated her subjects into grammatical categories with the same double relation to her medium, language. Groupings of characters were thought of as the elements of a sentence, and Stein actually plotted some of these interpersonal relations as sentence diagrams. "These diagrams were something like diagrams which used to be used in American schools for parsing sentences in graphicized form, except that her

8. Louis Vauxcelles, "Exposition Braque. Chez Kahnweiler, 28 rue Vignon," *Gil Blas*, Paris, 14 November, 1908, reprinted in English translation in *Cubism*, ed. Edward Fry (New York, 1966), p. 50. "Il construit des bonshommes métalliques et déformés et qui sont d'une simplification terrible. Il méprise la forme, réduit tout, sites et figures et maisons, à des schémas géométriques, à des cubes," p. 51.

9. Guillaume Apollinaire, *The Cubist Painters—Aesthetic Meditations* (New York, 1944), tr. Lionel Abel, p. 12.

diagrams were of people whose bottom or fundamental natures touched, if by ever so slight a line, and from there touched their friends and their friends' friends."[10] One such diagram, No. 107 (YCAL) (see figure 3), shows the 'main sentence line' running from "Matisse group" to "me" to "genial Pablo," with lines of dependency linking numerous other people in Stein's life. Terms like "independent" and "dependent" thus had not only a psychological, but also a spatial and grammatical value for Stein.[11]

The importance of the sentence diagram in Stein's first phase cannot be overstated, for all her basic notions of composition derive from it. The diagram is first spatial and simultaneous, and secondly rule-governed, and the sentence or character grouping which it represents has these same qualities:

> sentences as they have for centuries been written were a balancing a complete inner balance. . . . Sentences are contained within themselves and anything really contained within itself has no beginning or middle or ending, any one can know this thing by knowing anything at any moment of their living, in short by knowing anything.[12]

A sentence forms a unit of atemporal knowledge with an inner balance equivalent to the grammatical relations of the elements within it. This balance is also spatial when depicted as a sentence diagram, and it is rule-governed, a play with necessity. As Stein says, a sentence is dependent on "each part needing its own place to make its own balancing" (*Narration*, p. 23). In the same way, psychological laws determine what sorts of positions a person can fulfill in a

10. Janet Flanner, Introduction to *Two*, pp. xi-xii. Stein's actual diagrams are housed in the Beinecke Rare Book Library at Yale University, and have not as yet been published. Their impact on Steinian scholarship, thus, is limited to Miss Flanner's short note.

11. Stein sometimes spatialized her character relations in patterns not related to sentence diagrams. For example, in her manuscript notes to "Jenny, Helen, Hannah, Paul and Peter," a first-phase group portrait, she takes her five subjects' initials and groups them in a number of combinations which she then works out in her text (the initials are those of the real names of the subjects):

B. A. M. J. and M. B. A. Mrs. O.
A. Mrs. M. J.   B. A. M. J.
                        A. Mrs. M. J.

These are more or less ad hoc constructions, however, and it seems clear that Stein believed that the groupings related to sentence diagrams had a special authority.

12. Stein, "Lecture 2," *Narration* (Chicago, 1935), p. 20.

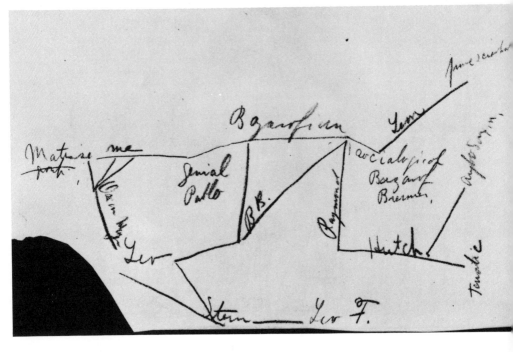

Figure 3. "Sentence diagram" of character relations in the "Matisse group."

grouping/diagram. The pervasiveness of this spatialization of character relations in Stein's thinking can be seen in the casual reference
Leo Stein made to their favorite type of figure painting. These works,
by Monet, Renoir, Degas, and Cézanne, were "all non-dramatic.
When figures are composed in a group their relations are merely spatial. At most they are relations of movement concurrent or opposite"
(Bridgman, p. 47).

This linking of a subject and his group to a functional element in
a sentence through their common translatability into a grammatical
diagram is analogous to the cubists' accommodation of the three-
dimensional subject to the picture plane through their common abstract organizational principles—geometry. Though neither grammatical nor geometric principles themselves ever became the subject matter of the two arts, for these works never were abstractions in the
sense of having totally abstract subjects, the public reacted to Stein
in much the same way as to such painters as Malevich. In the case of
Stein's writing, people thought it was too easy to depend so heavily
on the structural principles of the medium. What was the point of
repeating the same grammatical configuration over and over from
one sentence to the next with variations so small that they seemed
trivial? After all, just as it takes 'no skill to paint lines and circles on
a canvas,' 'anyone could turn out sentences full of "little" words
endlessly repeated,' and the number of parodies of Stein's first-phase
writing in magazines of the period testifies to the public's contempt.

Even though the cubists and Stein both turned to this "abstract-
ing" of their subject matter through the formative rules of their
media, the results of this common strategy in terms of mimesis were
directly opposite. In order to explain this, we must examine more
closely the work of the analytic cubists, and their work, according
to Erle Loran, can be understood only through its relation to the
technical innovations of Cézanne:

> the early period of Cubism was specifically an outgrowth of
> [Cézanne's] form. The Cubist phase was not merely eclectic, a
> formula based entirely on Cézanne's system of painting; the
> early Cubists arrived at their form through a close observation of
> nature or the subject. The shattered, interpenetrating, intersect-
> ing planes, and the gradations of dark to light, were based on a
> careful analysis of the subject. In such analysis they were also
> followers of Cézanne's ideology of art, which prescribed that
> creation must be based on the contemplation of nature. [p. 7]

The obsession with observation led Cézanne to feel that there was a
great deal of information not present in a specific view of an object
which nevertheless played a part in our perception of it. Our knowledge about the world is carried forward by our memory into every
perception we have of the world—what our eyes see is colored by
what our minds know.

Cézanne's psychological approach to perception impressed the
phenomenologist, Merleau-Ponty, as an almost scientific investigation
of the relation between perception and conception:

> By remaining faithful to the phenomena in his investigations of
> perspective, Cézanne discovered what recent psychologists have
> come to formulate: that lived perspective, that which we actually
> perceive, is not a geometric or photographic one. The objects we
> see close at hand appear smaller, those far away seem larger than
> they do in a photograph. . . . To say that a circle seen obliquely
> is seen as an ellipse is to substitute for our actual perception
> what we would see if we were cameras: in reality we see a form
> which oscillates around the ellipse without being an ellipse . . . it
> is Cézanne's genius that when the overall composition of the pic-
> ture is seen globally, perspectival distortions are no longer visible
> in their own right but rather contribute, as they do in natural
> vision, to the impression of an emerging order, of an object in
> the act of appearing, organizing itself before our very eyes.[13]

The similarity of this view to the notion of identity which Stein
drew from James is obvious. Both Stein in her first phase and Cézannean cubism depicted their subject matter as a function of time
and memory, as a thought element surrounded by mental "fringes."
By painstaking observation one would be able to know the essence of
the object emerging as a unified concept from the confused mass of
memory data.

The critical factor, then, for both Stein and Cézanne was time. For
the painter, the inclusion of temporal flow was an all but insurmount-
able problem for mimetic representation, since the canvas is a static,
unchanging object and since Renaissance perspective and *chiaroscuro*
implied that the painting was the visual field of a perceiver at one
dimensionless point of time. Cézanne's response was to discard

---

13. Maurice Merleau-Ponty, "Cézanne's Doubt," *Sense and Non-Sense* (Evanston, Illinois,
1964), trans. Hubert L. Dreyfus and Patricia Allen Dreyfus, p. 14.

partially the traditional conventions and to try to find means whereby the process of 'identification' (to use James's term) could be suggested on a static surface. Stein also chose to identify her subjects
with the process of perception, and since literature is a temporal art
this identification could have aided a mimetic representation. However, Stein's insistence on rendering each moment of present-percep-
tion as a dimensionless 'now' involved a reversal of the time status of
her medium. Thus, though Cézanne and Stein shared the same notion
of their subjects, they treated the problem of temporal flow in precisely opposite ways, and the mode of temporality which Stein chose
was on first view as little conducive to literary mimesis as Cézanne's
process-time was to mimesis in painting.

The fashionable term for the inclusion of time flow in painting during the early years of the century was the "fourth dimension," a
rather mystical concept as described by Apollinaire and his contemporaries. In his words, the fourth dimension "represents the immensi-
ty of space eternalizing itself in all directions at any given moment.
It is space itself, the dimension of the infinite; the fourth dimension
endows objects with plasticity" (p. 12). The "fourth dimension" implies for the perceiver a liberation from the fetters of his own static
position. He is to be able to see as a simultaneity what before was
visible to him only as a function of time. The picture frame and the
illusion of deep space imply that the painting is still a single visual
field at a moment in the perceiver's experience. But temporal sequence is implicit in the subject, because what is present on the
canvas cannot be present in a single direct perception of this subject,
but only through the superimposition of past views of it onto the
present. The subject is thus presented as a synthesis of a number of
temporally distinct perceptions. Such a treatment is conceptual; it
shows that the perception of an object is colored by previous knowledge about it.

The techniques used to achieve "emerging perception" were often
distortions of "normal appearances." Tabletops were tipped forward
in relation to the picture plane at an impossible angle, so that both
the front of the table and the tabletop with its contents could be
seen without extreme perspectival distortions (see figure 4). A distant but imposing mountain was greatly enlarged so that "the
psychological effect of enormous hills [would be] recorded in plastic terms" (Loran, p. 47). A building drawn from the front had both
its side walls visible, and different vertical and horizontal eye positions were implied by various aspects of the same object (as, for

Figure 4. Paul Cézanne, *Still Life with Peppermint Bottle*, 1868, oil on canvas, 26 x 32⅜ inches. (Courtesy of National Gallery of Art, Washington, D.C. Chester Dale Collection.)

example, in *Farm at Montgeroult*), as if the viewer were capable of
simultaneously travelling around the scene. As Loran notes, "The
effect of 'seeing around' the space, in a fourth-dimensional sense,
has thus been achieved and the planes of the buildings have simultaneously been brought into a more nearly parallel relation to the
picture plane. Paradoxically, the effects of three-dimensionality ('seeing around') and two-dimensionality . . . are thus simultaneously
increased" (p. 49). Cézanne's presentation of three-dimensionality
on a two-dimensional surface in fact stresses both dimensions. It
insists on three-dimensionality by showing several views of the depth
of the object; but it does so by partially destroying the relations
among them by flattening them toward the picture plane. The result
does not look precisely like reality, but it provides more information
about the reality than a conventional rendering. This non-mimetic
translation of three-dimensionality into two-dimensionality, with the
resemblance to reality still largely intact, is Cézanne's greatest achievement. This leads Loran to claim that "Cézanne's space may be taken
as the modern rebirth of the classical ideal of pictorial space, which
is three-dimensionality conceived in relation to the two-dimensionality of the picture plane" (p. 32).

Virtually every technique Cézanne developed helped to reconcile
the two visual modalities of volume and plane. For example, Cézanne
used large overlapping areas of color. Since they overlapped they implied relative depth in space and hence three-dimensionality; but
since they were "separate, unblended, and flat, and usually parallel
to the picture plane, *the color throughout maintains an essentially
two-dimensional character.* . . (p. 25). The famous invention, *passage*,
creates the same accommodation of plane and volume:

> At those parts of the contour of the volume where the value
> merges, or 'passes,' into the value of the background, there is of
> course no line; the form is open at that point. . . . Sharp contrasts
> and lines clarify the opposing planes and shapes, giving three-
> dimensionality; fused or lost edges create a merging of fore-
> ground with deep space, adding an element of two-dimensionality.
> [p. 26]

This drawing of the eye from the picture plane into deep space and
back was taken up by the cubists as a basic principle for organizing
space. But what for Cézanne was a means of suggesting the process of
perception in which multiple views of an object become fused into a

single visual identification was for the cubists the final mode of perception of the world; the interplay rather than the synthesis of
percepts was to constitute the total perception of objects. Winthrup
Judkins, in an enlightening analysis of cubist technique, lists a number of means by which his ambiguity is created:

> —planes which are at once transparent and opaque
> —tones of objects which "bleed" out and become background
>   tones so that the object is part of, and at the same time in
>   front of, the background
> —outlines which coincide with other outlines so that the contin-
>   uity may be read around either or across both
> —surfaces which recede behind other surfaces and project over
>   them simultaneously
> —shadows, mutually excluded by each others' light sources,
>   standing side by side
> —parts of objects shifted away from the whole and then changed
>   in tone so that the recognition of the original will be con-
>   stantly elusive
> —shadows which become substance
> —flat planes which disappear behind themselves
> —shapes created by arbitrary changes of tone competing with the
>   shapes of the recognizable objects within which they are de-
>   veloped
> —forms whose contours pass over other forms while their local
>   tones disappear beneath them. . . .[14]

Dr. Judkins concludes that the result of all these techniques in "A
Deliberate Oscillation of Appearances, A Studied Multiplicity of
Readings, A Conscious Compounding of Identities, *An Iridescence of
Form*" (p. 276).

This ambiguity of spatial relations is analogous to the ambiguity of
temporal relations in Stein's first-phase portraits. In such works, the
relation between the time of the portrait and the time of perception
of the subject is made as confused as possible, as is the temporal
status of each sentence-moment of perception to the next. Though
one sentence follows the next, it is not always clear that the grammatical reference of one sentence to a preceding one has any semantic

14. Winthrup Judkins, "Toward a Reinterpretation of Cubism," *Art Bulletin* 30 (December 1948): 275–76.

validity. Both the shifters indicating the time of the subject and those referring back and forth to elements of other sentences are made deliberately ambiguous. Stein gained by this disruption of temporal flow the possibility of representing her subject as an identity in a moment of realization complete in itself and exclusive of reference or relation to other moments. In contrast, spatial ambiguity allowed the cubists to escape the self-enclosed moment, because the various aspects of the object simultaneously present implied the passing of perceptual time. In effect, both Stein and the cubists reversed the treatment of temporality in their arts. Where the subject of a painting normally appears in an arrested moment of time, in cubist art the subject is definitely a temporal object. And whereas literature normally develops its subjects gradually from one sentence to the next, supplying new information as it proceeds, Stein's subjects were to be totally present, fully developed, in each atemporal sentence.

Connected with the ambiguity of spatial relations in cubism was the presence of small units of color which could not be directly related to any element of the represented object. These elementary units were borrowed from Cézanne, who had, according to Loran,

> invented the system of modulating a volume from its cool, dark side to its light, warm parts in chromatic nuances—that is, a series of steps or planes. The volumes attain by means of these tiny overlapping color planes a solidity different from that attained through mere dark-to-light modeling; it is a solidity based on the protruding character of warm color and the receding tendency of cool. . . . [p. 25]

As a result, the smallest integral units of the painting are non-mimetic and purely relational in effect (see figure 5). Solidity and light, the products of the interplay of these small units, are the result of "an abstract order" (p. 29).

These non-mimetic relational units found their way into cubism as the facetting of the late analytic stage. The forms of these facets "are not the recognizable parts of familiar objects whose manipulations can, for this reason, be followed with relative ease, but rather arbitrarily created facets or abstract planes whose behavior knows no norm" (Judkins, p. 277). Not only objects but the spaces between objects were divided into these arbitrary units, and it was their overlapping, their contrast or identity in color, that created the spatial ambiguity of the style.

Figure 5. Paul Cézanne, *Mont Ste. Victoire as seen from Bibmeus Quarry*, c. 1898-1900, oil on canvas, 25½ x 32 inches. (Courtesy of Baltimore Museum of Art, Baltimore, Md. Cone Collection.)

In the same way, the first phase of Stein's writing, with its emphasis on James's "transitive" or relational words, was an attempt to
eliminate representationality from its smallest independent units,
the word. The avoidance of nouns and adjectives and the abnormally
frequent use of pronouns, copulars, adverbs and other shifters led to
a purely relational word unit, the very relationality of which could
be manipulated to create ambiguity.

This emphasis on nonrepresentational, internally-relational units
for Stein and the cubists is relevant to the interest of both in the
structural rules governing their respective media, grammar and geometry. For syncategorematic words, shifters, or "pronouns" (in the
broad sense of internally-referential elements), are considered by
linguists such as Roman Jakobson, as "purely grammatical, relational
units."[15] This notion leads Jakobson to state that "The relation of
pronouns to non-pronominal words has been repeatedly compared
with the relation between geometrical and physical bodies." The
use of these words is thus equivalent to the articulation of the subject into two-dimensional color planes, since both "pronoun" and
plane relate directly to the abstract principles determining the two
media.

On the other hand, in both analytic cubism and Stein's first-phase
writing there are elements that are not purely relational. Even in
Picasso's difficult late analytic portraits such as those of Kahnweiler,
(see figure 6), Vollard, or Ühde, there are lines and planes that look
like features or parts of clothing, and the portraits bear an unmistak-
able resemblance to their subjects. Such mimetic units in the midst
of generally non-mimetic ones correspond to the occasional symbols
—nouns, verbs of action—in Stein's otherwise relational prose. In
either case, the artist is resorting to a limited number of elements
which signify in the mode normal to their medium—icons for painting and symbols for literature. The presence of even this small ratio
of "clues" seems to insure that the subject will be recognized.

The result of these clues in cubist painting is a mixed time sense,
for these direct resemblances communicate the subject immediately,
while the non-mimetic elements cause the subject to emerge by an
act of integration on the part of the viewer, and in fact to keep re-
emerging through all the ambiguities in his relation to the background.

15. Roman Jakobson, "Poetry of Grammar and Grammar of Poetry," *Lingua* 21 (1968):
606. This article supplies a partial history of sources for the association of grammar and
geometry.

Figure 6. Pablo Picasso, *Portrait of Daniel-Henry Kahnweiler*, 1910, oil on canvas, 39⅝ x 28⅝ inches. (Courtesy of Art Institute of Chicago. Gift of Mrs. Gilbert W. Chapman in memory of Charles B. Goodspeed.)

This mixed time sense, however, does not interfere with the intent of the painting to show the perception of the subject. The counterpoint of recognitions of the subject from the painting corresponds to the counterpoint of perceptions of the actual subject which are brought to bear by memory on any new identification of him.

However, in Stein's writing the presence of nouns, adjectives, and discrete verbs detracts from the time sense that she is trying to create. For these words, as symbols, refer to classes of objects and to characteristics which imply comparison and memory. In this way, they are consistent with the subject as identity, but not with the isolation of each moment of the perception of him in the present. The sentence cannot function in a self-contained present if the words within it make reference to a spread of time from the past to the present, and it was because of this contradiction, as we saw in the last chapter, that Stein made the changes culminating in the second and third phases of her portraiture. The presence of "clues," then, is a point of contact between Stein's work and that of the cubists, but one with opposite results in terms of the intents of the two styles.

The proportion of these representational elements to the nonrepresentational ones can be used as a way of discussing both the development of Stein's first-phase portraits and the analytic paintings, for both can be divided into early and late periods. We saw in chapter 3 that the late first-phase portraits such as "One. Harry Phelan Gibb" virtually eliminated nouns, adjectives, and adverbs, and used verbs only in the form of present progressives and verbals. The last chapter of *The Making of Americans* is another such work. Likewise, the paintings that Picasso produced between his summer at Cadaqués in 1910 and the beginning of the inventions leading to synthetic cubism in 1912 are much harder to "read" than the earlier ones because the relational elements of the painting are multiplied at the expense of the mimetic ones. In such paintings the tension between representational and purely compositional values is extreme, and the implications of this in terms of the subject matter are very interesting.

We have noted that both Stein's notion of the subject as an identity whose "bottom nature" was the defining trait of a "type" of person and Cézanne's concern with perception permeated with the knowledge of the perceived object carried forward by memory are consistent with James's notion of "identity." In fact, both conform to what Cassirer terms the psychological notion of the concept. According to Cassirer, the psychologist, like the Aristotelian, sees the concept "as the common element in a series of similar and resembling

particular things,"[16] and the process by which the concept is formed
is "the solidification of . . . features that agree, their fusion into a
unitary, indivisible whole, . . . a totality of memory-residues" (p. 11).
For most of Stein's first-phase works and for Cézannean cubism until
mid-1910, the subject was conceptual in this sense, although the
cubists were interested in the process of conceptualization while
Stein was concerned with the moment of its crystallization.

Cassirer contrasts to the psychological and Aristotelian notions the
"modern" notion of the concept. It defines the concept as the set of
relations determining specific phenomena rather than a common substance inhering in them. The concept is stated as a function of a number of abstract variables large enough to "generate" any individual
phenomenon to which it applies by the "plugging in" of particular
values.

The paintings of the late analytic period and Stein's late first-phase
writing seem to involve this "modern" treatment of their subject-con-
cepts. Implicit already in the 'grammaticization' of character, the
"modern" concept of the subject became dominant in Stein's work
when the typologies of, for example, "Julia Marlowe," gave way to
purely compositional balances within the sentence organized under
the complex of general headings of "working," "succeeding," "strug-
gling," and so on. In cubism, the switch was created by the translation
of aspects of objects, spaces between them, background, foreground,
into comparable, standardized units. The portraits of these two arts
of necessity included certain particulars, although these were restricted to verbals and present progressives in works like "One. Harry
Phelan Gibb," and to the merest suggestions of features and clothing
in, for example, Picasso's *Portrait of Daniel-Henry Kahnweiler.* In
the last chapter of *The Making of Americans,* however, everything is
stated in terms of variables—"one," "many," "all," "each," "some"—
relating to the most generalized activities—"being existing," "having
family living," "loving." This has led one critic, Max Bense, to speak
of such writing as an ontological treatment of existence. He quotes
Quine's criterion for existence: " 'Being is nothing other than the
world of a variable—to be is to be the value of a variable.' It seems
that Gertrude Stein in the last chapter of her novel has attained this

16. Ernst Cassirer, *Substance and Function* (Chicago and London, 1923), p. 9.

being-thematic plane of her epic theme."[17] A similar treatment of
the subject as a function of variables can be seen in a statement by
Roger Allard, a poet, critic, and close associate of the cubists:

> Thus the first postulate of cubism is the ordering of things—and
> this means not naturalistic things but abstract forms. Cubism
> feels space as a complex of lines, units of space, quadratic and
> cubic equations and ratios.
>
> The artist's problem is to bring some order into this mathe-
> matical chaos by bringing out its latent rhythm.
>
> In this way of looking at things, every image of the world
> is the point of convergence of many conflicting forces. The
> subject of the picture, the external object, is merely a pretext;
> the *subject* of an equation. This has always been true; but for
> many centuries this basic truth lay in a deep obscurity from
> which today modern art is seeking to rescue it.[18]

The treatment of the represented world as the subject of a geome-
trical-aesthetic configuration on the part of the cubists, or of a gram-
matical-aesthetic balance within the sentence by Stein is as close as
either came to an abstract subject matter. The tension or even competition between the represented subject and the schematic configuration for the role of "true subject" was the very essence of the
two styles. And there is no doubt that Stein was aware of this tension, as her riddling but very precise discussion of Cézanne's painting
shows:

> The apples looked like apples the chairs looked like chairs and
> it all had nothing to do with anything because if they did not
> look like apples or chairs or landscapes or people they were ap-
> ples and chairs and landscapes and people. They were so entirely

17. Max Bense, "Was erzählt Gertrude Stein?" *Probleme des Erzählens in der Weltliteratur*
(Stuttgart, 1971), p. 341. "Quine, der amerikanische Logiker, hat, einmal nach einem
Kriterium für Existenz gefragt, geantwortet, 'Sein' sei nichts anderes als der Wert einer
Variablen zu sein, 'to be is to be the value of a variable.' Mir scheint, daß Gertrude Stein im
Schlußkapitel ihres Romans diese seinsthematische Ebene ihres epischen Themas erreicht
hat."
18. Roger Allard, "The Signs of Renewal in Painting" ("Die Kennzeichen der Erneuerung
in der Malerei," *Der Blaue Reiter,* Munich, 1912), *Cubism,* pp. 70-71.

these things that they were not an oil painting and yet that is just what the Cezanne's were they were an oil painting. ["Pictures," *Lectures in America*, pp. 76-77]

Here the represented subject as phenomenon or appearance (apples, chairs, etc.), the represented subject as concept (they *were* apples and chairs . . .), the aesthetic factor (the "oil painting"), and the mode of signifying normal to the art ("looking like" or mimesis) are all present and all in conflict. It was the ability of both Stein and the cubists to keep all these factors in play, particularly by the inclusion of at least some "values" of the variables involved through the clues, the representational signs normal to the medium, that led to the new balance they created between aesthetic and representational values. This balance gave special prominence to the formal aspects of the work of art without turning it into an abstraction in the first sense of the term.

The similarities in theory and methodology between Stein's first phase and Cézannean cubism are thus quite marked. Both achieved a sense of composition in which every element was equally important in the whole design,[19] and where the abstract schemes of grammar and geometry were used to relate subject matter to the limitations of the two media. Both reversed the temporal modes of their media and de-semanticized the smallest units of their work by preventing them from signifying in the mode normal to their media. Finally, Stein and the cubists shared the notion of the subject as concept or identity, which created for Stein the contradiction of her first-phase writing. It was in the resolution of this contradiction that Stein's art became an abstraction in the second sense of the word.

The second meaning of "abstraction" applies to those works which do not have discernible subjects of any kind, or, if their titles indicate subjects, to works in which the relation between the work and the indicated subject is impossible to discover. An example of such abstraction in painting is abstract expressionism. These canvases, full of droplets and sprinkles of paint, do not look definitely like anything in reality. The usual responses to such art are that it is purely decorative, that it means something different to everyone who sees it, or that it is an aesthetic statement—perhaps that the modern artist is

19. See Leon Katz, "Matisse, Picasso and Gertrude Stein," *Four Americans in Paris—The Collections of Gertrude Stein and Her Family* (New York, 1970), p. 52, for a discussion of Stein's debt to Cézanne for her sense of composition.

liberating himself from direct representation, that he is illustrating
the role of chance in creation, or that he is showing in the most
dynamic way the relation between his generative act of applying
paint and the object thus generated. In each of these responses, the
sign-status of the work of art is denied. The decoration-hypothesis
denies the painting a *signatum*. The hypothesis of private meaning
suggests that a sign need not be sharable, a contradiction of the essential, social nature of the sign as fulfilling a communicative function. The reading of the "meaning" of a work as a meta-artistic
statement confuses the *signatum* of a sign with the connotation or
implications of its *signans*. It would be a similar mistake to say that
a tree, which is not a sign, "means" or "signifies" the creative power
of God or the skill of a gardener in tending it, although people have
always felt that the tree illustrated, implied, connoted such things.
Now, since a painting, unlike a tree, belongs to a class of objects
which normally do function as signs, we are predisposed to think of
it as meaningful. The facts that many abstract paintings are framed,
that the frame often "cuts off" sections of figures as if they were
not visible within the "visual field" of the picture, and that the
shapes and dabs "applied in a non-mimetic, uninterpreted whole re-
tain many of the qualities and formal relationships of the preceding
mimetic art" (Schapiro, p. 240) are other reasons for our tendency
to "read" such works with the same expectations as we read "conventional" paintings. Even when it is impossible for a group of
people to agree that an abstract impressionistic painting signifies
one particular subject, most people react to it as a suggestive, poten-
tially meaningful, or "numinous" object.

Cubism, of course, never became abstract in this second sense. Nevertheless, it carried the program outlined by Allard as far as possible without losing the represented subject altogether. As Edward Fry notes,

> After 1911 the cubists no longer worked directly from a model
> in nature; and in the *papiers collés* and paintings of 1913-14,
> which contain no illusionistic space, there was no prior Bergson-
> ian accumulation of knowledge through multiple perceptions in
> time and space. Instead the cubist proceeded directly to an
> ideational notation of forms that were equivalent to objects in
> the visual world without in any way being illusionistic represen-
> tations of those objects. [*Cubism*, pp. 38-39]

This "ideational notation" was, in effect, a number of arbitrary signs, symbols, used to suggest aspects of the subject. But the only way that the painting could indicate what the signs were, paradoxically, was to make them mimetic. For example, a table could be represented by the most unlikely means, but if the representation did not either look like wood, or a horizontal straight edge, or something with objects on it, there would be no way to understand that it was meant to suggest a table. This is the same situation as the symbolic representation of death in a painting by means of a painted scythe, where the scythe must look like a real scythe in order to operate symbolically. When enough of these mimetic synecdoches were composed on a canvas, the result could be quite unlike any aspect of visual reality, but the objects within it would still be recognized by visually mimetic clues (see figure 7). As a result, the smallest units of synthetic cubist painting were now mimetic, though they were arranged in such a way that there was no question of an overall imitation of normal appearances.

A similar switch can be seen from Stein's first to her second and third phases. In contrast to the "relational" language of the first phase, the later phases are full of symbols—nouns, verbs, adjectives, and adverbs—which, like the icons of synthetic cubism, are arranged in nonrepresentational patterns, as in the phrase "Give known or pin ware." There is no normal syntax to relate the referents of these words, so that by inventing the techniques of syntactical/semantic disruption discussed in chapter 3, Stein had created an "ideational notation" comparable to that of the cubists. And in both cases the smallest integral units were signifying in the mode normal to their media.

But whereas in synthetic cubism such a 'convocation' of elements could constitute a subject matter in itself, in Stein's prose the various referents of the individual words were not in themselves the subject. It was the person whose name appeared in the title of the portrait that was the proper subject, and the grouping of word referents in the portrait was meant to stand for the content of a mind perceiving that human subject. The prose that Stein produced was the result of the notion of the subject as "entity," an on-going 'now' unrelated to categories of thought. To accommodate such a notion, semantic fields and syntactic structures had to be disrupted in writing, so that a conjunction of words devoid of all but potential (or lexical) meaning could be achieved. But in isolating words in this way, Stein prevented them from signifying their ultimate subject.

The reason, then, that cubism remains representational even though

Figure 7. Juan Gris, *The Man from Touraine*, 1918, oil on canvas, 39½ x 25¾ inches. (Courtesy of Musée National d'Art Moderne, Paris. Gift of André Lefèvre.)

the disruption of its basic referential units is as thoroughgoing as that of Stein's later prose is that there is a central difference between painting and literature. The medium of literature, language, is itself a system of signs, which combine to form higher-level signs. And the referent of the individual language sign is of course not identical to that of the higher-level sign, the sentence. In painting, signs are created from non-significant material. The smallest units are neither fixed in meaning nor determinate in function. When the synthetic cubist makes each of his smallest integral units of paint look like something, he is using his medium in a conventional way, even though these units are not arranged in a conventionally mimetic way. But when Stein prevents her words from signifying on the sentence level, she is not allowing her medium to function normally. By preventing this, she achieves the same result as the abstract expressionists who did not permit any mimesis in their painting. By totally excluding the mode of signifying of her medium, Stein prevented her works from signifying altogether, reducing them to the status of "numinous" objects.

However, the creation of this fragmented, lexical language brought Stein's work very close in a technical sense to the synthetic cubists, with their isolated or disarranged forms. In fact, the similarities between the second- and third-phase techniques and those of the synthetic cubists are quite remarkable. Not only was the basic unit of the two arts now signifying in the mode normal to the two media (on the level of the individual word for Stein), but this unit was now deliberately polysemous. In *Man Leaning on a Table* (1915), for example, Fry identifies this new technique as "Picasso's use of condensed signs for the head, torso, and leg of the figure, and for the legs of the table: all the formal qualities of an object are 'synthesized' into a single characteristic, but highly conventionalized, new form" (p. 33). The pun functions in the same way in Stein's writing, as do Stein's beloved "mistakes," combining a number of possible referents or a number of different aspects of the same referent into a single sign.

A further contribution to this ambiguity or compression of meanings is the confusion which both Stein and the cubists established between the material and the subject matter of their respective arts. This began, in a sense, with the use of geometry and grammar in the earlier period, where the subject matter was conveyed in terms of the organizational principles of the medium. Whether these principles were signs of objects or subject matter in their own right was an essential ambiguity of this art. The discoveries precipitating the shift to synthetic cubism—*papier collé* and collage—opened new possibilities in this respect. When Braque glued a mirror to his painting, it both signified a mirror and was one. It also connoted the meta-artistic idea that art is a mirroring. Pastings of newspaper may be seen as representing newspapers, i.e., themselves, as commenting on the painting or the subject through the words printed on them, as connoting the fact that art has documentary value, and as fulfilling a purely aesthetic function by contributing to a particular formal balance in the composition of the work. In the same way, Stein frequently juxtaposed words as things to words as signifiers of things, as in the example "There can be no grammar without and and if if you are prevailed upon to be very well and thank you."[20] The words "and" and "if" are both the means and the object of expression. This ambiguity of medium and "message" in Stein's work makes it even more difficult to integrate the referents of signs in her writing, for the reader in constantly shifting from a reading of word as *signans* to word as *signatum*.

The relating of elements of the work of art for purely compositional rather than representational or "semantic" purposes is also common to Stein and the cubists. Fry notes that in the synthetic cubism of 1918, for example, "In addition to the usual cubist interlocking color planes, the individual synthesized signs are related to each other by a variety of other means, most prominent of which is visual rhyming . . . : morphologically similar elements, such as circles, are emphasized in the separate signs to which they belong" (p. 34). We noted in the last chapter the anti-semantic use of rhyme in Stein's second-phase portraits, where words without any semantic or syntactic relation were linked. Indeed, this technique becomes the primary organizational device in the late second-phase portraits such as "Jean Cocteau." By the third-phase portraits, when external reference is totally absent, this formal, internal set of correspondences is one of the numinous factors in the work upon which a 'descriptive interpretation' can be based.

One of the most obvious similarities between cubism and Steinian writing of all phases is the presence of metastatement. We think of the long ponderings in *The Making of Americans,* the masked

20. *How to Write,* p. 73. This example illustrates other ambiguities, as well, e.g., between "very well" as part of the idiomatic sequence, 'very well, thank you,' and as a pair of free lexical units.

statements of the transitional pieces, "Constance Fletcher" and "Mabel Dodge," the use of key theoretical terms such as "repetition" and "memory" in "If I Told Him," the epitomizing of the portrait situation in "Fourteen Anonymous Portraits," and again the presence of key-words like "grammar," in the late portraits. The same is true to a lesser degree of cubism, with its newspaper headlines commenting on the painting itself or on the attitude of the painter, for example, "La Vie Sportive" (Picasso, *Still-Life with Violin and Fruit*, 1913).

One particular type of cubist metastatement has a relatively direct analogue in Stein's early second-phase portraits. Professor Fry points out that in Braque's *Pitcher and Violin* (1909–1910) the facetting of form and the contrasting of light and shadow had become "completely subordinated to the demands of pictorial structure. As an indication of this new balance between art and reality, Braque painted an illusionistic nail at the top of the painting, as though to indicate by means of the shadow it casts that his canvas is simply a flat, painted surface which is tacked to a wall. This device is an example of the idea, which was becoming current by 1911, of the *tableau-objet*, the painting as object" (pp. 19–20). Braque's nail is mimetic in its shape, and its shadow implies a single light source. It thus employs the conventional means of representation in painting—mimesis as invented in the Renaissance—to deny the necessity or even the relevance of this mode of representation. In the same way, the first line of "Guillaume Apollinaire," "Give known or pin ware," is a rather teasing referential denial of reference. The line refers to the subject by imitating the sound of his name, though its components are, from the point of view of conventional language use, intransigently nonreferential. Like Braque's nail, it both refers to a conventional aspect of reality, here its subject's name, and stresses the independence of the artefact from making such direct references.

Another point of contact between Stein's post-1911 portraiture and cubism is the tendency to use 'visual' equivalents for devices which Stein had already adapted from the cubists. For she herself says that the generative problem of the second phase was the need to include "looking." Where before she had devised a purely literary equivalent for the cubist multiple perspective—the ambiguity of shifters displaced in relation to time—she now found equivalents which made reference to visual, spatial categories. For example, "Handing a lizard to any one is a green thing receiving a curtain" (*Geography and Plays*, p. 151) creates a multiple perspective through the two viewpoints involved—that of the person handing the lizard over and that of the lizard itself. This multi-perspective, stated as an atemporal equation between two spatially distinct views of the same fact, is of course created by purely linguistic means, since language cannot be visual in the literal sense of the word. Yet, in every detail, Stein evokes visual categories: the lizard's color is used to identify him and the act of handing is depicted as the dropping of a curtain.

Similarly, circumlocutions often function as a deliberate translation of non-visual into visual terms. For example, in the circumlocution cited in chapter 3, "There is an expression when contemplation is not connecting the object that is in position with the forehead that is returning looking," 'expression not based on visual perception' is given a concrete visual equivalent. The circumlocution dissects the referent into a set of visual components arranged in a somewhat unorthodox manner, and in this way it attempts a more direct carry-over of the dissecting of objects and the disruption of their spatial relations in synthetic cubist paintings than Stein's previous disruptions of syntax and semantics had achieved.

Nevertheless, despite the many similarities between cubist and Steinian technique, the later phases of the two arts were not finally analogous. For as we have seen, literary signs cannot be totally isolated and still refer to their subject. Stein had taken the idea of the *tableau-objet* at face value rather than as half of the tension between aesthetics and representationality essential to cubism. Her *écriture-objet* gradually lost every link to its subject until it ceased to signify anything in the proper sense of the word. In the case of portraiture, where the reference to a subject is a defining characteristic of the genre, Stein's desire for purely "mimetic" writing led to a logical contradiction.

Thus, the promise that people such as Alfred Stieglitz saw in Stein's portraits does not seem to have been realized. He said of "Matisse" and "Picasso," two first-phase portraits:

> These articles bear, to current interpretive criticism, a relation exactly analogous to that born by the work of the men of whom they treat to the painting and sculpture of the older schools.
>
> So close, indeed, is this analogy that they will doubtless he regarded by many as no less absurd, unintelligible, radical or revolutionary than the so-called vagaries of the painters whom they seek to interpret.
>
> Yet—they employ a medium in the technical manipulation of which we are all at least tyros.

They are expressed in words.

And hence they offer—to all who choose to examine them with an inquiring mind—a common denominator of comprehension, a Rosetta stone of comparison; a decipherable clew to that intellectual and esthetic attitude which underlies and inspires the movement upon one phase of which they are comments and of the extending development of which they are themselves an integral part.[21]

It is ironic that Stein's portraiture broke down precisely when it took the "Rosetta stone" analogy too seriously, when it tried to make a translation of cubist technique and psychological theory into a medium that was fundamentally different from paint and canvas, and from "raw perception." Rather than serving as a key to cubism, Stein's writing illustrates the very real barriers between painting and literature. And furthermore, where the cubists were satisfied with a compromise in overturning the norms of their medium, Stein insisted on trying the impossible. Her intransigence, however, should not be too harshly criticized, for the attempted translation of pictorial norms into literary ones, like all her failed experiments, reveals a great deal. It is a practical demonstration of ideas now being investigated by semioticians and structuralists, and as such, has much to contribute to our understanding of the relations between the arts.

21. Editorial, *Camera Work,* Special Number, August, 1912.

5

Portrait as Program: The Place of the Portrait
in Stein's Typology of Genres

This whole book now is going to be a detective story of how to write.

A play of the relation of human nature to the human mind.

And a poem of how to begin again.

And a description of how the earth looks as you look at it which is perhaps a play if it can be done in a day and is perhaps a detective story if it can be found out.

Anything is a detective story if it can be found out and can anything be found out.

Yes.

The Geographical History of America

As we have seen, the mimetic program of Stein's portraiture produced a series of partial 'solutions' culminating in an impasse. It is reasonable to ask at this point, then, whether the apparent dead end that Stein reached was peculiar to her portraiture alone, or whether all of her writing met a similar fate. This is to ask in effect what the relation is between Stein's portraits and her other genres. And it is a fascinating question, for her genres range through the whole expanse of conventional literature and beyond: essays or meditations, biography, autobiography, journalism, portraits, description, "geography," plays, operas, lyric poetry, aphorisms, advertisements, children's books, novels, "series," detective stories, romances, and even two films. "She always however made her chief study people and therefore the never ending series of portraits" (*Toklas,* p. 119), or so the 1932 persona of *The Autobiography of Alice B. Toklas* would have us believe. The centrality of the portrait genre within the corpus of Stein's work is a hypothesis that this chapter will attempt to explore.

A simple examination of Stein's bibliography is quite revealing in this respect. From a chronological point of view, the portraits must bow to the novel or novella as the earliest form of Stein's mature writing. *Q.E.D.* and *Three Lives* are extended fictive character explorations which contain a modicum of narrative. They are followed by the portraits in 1908 and several long pieces usually called novels,

most notably *The Making of Americans.* According to Stein, however, "In The Making of Americans I wrote about our family. I
made it like a novel and I took a piece of one person and mixed it
with a piece of another one and then I found that it was not interesting and instead I described everything."[1] The early novels are more
accurately termed descriptions of character and character relations,
and are directly connected with the concepts of character which
operate in the first-phase portraits. In fact all the texts written during
what we have termed the first portrait phase are dominated by the
portrait program.

In 1911, *Tender Buttons* appeared—"portraits of rooms and food
and everything"—followed by "descriptions," "geographies," and
plays in 1913. The first of each of these genres was, respectively:
"Scenes. Actions and Dispositions of Relations and Positions,"
"England," and "What Happened. A Five Act Play." And in 1914, a
related form arose, the series ("Series"). Despite their seeming diversity, description, geography, plays and series are intimately related to
the portraits of the second phase, and their appearance coincides
precisely with the emergence of the second-phase portraits.

In 1917, Stein's first journalistic articles appeared, "The Great
American Army" and "Relief Work in France." Such more or less
directly intelligible articles were also written during her trip to America in 1933–1934 and during the Second World War. They form a
group of audience-directed works, with *The Autobiography of Alice
B. Toklas* and the portraits of appreciation.

In 1918 in the gap in second-phase portraiture, another new genre
arose, the poem, as in "Selected Poems." However, this was certainly
not the first appearance of "poetry" in Stein's writing. The second
phase, with its accent on the visual, on things, was in fact a period
with poetry as its center. Poetry for Stein had a double sense—stan-
zaically organized writing and writing oriented toward objects.

In 1920 a number of interesting extensions of genres appeared.
"Ireland," for example, was a poetic variation on the nursery rhyme,
"Pease Porridge Hot," and suggests a link to Stein's children's books
of the late 1930s and early 1940s. 1920 also produced "A Movie,"
one of two works of its kind (the other is "Film. Deux Soeurs Qui
Ne Sont Pas Soeurs," written in 1929), which Stein included in her
collection of operas and plays. Also appearing in 1920 was the first
'biography,' "Next. Life and Letters of Marcel Duchamp," whose

1. *Everybody's Autobiography* (New York, 1973), p. 69 (hereafter referred to as *EA*).

standard Victorian biography subtitle and abbreviated length are almost a parody of the work's monumental precursors. It and others of its kind, such as "The Life of Juan Gris. The Life and Death of Juan Gris" (1927), seem to be merely versions of portraiture. The only long works that come near to being biographies, *Picasso* and *Four in America*, have interests other than the presentation of the chronological space of a life.

In 1923, Stein wrote "An Elucidation," a rather hazy attempt at an independent essay about her writing, and in 1926 in the transition between the second and third phases she produced a theoretical lecture called "Composition as Explanation." Though she had employed meta-literary statements and whole passages of theorizing as early as *The Making of Americans,* "Composition as Explanation" was the beginning of organized expository writing. It led to *How To Write, Lectures in America, Narration,* and *The Geographical History of America,* among others, and was to become the most important genre of all by the mid-thirties.

Four Saints in Three Acts. An Opera to be Sung, the first and most famous of Stein's operas, was written in 1927. The opera completed the genre group comprising plays and films, and less directly, description, geography and portraiture. In the same year Stein wrote *Lucy Church Amiably, A Novel of Romantic beauty and nature and which Looks Like an Engraving,* along with its very beautiful "Advertisement." Stein called the work a "romantic novel," a special category somewhere between the novel and pure description. It was one of a new group of novels appearing in the beginning of the third phase. The opera and novels all aimed, according to Stein, at the third-phase ideal of self-contained movement.

The last two genres to arise were among the most interesting— autobiography and the detective story. The first autobiography proper was *The Autobiography of Alice B. Toklas* (1932). The book indicated a new concern with character and identity; it not only explored these issues, but by its own public success launched Stein on a course of meditations on identity, genius, knowledge, and perception. It also marks the end of the dominance of the portrait genre, as is apparent in the paucity of portraits written after 1933, and thus it is both understandable and ironic that the centrality of portraiture is explicitly stated in this work, the culmination of, and point of departure from, the old program.

Closely associated with the notions of identity and character developing in the autobiographies was Stein's interest in detective

stories. She was an avid reader of these works and even went out on
night homicide patrol with the Chicago police during her trip to
America (*EA*, p. 209). She believed that the detective story was the
only possible form of narrative in the modern world because it eliminated character—the "hero" being dead at the start—and a plot developed chronologically from beginning to middle to ending. Stein's
first detective story was *Blood On The Dining-Room Floor* (1933),
and *The Geographical History of America* is full of them. Gradually,
Stein came to feel that every theoretical exploration was a kind of
detective story, a charting of the mind in its progress toward discovery.

The chronological survey of genres may be schematized as shown
in the accompanying diagram. It is apparent from the diagram that
the three phases of portraiture coincide with the beginnings of other
genres as well. The novel, for example, coexists with the portrait in
the first phase but disappears completely between 1913 and 1924,
during the second phase. The description on the other hand comes
into existence precisely in this period. And the play too begins at
1913 and continues virtually to the end of Stein's career, passing
through two phases, as we shall see, that correspond to the last two
phases of portraiture. The romantic novel appears near the beginning
of the third phase, and the theoretical essay occurs then too, growing
quickly into a major genre.

The conclusions suggested by this scheme are first that portraiture
was the most permanent of the genres, extending almost from the
beginning to the end of Stein's career; further, that its vicissitudes
marked, if not determined, the emergence and disappearance of
other genres; and finally, that after approximately 1933 this dominance shifted to other genres. An account of Stein's conceptualization of her genres tends to support this chronological evidence and
explains the portrait's fall from programmatic dominance after 1933.

Beginning with the second phase, we encounter a rather bewildering multiplicity of genres, especially after the uniformity of the first
phase. For after the period of portraits and portrait-like novels, 1913
brings us description and geography and series, plays, and poetry, in
addition to the second-phase portraits; 1925–1926, the essay and a
new phase of portraits, plays, and novels; and 1932–1933, the autobiography and detective story. We might simplify this list somewhat
by trying to see groupings within it, and the most obvious basis for
this grouping is the opposition between prose and poetry used by
Stein in the essays in *Narration*. The first-phase works are all prose,

Chronology of Stein's Literary Genres

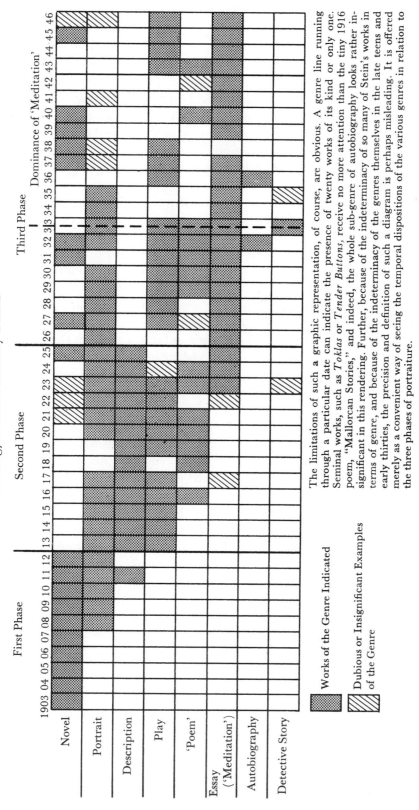

The limitations of such a graphic representation, of course, are obvious. A genre line running through a particular date can indicate the presence of twenty works of its kind or only one. Seminal works, such as *Toklas* or *Tender Buttons*, receive no more attention than the tiny 1916 poem, "Mallorcan Stories," and indeed, the whole sub-genre of autobiography looks rather insignificant in this rendering. Further, because of the indeterminacy of so many of Stein's works in terms of genre, and because of the indeterminacy of the genres themselves in the late teens and early thirties, the precision and definition of such a diagram is perhaps misleading. It is offered merely as a convenient way of seeing the temporal dispositions of the various genres in relation to the three phases of portraiture.

while the 1913 genres, including the plays, may be seen under the heading of poetry. The novels, autobiographies, detective stories, biographical portraits and theoretical meditations of the third phase are prose, all but meditations being "narratives" as well. The progression of the various genres turns out to be the gradual resolution of the poetic and narrative groupings into meditation, and in the process the loss of all subject matter beyond the acts of thinking and writing themselves.

Stein used the term poetry as an orientation in writing independent of form. It is an 'embroidering' on a name or noun. Though she had considered the noun inextricably related to memory, stasis, and identity, the second writing stage took up precisely the problem of how to create an immediate experience with a visual object—not a consciousness or an action, but a static object as it appears to a viewer. As Stein says, "my middle writing was painting" (*EA*, p. 180). She describes the switch from the avoidance of nouns in the early period as follows: "But and after I had gone as far as I could in these long sentences and paragraphs [of *The Making of Americans*] . . . I then began very short things and in doing very short things I resolutely realized nouns and decided not to get around them . . . and in that way my real acquaintance with poetry was begun" ("Poetry and Grammar," p. 228).

Many of the portraits of this period, such as "Susie Asado," and some of the descriptions and geography, such as "Accents of Alsace," are written in verse, and Stein herself declared that "Tender Buttons was very good poetry" ("Poetry and Grammar," p. 235). The primary concern of such works was "with using with abusing, with losing with wanting, with denying with avoiding with adoring with replacing the noun" (p. 231). Thus, poetry should not necessarily use nouns, but work around them. Stein speaks of this approach as "making it be a thing that could be named without using its name," as Shakespeare had created Arden forest "without mentioning the things that make a forest" (p. 236). At first in *Tender Buttons* and later in *An Acquaintance with Description* Stein tried "looking at anything until something that was not the name of that thing but was in a way that actual thing would come to be written" (p. 237). What she produced in a poem then was the complement of an imaginary sentence beginning "x is"; what the reader experiences is a set of perceptions which have fused around a thing. In the case of *Tender Buttons* where the things are named in the titles, the process is very much like that of portraiture where a group of perceptions

comes to define or describe a name. But whether the name is present
or not the effect of such pieces is a kind of riddle in which associations must be established between the description and the title, or
in which the title itself must be discovered. The only feature distinguishing the portrait from the 'poem' in general is the individuality
of the portrait subject, as opposed to the class character of the
poem's subject. The influence of the second-phase portrait program
on the other 'poetic' genres is obvious, then, particularly for the
descriptions.

The first experiments in visual description were *Tender Buttons*
("portraits of rooms and food and everything") and the portraits of
places. "I wanted to make portraits of places, I did. I did make them
of the Bon Marché, of the Galeries Lafayette, of a crowd at Mi-
Careme . . . Italians, and Americans . . ." ("Portraits and Repetition,"
pp. 186–87). The possibility of a portraiture of places or objects, as
we saw in chapter 1, is present in the origin of the genre, the *prosopopoeia,* and Stein developed this possibility in both the first- and
second-phase styles. It was only in the second phase, however, that
she portrayed totally inanimate subjects and it is on this basis that
the distinction between the description [2] (and geography) and the
portrait is made. Here the genre distinction seems to be purely a
question of subject matter.

Despite the effort to avoid the noun, however, the descriptions
inherited the portrait conflict between type and individual, between
the similarity among objects and their uniqueness. "In this natural
way of creating it then that it was simply different everything being
alike it was simply different, this kept on leading one to lists. Lists
naturally for a while and by lists I mean a series. . . . I began doing
natural phenomena . . . and natural phenomena naturally everything
being alike natural phenomena are making things be naturally simply
different. This found its culmination later, in the beginning it began
in a center confused with lists with series with geography with returning portraits . . ." ("Composition As Explanation," p. 27). The
depiction of the objects of the lists as "natural phenomena" suggests that Stein was trying to emphasize their existence as things-in-
themselves, self-contained and independent of human creation. In

2. The motivation for the description was Stein's desire to present the visual while main-
taining immediacy, i.e., avoiding memory, classes of objects, the noun. She was struck by
the fact that the name of a thing is "old" while the thing itself is always new in our perception. "What was there to do./I commenced trying to do something in Tender Buttons about
this thing" ("Poetry and Grammar," p. 237).

the same way, the lists themselves contained elements linked by part of speech and parallelism within the progression of the series, but intransigently individual, unique, single.

By 1926 Stein had developed the notion of the natural phenomenon into a theory of perception and composition. "The only thing that is different from one time to another is what is seen and what is seen depends upon how everybody is doing everything. This makes the thing we are looking at very different and this makes what those describe it make of it . . . the only thing that is different is what is seen when it seems to be being seen, in other words, composition and time sense" ("Composition As Explanation," pp. 21–22). Description then was the act of expressing the vision and time sense of a generation, and "composition" became both the vision of the time and its expression in writing. In this way the text and its subject were iconically related, both configurations to be perceived through the time sense of an era. The writer for Stein was one who was aware of the "composition" of his time and thus could translate it into a written composition. Unlike him, most people are unaware of the composition forming around them, and remain frozen in the view, and in the literary compositions, of the previous generation.

The generation, moreover, does not simply see its composition, but creates it. "The composition is the thing seen by every one living in the living that they are doing, they are the composing of the composition that at the time they are living is the composition of the time in which they are living" (p. 24). This simultaneous and reflexive perception and creation are taken one step further by the artist, who lives in his time and thus helps to "compose" it, sees the resulting composition, and describes or makes again the composition that he has helped to make in the first place.

Finally, the "natural phenomena" of this composition, its independent invariables, are the temporal categories within it: "The time when and the time of and the time in that composition is the natural phenomena of that composition" (p. 24). Each generation arranges in a new way the relations among these temporal categories, which are analogous to the givens in a physical composition—the rocks, trees, streams. Description then comes to mean much more than the depiction of inanimate objects—it is the perceptible form of perception itself, the composition of the temporal categories with which a generation perceives itself.

This extension of description to the act of composition was the culmination of the second period of Stein's writing. In the years immediately following she extended the category even further, seeing plays, operas and even novels as forms of description. "I found that since the landscape was the thing, a play was a thing and I went on writing plays a great many plays" ("Plays," p. 122). "In [the opera, *Four Saints in Three Acts*] I made the saints the landscape . . . all these saints together made my landscape" (pp. 128-29). "Lucy Church Amiably . . . quite definitely as a conception of what is seen was contained by itself inside it, although there it was a conceiving of what I was looking at as a landscape was to be itself inside in it . . ." ("Portraits and Repetition," p. 202). What set off this new extension of description into the other genres was a summer in the country in 1925. As Stein explains, "It was during this summer that Gertrude Stein began two long things, A Novel [of Thank You] and the Phenomena of Nature which was to lead later to the whole series of meditations on grammar and sentences. It led first to An Acquaintance With Description . . . She began at this time to describe landscape as if anything she saw was a natural phenomenon, a thing existent in itself" (*Toklas*, pp. 224-25). This procedure is closely related to the notion in the third-phase portraits of self-contained movement, a person (or object) totally relationless and yet having movement, being. Here the imminent disappearance of description as a separate mode is apparent. If anything can be presented as a thing in itself composed of a set of simultaneous and immediate relations, then any kind of subject matter can be a description and all entity writing is a mode of description. Any genre then becomes a form of description, and the term ceases to be a meaningful genre designation. From 1926 on, in fact, there are no more descriptions *per se*.

This decline of description is to be explained as well by the modification that occurred in the importance of vision and all the senses in Stein's thinking. Where before she had insisted upon presenting her simultaneous listening, speaking, and seeing, by the thirties she was denying the senses the association they had once had with knowledge as acquaintance, and thus with entity or the "human mind."[3]

Superstition is to believe what you see to believe what you hear and to see what you see.

---

3. The "human mind" by this time corresponded to 'entity' and "human nature" to 'identity.' The difference between the two sets of terms is that between faculty and mode of experience, respectively.

That makes superstition clear.
And in a way yes in a way it has nothing to do with human
nature or the human mind.
Superstition exists in itself because it is so true.[4]

That is, the data presented to the senses create "superstition." Its
absolute truth is the truth of facts, the truth, indeed, of what "exists
in itself," namely "natural phenomena." But the human mind (entity) is not concerned with this truth: "It is not concerned with being
or not being true" (GHA, p. 146). Truth is a relational concept involving a matching between statements and phenomena or ideas, and the
human mind is that mode of experience in which such relations are
not present. It is an immediate involvement in experience and not a
critical, analytic, or empirical mode. "The human mind knows what
it knows and knowing what it knows it has nothing to do with seeing
what it remembers . . ." (p. 63). In other words, what is available to
the senses is subsequently available to memory, and "superstition" is
formed out of such data. As a result, "Geography does not look like
it does in relation to the human mind" (p. 62). Thus an art that represents "geography" must not treat it as it is, but as the human mind
knows it. What it will represent finally is the action of the human
mind itself, and not the thing at all. Subject matter at this stage is
not distinct from the mental activity directed toward it. Description,
geography, portraiture—any focusing on things—becomes irrelevant
and these genres melt into the general program for a self-reflexive
art of the human mind.

    The second major genre that appeared with the break-up of genrolo-
gical unity in 1913 was the play. It too had its origins in portraiture,
specifically, the 1912 portrait, "M. Vollard et Cezanne." But Stein
claims that the theater had held an important place in her thinking
for a very long time. In "Plays" (Lectures in America), she gives a
history of her experience with the genre, from her earliest visits to
the theater to the time of the writing of the essay, 1934.
    What had initially struck her about drama was that the emotion of
the audience was always ahead of or behind the action on the stage.
She calls this a "syncopation" ("Plays," p. 93) of the audience's
emotion to the stage action. Being a profoundly mimetic writer, she

---

4. *The Geographical History of America or The Relation of Human Nature to The Human
Mind* (New York, 1936), p. 146 (hereafter referred to as *GHA*).

found this temporal discrepancy aesthetically distasteful, and one of the most important considerations in her own playwriting became the maintenance of a complete unity between the immediate action on the stage and the audience's experience. Stein spoke of a play later as "a thing I do not see but it is a thing somebody can see that is what makes a play to me" (*EA*, p. 193). This accent on vision is vital, for it implies a direct and immediate relation between the audience and what they see, without the entrance of memory or anticipation. It also ties the plays directly into the visual program of the second phase.

Stein describes in "Plays" the stages in her reading of drama as a child: "there was in reading plays . . . the necessity of going forward and back to the list of characters to find out which was which and then insensibly to know. Then there was the poetry and then gradually there were the portraits" ("Plays," p. 110). This progression, though Stein does not explain it, may be paraphrased as follows: first the identities of characters and their relations are remembered; then the language itself, the sound and pattern of the words, become apparent; finally this language creates an immediate experience with the characters, as in portrait perception. This process obviously takes some time and depends upon the reader's ability to return to the beginning, to the *dramatis personae*. But in live drama no such possibility exists. There "the things over which one stumbles . . . and there it was a matter both of seeing and of hearing were clothes, voices, what they the actors said, how they were dressed and how that related itself to their moving around. Then the bother of never being able to begin over again because before it had commenced it was over, and at no time had you been ready, either to commence or to be over" (pp. 114-15).

All these problems were solved for Stein when she went to see Sarah Bernhardt and a French company of actors. "The manners and customs of the french theatre created a thing in itself and it existed in and for itself as the poetical plays had that I used so much to read, there were so many characters just as there were in those plays and you did not have to know them they were so foreign, and the foreign scenery and actuality replaced the poetry and the voices replaced the portraits. It was for me a very simple direct and moving pleasure" (p. 116). What happened in this experience was that Stein did not "understand" the play in the normal sense of the word, but instead participated in it through something close to direct perception. Because of this, Stein says, she became interested in melodrama: "as what the people felt was of no importance one did not have to realize what was said" (p. 116). And one of her very latest plays, as we shall see, was a melodrama.

This notion of the play as a form of direct visual experience was expressed in Stein's comparison of plays to the dance and to various sports. One of her plays, *A Wedding Bouquet,* was produced, in fact, as a ballet, and Stein claims that she became interested in writing plays in the first place after seeing "Isadora Duncan and then the Russian ballet and in between Spain and the Argentine and bull-fights and I began once more to feel something about something going on at a theatre" (p. 118). This set of comparisons is developed more fully in *Everybody's Autobiography*, where Stein discusses the saints in her opera, *Four Saints in Three Acts,* as moving but doing nothing. "Later on when I saw them playing football they did the same thing they moved some and they did nothing" (*EA*, p. 194) (a comment that certainly could not have gratified her American hosts at the game). The dance and war, moreover, are related in that they are seen: "That is what they are for that anyone living then can look at them. And games do do both they do the dance and war bull-fighting and football playing. . . . That is the reason that plays are that, they are the thing anybody can see by looking." Plays then, like games, are both dance and war in that everyone moves about a lot but does nothing purposeful, and all this goes on in such a way as to be seen by an audience. A play for Stein is plotless; it is pure, visible activity.

The metaphor of the game suggests that Stein was using the word "play" as a pun—*ludus* as well as drama. In fact Stein eventually exposes this joke in *The Geographical History of America*:

Play I

The human mind.

The human mind at play.

[p. 155]

Here a play becomes synonymous with the play of the "human mind," which is precisely that degree of immediate seeing and hearing, disjoint from memory and anticipation, that Stein sought to create in the readers of her plays. In other words, a play eventually became a representation of the experience of entity, a movement that was not doing anything but was simply being. This, of course, is precisely what the later portraits were, except that in the portraits there is an object toward which the playing is directed while the play focuses on the essence of the play-ing. Thus a play creates an audience for the human mind of its author.

The distinction between the portraits and plays is explained by Stein as follows: "in my portraits I had tried to tell what each one is without telling stories and now in my early plays I tried to tell what happened without telling stories so that the essence of what happened would be like the essence of the portraits, what made what happened be what it was" ("Plays," pp. 121–22). In the early stages this distinction perhaps was meaningful, but as "what happened" became more and more internalized, with entity conceived as a self-contained movement, the opposition became illusory.

Another way that Stein differentiated portraits and plays is perhaps more promising. We saw this in chapter 3 where Stein was quoted as saying that portraits represented the essence of individuals, while plays represented the essence of the relations between individuals. Sometimes these relations are depicted through the interchanges of characters in Stein's plays, but frequently characters are completely lacking. As Stein says, "anything that was not a story could be a play and I even made plays in letters and advertisements" (p. 119).

Out of such experiments came the idea that a play was analogous to a landscape: "I felt that if a play was exactly like a landscape then there would be no difficulty about the emotion of the person looking on at the play being behind or ahead of the play because the landscape does not have to make acquaintance" (p. 122). The elements of the landscape do not have an inner life, an identity or history which can take the reader out of the immediate experience of the landscape as a whole. Further, the landscape is most essentially a configuration, a set of relations. "The landscape has its formation and as after all a play has to have formation and be in relation one thing to the other thing . . . the landscape not moving but being always in relation, the trees to the hills the hills to the fields the trees to each other any piece of it to any sky and then any detail to any other detail . . . the relation is there anyway. And of that relation I wanted to make a play and I did, a great number of plays" (p. 125). This notion of the play as the essence of what happens, and of what happens as simple visual relationship, as immediately perceptible as in a landscape, brings us very close to the early groupings of character as diagrams of interrelation. It sounds like the project of *A Long Gay Book*—to describe "what anyone feels acts or does in relation to any other one" (p. 92), except that the visual revolution of 1911–1913 had transformed the feelings, acts, and doings of the elements of the relation into essences with the immediacy of visual data. In a sense, the play became the genre in which relationality could be preserved without allowing memory to enter. It was a projection of the elements organized as types in the early portraits into an accidental and immediate configuration.

The analogy between play and landscape marked the second stage of operas and plays stemming from the summer of 1925 when Stein began to describe landscape as if anything she saw was a natural phenomenon, a thing existent in itself; "and she found it, this exercise, very interesting and it finally led her to the later series of Operas and Plays" (*Toklas*, pp. 224–25). By 1935 Stein was simply claiming that "A play is scenery. / A play is not identity or place or time but it likes to feel like it oh yes it does. . . " (*GHA*, p. 238). This simple equation is possible because Stein had pared down the play to its essentials— the play of the human mind as a thing in itself. In explaining why a play can get along without identity and place and time, Stein goes right back to her earliest problem with plays, the remembering of the characters' names and the time disjunction. "There need be no personages in a play because if there are then you do not forget their names and if you do not forget their names you put their names down each time that they are to say something. The result of which is that a play finishes" (p. 233). That is, if speeches become attached to finite characters that live by virtue of the play, they and the play of words, relation, and perception that they carry will cease to exist at the end of the play. If the "play" is simply an engagement of the "human mind," if it helps the audience to experience in the mode of the human mind, then the temporal perception of beginning, middle, and end will be impossible.

Aside from the theoretical relations that exist between the plays and portraits, there is a general formal similarity between contemporary works of both genres. The most striking feature, of course, is the division of both into lines that frequently do not delimit utterances. The lines give the impression of a dialogue, but the inclusion of different responses within one line or the breaking of a single utterance into several lines is rather puzzling. As I mentioned in chapter 3, this practice creates a rather arbitrary relation between voice and utterance, which is obviously what Stein was aiming at in her plays. William Gass demonstrates how such a transformation of a normal utterance into a Steinian dialogue can come about. First the

simple sentence is rearranged and its elements repeated until enough
variations have been produced for a paragraph or long sentence of
the early style. "Think next what might happen if we considered the
sentence to be composed of various voices: in short a play. For what
else is a play? It simply cites the separate sources of its sentences."[5]
Now if a Steinian play is stating the separate sources of its sentences,
but those "sentences" are really parts of a single sentence, then those
sources are in some sense grammatical functions. This seems to be
another way in which character and grammar are associated by Stein,
a variation on the use of sentence diagrams to depict character relations which we saw in the first phase.

Gass compares the breaking of the sentence into separate voices to
the techniques of choral music and cubist painting. "A musician
would have no trouble in seeing how a single sentence might be
treated as the consequence of a chorus, nor would a modern painter
find it hard to imagine the dissolution of his plate, bread, vase, and
fish, into plastic elements he then rearranged in a new, more pleasing
way" (p. 30). These two analogies are provocative. The choral analogy in fact is hardly an analogy at all, for the opera was not a distinct
genre from the play in Stein's thinking,[6] and it is with the musical
line and the different voices of the operas that Stein's dramatic productions make the most obvious and enjoyable sense.

The painting analogy sets up a parallel between a still life or landscape and a sentence, the artist being at liberty in either case to rear-
range the elements as he sees fit. In both the painting and the sentence,
an element other than disorder is introduced by this reshuffling—for
the painter, some comment on perspective, light and the violability
of form; for the writer, a comment on the relation between identity
and utterance and on the violability of grammatical form. Here we
have a kind of attenuation of consciousness across characters on the
basis of grammatical continuity, or else a superimposition of characters through the uniting of different grammatical utterances into one
"speech." This extension of consciousness across the boundaries of
identity is one of the ways in which Stein's notion of entity and the
human mind was realized in the plays. Here it is grammar that not
only defines the nature of the voice but shrinks or stretches its limits.
And the composition that the artist makes of these cropped, juggled,

5. William Gass, Introduction to *GHA*, p. 30.
6. In speaking of *Four Saints in Three Acts*, for example, Stein uses the word *play* rather
than *opera* in "Plays," p. 129.

and extended voices is very precisely a play with relationality. This interweaving of characters is also of great importance in *The Autobiography of Alice B. Toklas*.

A clear example of the effects of such ideas in playwriting can be seen in the late piece, "Three Sisters Who Are Not Sisters A Melodrama" (1943). The three sisters who are not sisters turn out to be three orphans who are unrelated, except by their common lack of parents. They are joined "on stage" by a pair of male twins. The characters quickly announce their states—e.g., "We are three sisters who are not sisters"—without a context or situation for their meeting, their present purpose, their background. The nature of the female and male groups calls into question precisely the notions of identity and interrelation mentioned above: what is the difference between relation and identity (the twins)? what does it take to create a relation (the sisters who are not sisters)?

These problems are exacerbated by the "action" which follows. The characters decide to find something to do—not, as they insist, something to do about the fact that the three sisters are not sisters but just "something to do." Here purposeful activity related to identity is being contrasted to "pure activity." The perplexity is solved when Samuel says, "I have an idea a beautiful idea, a fine idea, let us play a play and let it be a murder" (I, i). The activity is to be a play—a playing of a play in fact—and the object of the play is murder, the obliteration of an identity. And the characters perform this act with a vengeance. The lights go out mysteriously and when they go on again a dead body is lying on the floor. Nobody knows who the murderer is, including, ostensibly, the murderer himself. The lights go out again; again a corpse is found; and again, none of the survivors knows which one the murderer is. It is quite immaterial which ones are dead and which survive, since the characters are not individuated in any way. They are simply interchangeable corpses—or murderers—and though the survivors after each murder make a great cry about who the murderer is, his identity is quite irrelevant from the audience's point of view. After the fourth murder, the surviver realizes that she must be the murderess, and poisons herself. Then the lights go on again and everybody is alive. They reassert their identities—"three sisters who are not sisters,"—have a short argument about whether or not they are dead, and then decide to go to sleep. Here the relation of playing to being is "dramatized" in a very direct way. In play, discrete identity is destroyed (literally, through the murders, and in a different sense through the interchangeability of the characters);

it is only when the play-ing is over that the question of identity and relationality is again an issue.

A coincidence of title brings us to the final sub-genre of the play, the film. For one of Stein's two films, interestingly enough, is entitled "Film. Deux Soeurs Qui Ne Sont Pas Soeurs" (1929). It makes a revealing contrast to the later melodrama in terms of technique. For where the stage action contains all the classical unities, the film constantly defies them. It consists of three episodes, each one paragraph in length, which are separated by a number of hours or days. There is no dialogue, and the entire piece is made up of sequential statements of action. Within these, there is no ambiguity whatsoever about the relative temporal ordering of actions.

In the first episode a laundress carrying a package of laundry for delivery stands on a corner outside Paris, looking "avec ardeur"[7] at a photograph of two white poodles. Two ladies get out of a two-seater car and ask to see the photo. As they admire it, a young woman with her hair done as if for a beauty contest wanders past, gets into the car, and starts to cry. The two ladies throw her out of the car, in the course of which calamity she bumps against the laundress. The ladies drive off. The laundress realizes that she no longer has the photo, sees a young man, and tells him the whole story. Throughout this first "scene" and the film as a whole there is no attempt made to explain the motivation behind these acts. One event simply follows the next, and the action, like the photo, passes from one character to another.

A few hours later in front of a placement office, a younger laundress stands with her package of laundry. The two ladies drive up and show her the photo, which she looks at "avec plaisir et excitation, mais c'est tout." The beauty queen passes and runs toward the car. The two ladies get into their car, dropping a little package in the process but keeping the photo. They drive off.

Two days later ("le surlendemain") the first laundress stands in her street with a package of laundry and sees the beauty queen approaching with a little package at the same time as the young man comes toward her. The three suddenly see the car in which sit the two ladies and a real white poodle holding a little package in his mouth. "Les trois sur le trottoir le regarde passer et n'y comprennent rien."[8]

7. *Operas and Plays* (Paris, 1932), p. 399.

8. *Ibid.*, p. 400. The same peculiar story turns up in a late novel, *Ida* (New York, 1941), pp. 21–23. But here the narration centers upon the beauty queen who is a projection, an alter-ego or "twin," of Ida herself. The loss of the dog, car, and package to the ladies is very unsettling to Ida.

What is "happening" in the film is an apparent victory for the ladies in their turning the picture of the poodles into a real poodle and in their regaining the lost package. The laundresses, on the other hand, are deprived of their photo, the beauty queen of the car she presumably wants, and all the sidewalk characters of an understanding of how the transformation of picture into poodle has taken place.

However, the real "happenings" of the film are the plays on numbers and roles. There are two ladies, two laundresses, two days, two seats in the car, two poodles in the picture, and two young "supporting characters," the beauty queen and the young man. There are three episodes, three packages of laundry, and two groups of three characters at the end. The photo of the two poodles occurs in the first two episodes and is replaced by a real poodle in the third; the loss of the package is paralleled by the loss of the photo, both of them restored by the end in the figure of the poodle with package. The action is reciprocal—the photo, car and package on the one hand, either stolen, threatened by theft, or lost, or on the other, regained, defended, found. The bewilderment of the laundress and the others at the end is balanced by the apparent triumph of the ladies.

If this piece seems somewhat surrealistic, with its play on numbers, its juxtaposition of unexplained acts, and its undeveloped characters appearing in strangely coincidental fashion, the reader should not be surprised.[9] For Stein's notion of film was largely influenced by the surrealists; she claims, for example, that Jacques Viot told her: "you have to remember in writing film stories that it is not like writing for the theatre the film audience is not an audience that is awake it is an audience that is dreaming . . ." (*EA*, p. 210). The sudden spatio-temporal jumps and incomprehensible 'symbolic' acts of dreams can be seen in this "film" and force the reader to experience them with the immediacy of a dream. The lack of logic makes anticipation, synthesis, and even remembrance virtually impossible.

Despite their differences in temporal continuity, the film and the melodrama discussed here have much in common: the groupings of characters who are related but dissimilar, e.g., the sisters who are not sisters (here, the laundresses? the ladies? the beauty queen and the younger laundress? the two poodles in the picture?) as well as the constant plotting and rearranging of interconnections. The problem of temporality and knowledge comes in as well, the audience in

9. This, despite her statement in the Catalogue to Allan's paintings (quoted in T. Wilder, Introduction to *Last Operas and Plays*) that surrealists are pornographers.

neither work being able to anticipate what will happen, and the characters not understanding anything more, apparently, than the audience. With the film as with the melodrama, actions *per se* are unimportant since they are incomprehensible. They are significant only symbolically, as losses, gains, aggression. Stein herself asserted this similarity between the two genres: "the thing which has induced a person like myself to constantly think about the theatre from the standpoint of sight and sound[10] and its relation to emotion and time, rather than in relation to story and action is the same . . . general form of conception as the inevitable experiments made by the cinema" ("Plays," p. 104).

The play, opera, and film are thus variations within the major genre of the play, which appeared within Stein's work from 1913 to 1926, and then with modifications until the end of her career. Since, as we have seen, its definition was not dependent on specific subject matter but on essential relationality, it avoided the fate of the portrait and other descriptive modes. Nevertheless, the play after the early thirties became synonymous with the play of the human mind, and as such its formal characteristics, such as act and scene divisions, are often to be found in theoretical essays.

In 1918, at the beginning of her first hiatus in portrait writing, Stein began to write poems proper—short compositions with recognizable meters, rhyme schemes, stanzaic patterns, and often elaborate sound repetition. These are related to a rather tantalizing statement in "Poetry and Grammar" that counting is important to poetry:

> After all the natural way to count is not that one and one make two but to go on counting by one and one as chinamen do as anybody does as Spaniards do as my little aunts did. One and one and one and one and one. That is the natural way to go on counting.
> Now what has this to do with poetry. It has a lot to do with poetry. [p. 227]

Though Stein never explains what the connection is, it is clear that this "natural" counting is related to insistence, a constant returning to an element, a name for example, a constant beginning. Such "counting" creates the repetition, rhythm, and equivalent units

10. "Deux Soeurs" is a silent film. The earlier attempt at the genre, "A Movie" (1920), has dialogue.

(lines) that characterize poetry. Further, Stein later decided that counting was the religion of the modern world, for in the absence of a world beyond, people focus on life on earth and spend their time counting astronomical sums of money.

Stein, however, was more interested in small numbers:

> I always like counting but I like counting one two three four five six seven, or one little Indian two little Indians three little Indian boys counting more than ten is not interesting at least not to me because the numbers higher than ten unless they are fifty-five or something like that do not look interesting. . . .
> The queen was in her parlor eating bread and honey the king was in his counting room counting out his money. [*EA*, p. 120]

The connection between poetry and counting thus is most apparent in nursery rhymes. And Stein's poetry proper is certainly closer to jingles and Mother Goose than to any other form of poetry. Indeed, nonsense and children's literature have an important place in her work, because of their obsessive internal patterning independent of any relation to reality. One of her children's books, *To Do. A Book of Alphabets and Birthdays,* for example, is organized as a form of counting, with jingles and stories arranged within the rigid framework of the alphabet. This notion of poetry as repetition was the sense of the word normally used by Stein in the mid-thirties. Thus she says that the portrait "George Hugnet," with its extraordinary redundance and repetition, "made me realize what poetry really is" ("Portraits and Repetition," p. 203).

With the elimination of plot in narrative, however, the distinction between poetry and narrative became a problem. For poetry had been, in fact, a kind of narrative: "If poetry is the calling upon a name until that name comes to be anything if one goes on calling on that name more and more calling upon that name as poetry does then poetry does make of that calling upon a name a narrative it is a narrative of calling upon that name" (*Narration*, p. 26). But since prose has ceased to be a narrative and since a name, especially a narrative of a name, is no longer viable, "now it is coming that once again nobody can be certain that narrative is existing that poetry and prose have different meanings" (p. 28).

For all the genres begun in 1913, genre definitions became more fluid with each successive stage in Stein's development. Descriptions could be seen as plays and plays as descriptions by 1925; by the early thirties they were simply different orientations toward the immediate

activity of the human mind. Poetry, too, became indistinguishable
theoretically from prose. This loosening of genre boundaries and
even the prose/poetry distinction is a result of the shifting of the
subject matter of all the genres to the same thing—the human mind.
Differences among plays, portraits, descriptions, and poems after
that could only be determined by form, as by the act-headings of
plays or the stanzas of poems.

The same progression is visible in prose, particularly in the family
of "narrative" texts—the novel, biography, autobiography, romance,
and detective story. However, the word narrative must be used ad-
visedly in characterizing Stein's work, for she distinguished strictly
between the world's narratives and her own. The problem with narrative, and with its arch-exemplar, the pre-twentieth-century novel,
was that it depended upon memory; it involved the reader in a virtual
history tied inextricably to remembrance and thus created a disjunction between the time of the reading and the time in the reading:
"novels are soothing because they make anything happen as they can
happen that is by remembering anything" ("Portraits and Repetition," p. 181). We might compare this statement to Suzanne Langer's
view that fiction, unlike the film or theater, makes "a past."[11] As
with the portraits and plays, the novel must capture an essence rather
than tell a story: "everybody hears stories but the thing that makes
each one what he is is not that" ("Plays," p. 121). "A thing you all
know is that in the three novels written in this generation that are
the important things written in this generation, there is, in none of
them a story. There is none in Proust in The Making of Americans or
in Ulysses" ("Portraits and Repetition," p. 184).

Stein felt that the old novel was outmoded as well because it dwelt
on the imagining and developing of characters. "It is funny about
novels and the way novels now cannot be written. They cannot be
written because actually all the things that are being said about any
one is what is remembered about that one or decided about that one.
And since there is so much publicity so many characters are being
created every minute of every day that nobody is really interested in
personality enough to dream about personalities" (EA, p. 69). Further, "characters in books do not count in the life of the reader the
way they used to do and if they do not the novel as a form is dead"
(p. 102). The reason for this change in the reader's reaction to

---

11. Suzanne Langer, "A Note on the Film," *The Oxford Reader: Varieties of Contemporary Discourse,* ed. Frank Kermode and Richard Poirer (New York, 1971), p. 577.

character, like that to the story, is the role of the news media. In fact Stein cites this explanation so often that one begins to wonder whether she is not building on the etymological relation between "novel" and "news."[12]

Stein works the demise of character and plot into an elaborate theory of the difference between British and American literature. "Always before the language of each nation who had a narrative to make a story to tell a life to express a thing to say did it with a language that had gradually become a language that was made gradually by them to say what they had to say. But here in American because the language was made so late in the day that is at a time when everybody began to read and to write all the time and to read what was written all the time it was impossible that the language would be made as languages used to be made to say what the nation which was coming to be was going to say. All this has never happened before. History repeats itself anything repeats itself but all this had never happened before."[13]

The American language did not develop gradually through time, and hence it expresses, according to Stein, the immediacy of the modern world. As a result, the proper American—and hence modern—novel is not one which attempts to tell a story through its plot or to create interest in characters. The new novel should deal in knowledge rather than emotion, because knowledge is created by simultaneity, while emotion is created by sequence. "A narrative can give emotion because an emotion is dependent upon succession upon a thing having a beginning and a middle and an ending. That is why every one used to like sequels . . . but actually in modern writing sequels have no meaning" (*Narration,* p. 22). Modern writing must operate immediately, like sentences: "Sentences are contained within themselves and anything really contained within itself has no beginning or middle or ending, any one can know this thing by knowing anything at any moment of their living, in short by knowing anything. How do you know anything, well you know anything as complete knowledge as having it completely in you at the actual

12. Novels, like the news, deal with that mode called identity in the early phase and human nature in the later years, a mode in which memory is present. For Stein, proper novels should not be like the news but instead like an almanac, which "has a relation to the human mind because every day it tells what it is./An almanach has no relation to human nature because every day human nature tells what it was" (*GHA*, pp. 141–42).

13. "English and American Language in Literature," *Life and Letters Today* (September, 1935), p. 22.

moment that you have it. That is what knowledge is, and essentially therefore knowledge is not succession but an immediate existing" (p. 20). This is the kind of knowledge that we have associated with James's term, "acquaintance."[14]

The new narrative, to create this immediacy, would have to do away with succession. But this need brought Stein up squarely against the basic units of English prose—the sentence and the paragraph. Here her famous maxim that "A sentence is not emotional a paragraph is" (How To Write, p. 23) becomes understandable, for since a paragraph is a succession of sentences it contains the same emotion as a succession of events. Or, as Stein specified, "Paragraphs are emotional not because they express an emotion but because they register or limit an emotion" ("What Is English Literature," Lectures in America, p. 48). Thus, Stein felt compelled to do away with the successivity of the paragraph, to make it a unity of knowledge like the sentence. In order to do so, she first created the long meandering sentences seen in the early portraits and The Making of Americans. These sentences "had no longer the balance of sentences because they were not the parts of a paragraph nor were they a paragraph but they had made in so far as they had come to be so long and with the balance of their own that they had they had become something that was a whole thing and in so being they had a balance which was the balance of a space completely not filled but created by something moving as moving is not as moving should be. As I said Henry James in his later writing had had a dim feeling that this was what he knew he should do" ("Poetry and Grammar," p. 225). Henry James was sometimes a kind of touchstone for Stein's notions about writing, and this idea of the self-enclosed sentence as a unit of immediate knowledge is a very provocative point of contact between them. In the early period of Stein's art, the merging of sentence and paragraph by a running-together of separate grammatical sentences and clauses into one super-sentence was Stein's method of creating a constant state of acquaintance within a long text. All the dislocations of tense and grammatical categories noted in connection with the first-phase portraits were used in this writing.

In 1913 with the coming of Stein's concern with visuality and things, the novel disappeared altogether, and did not reappear until 1925 (A Novel of Thank You), when Stein was entering on her third

---

14. William James, of course, considered the sentence a basic unit of "knowledge-about." For clarification, see chapter 2.

portrait phase of self-contained movement. At this time a new solution to the problem of the novel arose—the romantic novel.[15] The major work of this type is *Lucy Church Amiably* (1927), an attempt to creat a novel of self-contained movement involving the descriptive visuality of the previous period and the progression of knowledge normal to narrative. The subtitle of the book, "A Novel of Romantic beauty and nature and which Looks Like an Engraving," reflects Stein's intent to translate the novel into a descriptive mode. But where the description in the early novels was dictated by notions of character types, that of the late novels was a translation of the visuality and enclosure of the second-phase portraits into a longer form. Stein in fact speaks of the romance as the culmination of the path from lists and series to "natural phenomena" where "naturally everything being alike natural phenomena are making things be naturally simply different" ("Composition As Explanation," p. 27). "Romanticism is then when everything being alike everything is naturally simply different, and romanticism" (p. 28).

However, the romantic novel was finally not a mode of writing belonging either to identity or to the "human mind." It is true that it had no novelistic succession within it, just as description or "scenery" had none: "Now scenery has no beginning and middle and end, and that is what makes scenery romantic" (*GHA*, p. 218). But like description, the romantic novel was too closely tied to spatiality: "The human mind has to say what anything is now. Not ever where anything is that is romance but has to say what anything is now oh yes yes yes that is the human mind" (p. 173). The human mind has no relation to spatiality, the physical; it is simply involved in the immediacy of each moment. Thus, though description and "romance" both avoid the temporal flux that destroys this immediacy, they are too much involved with relationality and physical contexts; they prevent the enclosure of the experience which characterizes "entity" or the "human mind."

In fact, Stein decided that romance was merely a symbol of the human mind, like money, like words, and like the weather. This linkage can be seen in the following series of quotations:

> It is an obligation to have money connect itself with romanticism because that too is not human nature but scenery. . . . [p. 220]

---

15. As with the etymological association of "novel" and "news" mentioned earlier, one suspects that Stein is suggesting through the term "romantic" its etymological relation to "*roman*."

> Money is what words are.
> Words are what money is. [p. 201]

weather and money have nothing to do with events or with
human nature, they have to be the symbols of the human
mind and the human mind is what it is and it writes that.
[p. 105]

The problem with all these symbols—words, money, weather,
romance—is that they are symbols and not equivalents. Stein was
constantly urging that the word, or name, be replaced in writing by
the thing, that all these symbols, these signs pointing toward things,
be replaced by a writing of things—the *écriture-objet* discussed in the
previous chapter. "What is money and what is romanticism it is not
like human nature because it is not finishing it is not like a master-
piece because it has no existing" (p. 230). Symbols have no "existing"; they are not self-contained movement. And at this point the
long development of description from the early descriptive novels
to *Tender Buttons* to the romantic novel finds a dead end. No matter what technical advances the 'pure' description made possible, it
lacked the essential life, the living, necessary for a masterpiece.
Such living could only come from a writing involving a human
subject.

The logical solution, then, was a narrative of people, and in particular, one tied closely to the play of a person's mind—the autobiography. Of course, Stein considered the conventional autobiography,
like the conventional novel, an illegitimate form in the modern
world since it told a story: "It is of course perfectly natural that
autobiographies are being well written and well read. You do see anybody can see that so much happens every day and that anybody
literally anybody can read or hear about it told the day that it happens. . . . Novels then which tell a story are really then more of the
same much more of the same [telling of what happens] , and of
course anybody likes more of the same . . ." ("Portraits and Repetition," p. 184–85). However, Stein's own autobiographies did
not fall into this category: "I write plays and not novels. An
autobiography is not a novel no indeed it is not a novel" (*EA*,
p. 194).
   Stein's first work of this genre was *The Autobiography of Alice
B. Toklas* (1932), in which she set out to write the autobiography
of Toklas "as simply as Defoe did the autobiography of Robinson

Crusoe."[16] That is, the same relationship was to exist between Stein and the first-person narrative of her fictional creation, Toklas, as that between Defoe and the first-person narrative of Crusoe, and further both works were to be seen as "autobiographies." This puzzling comparison of a living person to a fictional character, of an autobiography to a novel, makes sense, however, if we keep in mind Stein's notion of the relation between fiction and nonfiction in the twentieth century:

> There is no real reality to a really imagined life any more.
> Nothing I like more than when a dog barks in his sleep.
> That is a reality that can be known not by listening but by the dog who is asleep and feels like barking, he barks as if he barks and it is a bark it really is a bark although he is only dreaming. How much does he know that he is barking. . . .
> What is the difference between remembering what has been happening and remembering what has been as dreaming. None. [*GHA*, p. 74]

That is, the distinction between the fictional and nonfictional is now nonexistent. Real characters have a greater imaginative force than imaginary ones because the modern media are removing all motivation for imagining characters. "Since there is so much publicity so many characters are being created every minute of every day that nobody is really interested in personality enough to dream about personalities . . . how can you dream about a personality when it is always being created for you by a publicity, how can you believe what you make up when publicity makes them up to be so much realer than you can dream. And so autobiography is written which is in a way a way to say that publicity is right, they are as the public sees them."[17] The autobiography is then the validation of the force of the media in raising nonfiction to a dominant form.

The Robinson Crusoe comparison also suggests that Stein thought Defoe was talking about himself by inventing a character who spoke

16. *Toklas*, p. 252. Stein expresses a similar idea in another work of this period: "Robinson Crusoe and the footsteps of the man Friday is one of the most perfect examples of the non-existence of time and identity which makes a master-piece . . . There is no time and identity in the way it happened and that is why there is no fright" (*What Are Masterpieces*, p. 93).

17. *EA*, p. 69. We might note that the vast majority of Stein's genres are nonfictional. It is interesting that the breakdown of the boundary between fiction and nonfiction created by the mass media was hailed thirty years after Stein's observations as the original insight of McLuhan, Tom Wolfe, *et al.*

in the first person. That is not to say that every first-person novel is
an autobiography, but rather that every autobiography involves the
creation of a semi-real character separate from the writer. The selec-
tion of Toklas as this character immediately focuses attention upon
the special relation between her and Stein. For if the hero of a novel
is a creation if not a projection of its author, then the narrator, Toklas, though existent in her own right and treating the author Stein as
a character in her narrative, is also a creation and a projection of
Stein. The implications of this continuity of self over other, over
one's companion, one's audience, are rather mind-boggling. However we saw something like this before in the plays, where characters
merge into each other through their speeches. And in portraiture
such a merging of subject and writer is essential, the writer recording
his perceptions of another and in so doing recording himself. *Toklas*
is one stage more complex: the writer records another's perceptions
of her and in so doing creates the other who is then found to be the
writer herself. This game of hide and seek between author and persona, self and other, perceiver and perceived, essence and audience,
propelled Stein's final portrait conception of character out of its
secure situation. Character had again become a problem. The precision and succinctness of the portrait form as well had been left
behind in this long discursive text.

The doodle, "Gertrice/Altrude," in the manuscript of "Lend a
Hand" (YCAL, No. 269) suggests just such an intermingling of character. The same doubling can be seen in the manuscript of *Toklas*
itself, where large stretches appear in Toklas's handwriting. I do not
believe as some critics (e.g., Bridgman, p. 209) have suggested, that
she in fact composed large parts of the work, Stein hiding this fact
in her joy at producing a comprehensible, saleable piece of writing.
Toklas was probably transcribing Stein's dictation, thus creating in
real life the same confusion of identity upon which the artful *Toklas*
is based. Indeed, the realms of reality and fiction were not discrete.

The book is structured around two principles which are suggested
in the following paragraph: "But to return to the beginning of my
life in Paris. It was based upon the rue de Fleurus and the Saturday
evenings and it was like a kaleidoscope slowly turning" (p. 89). The
"return" and the "kaleidoscope" are temporal and spatial symbols of
the treatment of experience in the autobiography. The reader is constantly returned to events in such a way as to superimpose the
present onto the past, to destroy linear temporality. At the same
time, any single event is at the center of a constantly shifting set of

accompanying events or associations, like a kaleidoscopic image. The pattern keeps changing, and virtually anything can be incorporated into the design.

The element of randomness and chance suggested by the kaleidoscope metaphor not only relates to the free association of events, but characterizes the events themselves. People are reported as doing all kinds of peculiar things, without any indication of surprise or disapproval (except for a few incidents, such as that with Hemingway) from the narrator. In the famous birthday party for Rousseau, for example, an extraordinary sequence of events transpires—fights, drunken dancing on a table, the recitation of poems, the request for Toklas to sing American Indian songs!, the eating of the decoration on her hat by a drunken poet—but these are told with a kind of deadpan good humor that does not judge. The only hint of reaction is Toklas's displeasure at losing her hat ornament. The clearest statement of this randomness of events and the passive observation of them comes after the persona has gone through a long list of important people who visited the atelier: "It was an endless variety. And everybody came and no one made any difference" (pp. 123-24).

The only thing that does seem to make a difference in the book—beyond the initial meeting of the two women (marked by a symbolic earthquake on a notebook cover, like the San Francisco earthquake which led to Toklas's trip to France), and perhaps the outbreak of World War I—is Stein's success as a writer. Like *A Moveable Feast*, the autobiography chronicles the development of a career up to the point of widespread recognition, except that, whereas in Hemingway's book the history is written after the fact, Stein's autobiography is itself the culmination of her rise to fame. She leads up to this success in the last six pages or so with descriptions of her Cambridge lecture, the printing of various long neglected pieces such as *The Making of Americans* by commercial publishers, the forming of the Plain Edition by Toklas, and the translating and publishing of her work in French. Then as the final stage in this rise to fame, "for some time now many people, and publishers, have been asking Gertrude Stein to write her autobiography and she had always replied, not possibly." The request for the autobiography is the culmination of Stein's success, and the ruse of Toklas as autobiographer is the mechanism that finally brings the book into being. The narrator reports Stein's words at the end of the work: "I am going to write it as simply as Defoe did the autobiography of Robinson Crusoe." And then the narrator becomes the first person again, making Stein the third: "And she has and this is it" (p. 251). These last words merge the writing of the book into the book itself, and move it from the past into the present. The book is self-reflexive and the writer's identity becomes realized in the culmination that the book both represents and is.

A similar ending can be seen in *Everybody's Autobiography* (1936), in which many of the problems about identity raised by *The Autobiography of Alice B. Toklas* and Stein's ensuing fame are discussed. She ends that book: "perhaps I am not I even if my little dog knows me but anyway I like what I have and now it is today" (p. 318). Here the question of identity, the relation of identity to autobiography and the equating of the time of the subject to the time of the autobiography are again present.

In *Everybody's Autobiography* however Stein indicates a certain dissatisfaction with the previous autobiography:

> I had really written poetry and I had really written plays and I had really written thinking and I had really written sentences and paragraphs but . . . I had not simply told anything . . . I would simply say what was happening which is what is narration. . . .
>
> And now I almost think I have the first autobiography was not that, it was a description and a creation of something that having happened was in a way happening not again but as it had been which is history which is newspaper which is illustration but is not a simple narrative of what is happening not as if it had happened not as if it is happening but as if it is existing simply that thing. [pp. 302–303]

In other words, *Toklas* was still a story and thus was "soothing" because it involved memory and a disjunction between the time of the reader and the time of the events.[18] Somehow, Stein believed that this discrepancy could be overcome—had been overcome in *Everybody's Autobiography*—by turning a sequence into an object. This is the intent of the kaleidoscope image, but its realization was another thing.

18. Stein seems to blame this 'failure' on the motivation behind the writing of the book. In "Portraits and Repetition" she claims that it was written with an audience in mind, unlike the works of entity in which there was no interference with the unity of the act of writing and the work being written (p. 205). In *EA*, p. 41, she implies that *Toklas* was motivated by a desire for money: " . . . men because they are like animals in everything except in having money always have to have what they do not have, and so I wrote the Autobiography."

Stein set about this problem in *Everybody's Autobiography* with a 'genuine' first person and a 'conventional' history to tell—what happened as a result of the success of *Toklas*, in particular, her trip to America as a celebrity. Here the interpenetration of an autobiography and the life it depicts is apparent, for Stein's printed history had profoundly influenced her subsequent lived history. The word "autobiography" is used deliberately ambiguously in *EA* to refer both to the book and to the life.

The change in Stein's relation to her audience created by *Toklas* is expressed in the central conceit of the book—that it is everybody's autobiography:

> Alice B. Toklas did hers and now everybody will do theirs.
> Alice B. Toklas says and if they are all going to do theirs the way she did hers. [p. 3]

The "way she did hers" of course was to be the creation of Stein, or alternately to be the creator of Stein through her function as audience. In the same way, with Stein now a universally recognized celebrity, she was both the creator of her audience's voice and its creation. The relation between self and audience became of consuming interest to her in the years between the two autobiographies, and is discussed most clearly in *The Geographical History of America* (1935). There Stein states: "being I I am I has really nothing to do with the little dog knowing me, he is my audience, but an audience never does prove to you that you are you" (p.113). Stein goes on to say that "there are no witnesses to the autobiography of any one that has a human mind" (p. 90). But the whole genre of autobiography is based precisely upon such a witnessing, such a disjunction between a life and its appearance, even to the one whose life it depicts. The autobiography in effect splits its writer/subject in two, making him his own audience, a state of affairs that Stein had always deplored as inhibiting genius and hence masterpieces:

> identity is funny being yourself is funny as you are never yourself to yourself except as you remember youself and then of course you do not believe yourself. That is really the trouble with an autobiography you do not of course you do not really believe yourself why should you. . . . You are of course never yourself. . . . [*EA*, p. 68]

Stein attempted to overcome this problem by merging her audience with herself as the subject of the autobiography, and by weaving her experiences of people into an even more disjointed web of associations than in *Toklas*. [19] However, this strategy was only partially successful, and large sections of *EA* read like a simple narrative of her adventures in America and the ideas that became clarified along the way. Her ambivalence about the possibilities of the genre are apparent in the following key passage of *The Geographical History of America* in which she warns against the trio of anticipation, causality, and identity: "become," "because," and "be":

> Become Because.
> Beware of be.
> Be is not what no one can be what no one can see and certainly not what no one can say.
> Anybody can say be.
> Be is for biography.
> And for autobiography.
> No not for autobiography because be comes after.
> So once more to renounce because and become. [p. 192]

Autobiography is perhaps prior to or outside of identity and the concerns that destroy the immediacy of experience and of writing. But its status seems rather insecure here. Indeed, the final autobiography which Stein produced, a short piece called "The Autobiography of Rose" (1936), is more like a portrait than an autobiography, treating the girl, Rose, in the third person and not referring directly to Stein's life. The autobiography does not seem to have been possible to render as "it is simply a thing."

The last generic solution to the problem of narrative was the detective story. Stein decided that this was the only valid form of the

19. E.g., "in America and in England too Alice B. Toklas was more than Alice Toklas [a comment on the difference between the French and English titles of *Toklas*]. Alice Toklas never thought so and always said so.

"That is the way any autobiography has to be written which reminds me of Dashiell Hammett.

"But before I am reminded of Dashiel Hammett I want to say that just today I met Miss Hennessy and she was carrying, she did not have it with her, but she usually carried a wooden umbrella" (p. 3).

novel now that the mass media and mass population had invalidated
fictional characters:

> the earth now is all covered over with people and . . . hearing
> anybody is not of any particular importance because anybody
> can know anybody.
>   That is really why the only novels possible these days are detec-
> tive stories, where the only person of any importance is dead.
> [*EA*, pp. 101–102]

Furthermore, the fact that the hero is already dead means that the
event, the "story," happened before the book began; thus "there can
be no beginning and middle and end because he is dead" (p. 123).
The detective novel solves the problems of character and successive
plot, since the "action" of the novel is the gradual growth in understanding—knowledge—of the reader in relation to the central, unchanging situation. "Any detective story is ready to be told. And as you
know it you know it" (*GHA*, p. 127). Again, Stein's relation to Henry
James is apparent, the novel being conceived as a charting of the
reader's understanding, as much as any detective's, in relation to an
unchanging fact. Stein noted that this play of the mind, and not the
crime with which it played was the real point of the detective novel, for
the crime was a question of "motive" or necessity, a function of
human nature, while detection was a question of the "reason why"
(p. 123) which belonged to the human mind:

> in the story it is the detection that holds the interest and that is
> natural enough because the necessity as far as action is con-
> cerned is the dead man, it is another function that has very little
> to do with human nature that makes the detection interesting.
> ["What Are Master-Pieces," p. 88]

Stein deliberately contrasted the notion of character used in the
detective story with that in her first phase of writing. In this period
she had believed that "every one was in a group and a group was
separated from every other one, and so the character of every one
was interesting because they were in relation but now since the earth
is all covered over with every one there is really no relation between
any one. . . . That is what makes detective stories such good reading,
the man being dead he is not really in connection with any one. If
he is it is another kind of a story and not a detective story" (*EA*,

p. 99). It is the isolation, the essential isolation, of people that is interesting and not their relations to others. The switch in character conceptions from identity to entity, from type to individual, is an expression of the radical isolation of people, and is represented by the isolation of the hero in death, this posed as a problem in the detective story, an immediate fact to be confronted head-on. Interestingly, this is the opposite situation from the autobiography, where the relation of self to other is definitional.

The possibility of such a presentation of character arose, according to Stein, as an essentially American phenomenon, and it is here that her theories of the relation between geography and the national character can be seen most clearly. Stein had flown all over America during her visit of 1933–1934, and had been impressed by the immense stretches of flat land and the straight lines marking roads and territorial boundaries. She said that it was seeing the squared-off countryside from a plane that made her know that cubism was in fact an accurate picture of the modern (*EA*, p. 192). Furthermore, she claimed that the American countryside was uniquely suited to wandering, the activity of saints and the symbol of the movement of the human mind:[20] "Wandering around a country has something to do with the geographical history of that country and the way one piece of it is not separated from any other one . . . the straight lines on the map of the United States of America make wandering a mission and an everything . . . really wandering has something to do with the human mind" (*GHA*, pp. 92–93).

It was precisely this fostering of the human mind by American geography that made death what it is in American literature:

> Writing is neither remembering nor forgetting neither beginning or ending.
> Being dead is not ending it is being dead and being dead is something. Think of any crime of course being dead is something.
> Now and that is a great American contribution only any flat country has and can be there that being dead is actually something. [p. 150]

The use of death as "something" in literature is to be seen in the history of American mystery and crime stories, beginning, according to

20. Stein claims that Spain is also a country for wandering and thus has produced the most important saints.

Stein, with Mark Twain, who "did make a dead man dead. I think he was the first man to ever do that and it was a great American thing to do."[21] Though Stein never discloses precisely which works of Twain's she has in mind here, perhaps she is referring in particular to *Tom Sawyer*, in which Tom watches his own funeral, having a view of his character presented to him which is utterly out of keeping with anything anyone has previously said to him. In any case, in this rather puzzling notion of the function of death in American literature, Stein associates the elimination of a dynamic character with the release of the human mind in writing.

The problem with the detective novel, however, is that the characters within it spend their time trying to establish the identity of the corpse and tracing the relations with other characters that led to his death: "About detective stories is the trouble with them that the one that is dead has no time and no identity for him to them and yet they think that they can remember what they do not have as having it without their having it for them" (*GHA*, pp. 213–14). This is an incorrect approach to a mystery for Stein, who claimed that she never tried to anticipate the solution and hence found the immediate experience with the book very exciting. "I would like to read a detective story every day and very often I do" (p. 214).

Gradually, however, Stein extended the category of the detective story to all forms of writing in which the writer and reader are engaged in immediacy and discovery. In the largely theoretical book entitled *The Geographical History of America*, Stein wrote a number of "detective stories," for example,

> Detective story number I. About how there is a human mind. And how to detect it.
> Detective story number I.
> The great thing to detect in a detective story is whether you have written as you have heard it said. If you do write as you have heard it said then you have to change it. [p. 123]

The act of writing itself is being discussed as a detective story and the detective story is about detecting in writing. What is detectable there is the existence of the human mind, for it is only through this faculty that masterpieces come about. The act of judging writing, then, is a constant alertness toward what is essential and immediate in thinking,

21. "Mark Twain Centenary," *Painted Lace and Other Pieces* (New Haven, 1955), p. 316.

and a rejection of what belongs, instead, to human nature. It is at this point in Stein's writing that the "narrative" mode finds its culmination, for in the explanatory writing of the mid-thirties, subject and writing become inextricably fused and a book is a constant discovery of what one is immediately experiencing. Writing and reading are seen as pure acts of the human mind in its experience with its own experience. This possibility of infinite self-contained reflexiveness is the completion of the novel genre, and at the same time, the logical aim of the theoretical essay.

The subject of the essay brings us back to the beginning of the third phase—1926—when a lecture was commissioned by Cambridge University. Its title, "Composition As Explanation," could serve as a motto for all of Stein's essay writing, for she was almost always exemplary rather than discursive in her theorizing; the compositions were themselves demonstrations of what they supposedly explained. They are definitionally reflexive texts, although this reflexiveness was only partially developed at the beginning.

Stein was obviously bothered in this first lecture by the problem of the audience. *The Autobiography of Alice B. Toklas* describes her great nervousness in preparing "Composition As Explanation," and in fact she contrasted the kind of writing that goes into portraiture to that of lecturing: "as I write the movement of the words spoken by some one whom lately I have been hearing sound like my writing feels to me as I am writing. That is what led me to portrait writing. However lecturing is another matter" (*EA*, p. 88). As a result of her awareness of audience, Stein's lectures are much easier to understand than the theoretical works that were written without any physical audience in mind, such as *How To Write*. The illustrations from her other texts seem 'artistic' compared to the discursive body of the lectures, and as a whole the lectures are surprisingly clear and consistent. In fact, Stein's statement that "I had always liked Poe I liked his explanation of the Raven . . ." (*EA*, p. 248) suggests a possible model, and a super-rational one at that. Stein certainly did not explain her writing in as clear terms as Poe—temporal sequences in particular are difficult to recover from her accounts—but there is the same enigmatic simplicity in "The Philosophy of Composition" as in many of Stein's essays, both talking quite matter-of-factly about complex procedures as if their enactment in art were merely a question of a few ideas and some mechanical techniques for putting them across.

With *How To Write* and other reflexive essays, the reader is involved in a different process. He is constantly shifting from statement as reference to statement as example or thing, a device which we saw in the second- and third-phase portraits, typical as well of cubism. But in the essays, it is writing and thinking *per se* that undergo this semiotic shifting, making the act of writing and its product precisely equivalent. Here Stein's aim of simultaneous talking and listening and of self-contained movement seems to find one of its best fulfillments, for the interference of the demands of subject matter, as in portraiture and all the other genres, is eliminated. In such works avowedly about the mind as it acts in writing, there is never the kind of contradiction posed by the external/internal clashes of portraiture. Further, needless to say, these works do not depend on the projection of any characters or plot: "I tell all the young ones now to write essays, after all since characters are of no importance why not just write meditations, meditations are always interesting, neither character nor identity are necessary to him who meditates" (*EA*, p. 102).

As Stein's ideas about the various genres became more and more abstract in the thirties, theoretical reflexiveness began to characterize all of them, and all of them became, in a way, versions of the essay. This development came to a head in a key passage from the major theoretical piece of the thirties, *The Geographical History of America*:

> This whole book now is going to be a detective story of how to write.
> A play of the relation of human nature to the human mind.
> And a poem of how to begin again.
> And a description of how the earth looks as you look at it which is perhaps a play if it can be done in a day and is perhaps a detective story if it can be found out.
> Anything is a detective story if it can be found out and can anything be found out.
> Yes. [*GHA*, p. 120]

Here the genres are not defined formally in connection to texts, but are different perspectives on the same text. A genre is simply an orientation toward a piece of writing. Hence, a theoretical exposition can be seen as a detective story if it is a search after knowledge; as a play if it depicts the relation among the elements involved; as a poem if it constantly returns to its focus and elaborates a single issue; as a description if it creates a simultaneity between the perception and the perceived; again as a play if it respects the Aristotelian unity of time between the "action" and the artistic experience; and again as a detective story if it itself is the object of knowledge. The assurance that "anything can be found out" implies that anything, or any piece of writing, can be a detective story, regardless of form or ostensible content. Thus Stein's writing about writing can be seen from all these different standpoints. The literary essay becomes the essential core of writing upon which all the genres are based. `

Perhaps the most explicit demonstration of this fact is a group of texts centered upon the problem of identity, which were written at the same time as *The Geographical History of America* and in fact duplicate many of its ideas. They are "Identity A Poem A Story and A History,"[22] and its companions, "Identity A Tale" (see appendix 1, below) and "Identity A Play" (the latter published in *What Are Masterpieces* under the title, "Identity A Poem"). These three texts appear in quite a few versions in manuscript. Stein was clearly unsure about how to approach the topic and tried over and over, using different genres, without being satisfied with the results. The versions that we shall consider seem to have struck her as more satisfactory than the others, since "Identity A Play" and "Identity A Poem" are finished pieces which eventually found their way into print and our version of the other text got as far as a typescript. The most satisfactory version of all, of course, must have been that incorporated into *The Geographical History of America.*

The themes of the three versions are the direct relation between identity and human nature, their opposition to the human mind, and the role of audience in the creation of identity. This opposition between audience-created identity and true creative being goes all the way back to Stein's identity versus entity and ultimately to James's knowledge-about versus acquaintance. Stein insists in *Narration* that human nature is the subject of masterpieces, although it has nothing to do with their creation, and in the three pieces on identity this idea is being worked out in a pure form: identity is the subject, and is to be presented by way of the major genres of the human mind.

Despite their titles, "Identity A Tale" and "Identity A Poem A Story and A History" are virtually the same. "Identity A Tale" contains nearly all the generic divisions of the other text, but

23. Written in several manuscript versions with "A Pun" as one of the genres of the title, although the bibliographies do not list the title as such.

elaborates many of them and places them in a narrative frame concerning the vicissitudes of "Sweet William," his genius, and "his
Lilian."

The "Tale" begins with the general observation found in several
of Stein's works of this time: "Since there are no men in existence
anywhere except here on this earth being men is not an easy thing to
happen." Then, in a new paragraph we are introduced to one of these
men, Sweet William, who has his genius and therefore has not had to
look for it. He has just found his Lilian, moreover, after looking for
her. The sound similarity between "William" and "Lilian" suggests
that they are versions of each other; more precisely, Lilian is William's identity which must be sought outside himself. His genius, his
essence, on the other hand, is part of him and hence does not involve
him in relationality, in going outside himself. The difference in sex
between the two "characters" and the sexual suggestion in "and then
he had Lilian" begin to imply that love is an analogy for the creation
of identity, the lover acting in a sense as an audience, and we have
seen how this notion operates in *Toklas*.

This introductory section establishes the "characters" of the tale,
who are in fact aspects of every character; the piece is a kind of
psychodrama. Further, though the genre here is the "tale" or short
narrative, the text is clearly a theoretical meditation; the genre is
simply a special approach or perspective on a metaliterary problem.
That is, identity will be treated as "what happens," and the narrative
frame will organize the other generic approaches to the same issue.

Immediately after the introductory exposition, the division entitled "A poem" takes up the same issues, or what can be discovered
to be the same issues. With the simplicity and repetition of a nursery rhyme, it begins, "It is natural that there are many / It is natural
that there are few." The meaning of this couplet goes back to the
introduction in that the "many" are the plural "men"; and it leaps
ahead to a later occurrence of the introductory sentence, "Since
there are no men in existence anywhere except here being men is not
an easy thing and therefore masterpieces are so rare." Thus "it is
natural" that there are very few masterpieces. This idea is repeated in
many of Stein's works—most notably in "What Are Master-pieces and
Why Are There So Few of Them." Its appearance in "Identity,"
before the reader has sufficient information to interpret it, is typical
of Stein's writing at this time. Every sentence in this text is based on
a simultaneity of ideas; every expression is tied to all of the others.

The next two lines of "A poem" rhyme with the second line of the preceding couplet: "A city says how do you do / And sometimes one or two." Perhaps the city's greeting is Stein's reception in various American cities, especially in New York, where she was welcomed by lighted messages on various buildings.[23] As such, the greetings are another version of audience, the external accompaniment of the self that creates identity. The "sometimes one or two" could go back to the "few" of the first two lines, or could refer to the two states of the self as a unity or a duality. The continuation of "A poem" in "Identity A Poem A Story and A History" supports this interpretation: "Listen to me and they do. Anybody has no identity but not for you." That is, when one is talking to an audience one is operating through identity; the identity-free being cannot be for another.

After "A poem" the narrative continues. But in fact "what happens" is implicit in what has "already happened." We learn that "Now Sweet William had his genius and so he could tell a careful story of how they enjoyed themselves. But he did not have his Lilian, he looked for Lilian and so he could not tell a careful story of how they enjoyed themselves." In other words, if one operates through genius or essence one can produce masterpieces, "careful stories"; identity, however, inhibits their creation, since one is constantly looking for completion outside oneself.

Next we find "A conversation" between a "he" and a "she," presumably, William and Lilian: "Well well who is a genius he said and she said well well. Well well who is the genius." In this first conversation paragraph the two are competing over who is the genius. It should be noted that the configuration of elements—the "well well"'s, pronouns, and the words spoken—is asymmetrical here, whereas in the next verse paragraph where there is no conflict the configuration is perfectly symmetrical: "What is a genius she said and he said what is a genius. And they both answered at once who is a genius. When they both answered at once they answered well well what is a genius." Their unanimity is expressed here as simultaneity—they both answer at once. The answer they give is a question, "who is a genius," a favorite Steinian device. The last sentence of the conversation paragraph is open to a double interpretation: when they both answered at once they answered well by asking another question, 'well what is a genius,' or they answered the question, 'what is a genius,' well. That is, being a simultaneity, acting every moment in the present, is what it is to be a genius.

23. *EA*, p. 175: "and then we saw an electric sign moving around a building and it said Gertrude Stein has come. . . . "

However, after this promising moment, "Then there was a pause and Sweet William looked for Lilian." The pause is a moment unfilled with this unity, a break in simultaneity, and, as we have seen so often before, the antithesis of the "now" of entity. After this, William is upset and has an apparent disagreement with Lilian: "He says oh no she says oh no it is so." The symmetry, the unity symbolized by the "conversation," is gone, and now the second meaning of "converse" —'opposite' or 'opposed'—is dominant.

Next we learn that "Sweet William forgot nothing. To forget is not to remember but to remember is not to forget." To interpret this convoluted play on the negative we must turn to the following section, "A motto." "Why should alas be near to nothing." The narrative continues, "And so Sweet William was nervous as was his habit." Stein explains in *The Geographical History of America* that time disjunctions create nervousness rather than the excitement of the human mind. Sweet William is apparently back in the throes of identity. "Alas" or regret is next to "nothing" because it is an emotion that looks back into the past and hence creates a mixture of time senses. Thus, when "Sweet William forgot *nothing*" he was forgetting his regret; he was thus not forgetting and forgetting at the same time. He was involved in a contradiction in time sense, the source of his nervousness. In terms of genre, the "conversation," like a play, puts the various parts of the situation—he, she, genius, memory—into a set of immediate relations. The "motto," "Why should alas be near to nothing," quite properly provides the clue to understanding what has come before.

Now a motto normally comes at the end of a "tale" and summarizes what is to be learned from it. But here the motto gives the same information that was present in every other generic division of the tale, and moreover comes in the middle of it. However the motto does mark the end as far as Sweet William and Lilian are concerned. What follows simply retells the "story," such as it is, in different terms.

First comes "An aphorism," which declares that "It is always well to tell what it is that is done." Presumably, the tale has been doing just that, but since "It is always well" to do so, Stein proceeds to talk about "what it is that is done" in a different way. She explains in the next paragraph that stories are not interesting because they have made-up endings that do not provoke the audience to cry anymore. "And so there is no ending. That is what makes stories what they are and now I will tell one." That is, modern stories cannot have an ending because they cannot involve people now that character and action are irrelevant. Since they cannot end, her own story, the "Tale," cannot end either, and so she has to start over again with "Identity a story." Here we learn that it is only through masterpieces that men exist, for they exist then as geniuses. The "story" simply repeats the rest of the "tale."

The very end of the tale is taken up with the narrator's feelings about words of one syllable. As Bridgman points out (p. 285), these words are a sign of unity for Stein, although one which is impossible of realization. Perhaps this is why Stein says that "I wish words of one syllable were as bold as told." Apparently Stein is noting a contradiction between the unity of consciousness and the power of narrative, a contradiction which is denied at the same time that it is stated ("told" *is* a word of one syllable). Nevertheless, Stein declares at the end that she "will tell in words of one sylable [sic] anything there is to tell not very well but just well." This promise to tell as best she can about sequences through unity is of course her program as a writer: to tell of human nature (sequence, memory, identity) through the human mind (unity, simultaneity, entity). She will tell it "just well" rather than "very well" because "very" has more than one syllable, that is, because excellence in narrative creates a temporal disjunction. This promise to tell on, as it were, is also found in "Identity A Poem A Story and A History" where Stein concludes with a "Meditation": "And now I am going to tell the story of anybody's life. And begin with any one."

Thus the stories and meditations never end because they project out into the future, return to their own beginnings, and in fact say the same thing at every stage in their own "progression." The different orientations to each of these stages is created by the difference in the genres involved. Stein takes us through a genrological kaleidoscope of views of the same idea. In fact, this is cubist multiperspective worked out on a literary-theoretical level, as if Picasso had rendered his approach to color or time through a canvas simultaneously containing still life, portrait, landscape and historical scene.

Finally in "Identity A Play" ("Identity A Poem" in *What Are Masterpieces*) the whole "cast" of factors of the self is present: the human mind, human nature, the little dog (audience), "I," and memory. The piece begins with the rather haunting words, "I am I because my little dog knows me. The figure wanders on alone." Here identity is postulated as a function of audience, while true being or

entity is separate from this mode of consciousness. This statement is
the first in "Play I," a group of paragraphs exploring the relations
among the various facets of character. These paragraphs proceed as
a kind of logical exploration, with postulates, if-then statements,
conclusions, and illustrations. At one point they break up into something resembling a theatrical script:

The human mind.	The human mind does play.
The human mind.	Plays because it plays.
Human Nature.	Does not play because it does not play again.

Here what begins as a play—the 'character,' the human mind, named
before his speech—changes into a 'meditation' in the next line, where
the "human mind" becomes the subject of its predicate/speech. The
relation between the character and his words on the one hand and
the grammatical subject and its predicate on the other is being dramatized. This change eliminates the situation of the human mind's
talking about itself—a doubling of consciousness linked to identity.
Instead of talking about itself as playing it simply plays, and its talk,
its expression, is thus play: the speaking and the doing are one.

This flow of ideas, plays, and demonstrations of ideas continues
throughout "Identity A Play." New plays begin following out the
argument of what identity is and what the self is. The "voice" shifts
back and forth between an unidentified third-person narrator who
speaks in the first person as well, to characters with speeches, such
as "Chorus," "Tears," "The dog." These speakers are all aspects of
the problem of self-definition, and all come in for separate scrutiny
in the argument.

The end of "Identity A Play" is the reaching of a quasi-solution. "I
am I has really nothing to do with the little dog knowing me, he is
my audience, but an audience never does prove to you that you are
you." That is, one's identity is independent of audience. But the next
paragraphs seem to revive the little dog's value, for we learn that "He
can almost say the b in bow wow." "b" is clearly a play on "be," so
that in speaking, in making its noise, the dog is almost expressing its
being. Further, its noise is a case of "insistence," repetition with a
difference. The dog's near ability to make the sound differentiating
"bow" from "wow" means that the audience has some positive virtues as well as negative effects.

Stein then makes a very assured statement about her identity: "I

am I yes sir I am I," but follows this by posing the same idea as a
question: "I am I yes madame am I I." The same question is repeated
—"When I am I am I I"—followed by the positive assertion, "And my
little dog is not the same thing as I am I." Apparently identity and
audience can be definitively separated. But immediately the Chorus
asks, "Oh is it." And presumably the first voice takes this question
up, "With tears in my eyes oh is it. And there we have the whole
thing / Am I I."

At the very end of "Identity A Play" this dilemma is tied to the
act of writing. "Scene II / An end of a play is not the end of a day. /
Scene IV / After giving." The lines suggest the same continuity
beyond the finite limits of the text that we saw in the other two versions of "Identity." It depicts the act of writing, or of this special
writing, as "giving," an offering to the outside, presumably to the
audience. This reaffirmation of the audience's validity for the writer
—even the writer operating through the human mind—was prepared
for by the preceding lines, but nevertheless comes as a rather moving
conclusion to the previous agonizings over the conflict between
authenticity and audience-directed existence. It is a kind of truce
with the audience that contrasts pleasantly with the starkness of the
lone, wandering figure with which the work began.

If we place "Identity A Play" together with the other two "Identity" pieces we have a complete range of genres (except for the portrait, which by this time was virtually defunct) brought to bear on
the same thematic problem. The transformation of concepts into
characters, the linking of character and speech to subject and predicate, and the constant grouping and re-grouping of the elements of
the theme are the play-genre's means of exploring an issue. The
results are identical to the genre shifts in the other two pieces; with
each we look at a problem through the filter of a different genre.
This complex of texts is a graphic demonstration of Stein's conception of genres as forms of knowing, epistemological approaches to
the essential issues of art and consciousness.

Further, we might note how clearly the "Identity" texts sum-
marize the final state of Stein's experimentation. We have already
seen how the rise of the meditative essay, solving the disjunction
between subject matter and the act of writing, turned Stein's writing
inward, eliminating genre distinctions according to subject matter
and leaving only formal differences. It did away with the portrait
contradiction of a self-enclosed text that is at the same time definitionally referential, and joined all the other genres into a common

end—the exploration and expression of the "human mind." The essay healed the split dramatized in "Identity A Play" between the writer as the lonely figure locked in his own genius and the writer as "giver," for the essay was available to its audience in a way that the third-phase portraits were not.

However, the dominance of the meditative essay created a different kind of isolation from that previously experienced by Stein. From an author whose work was unsharable, she became an author who could write only about her own mind or her writing itself. The extension of the artist into the world, dictated definitionally by the portrait, was now impossible. Thus, the meditations of the thirties rationalized, in both senses of the word, the contradiction of non-representational portraiture, easing Stein into the compromise of communication, but with a severely limited sphere to communicate. The strain created in her by this limitation is dramatized in the "Identity" texts, and virtually all the rest of her writing is caught between audience-directed referentiality and self-reflexive isolation. The mimetic representation of reality epitomized by the portrait had been proven an impossibility.

At this point we might recall Ortega y Gasset's program for modernist portraiture with which chapter 1 closed: "What if the painter . . . decided to paint not the real person but his idea, his pattern, of the person? Indeed, in that case the portrait would be the truth, and failure would no longer be inevitable. In foregoing to emulate reality the painting becomes what it authentically is; an image, an unreality." In producing portraits consistent with Ortega's program, such as "George Hugnet," Stein had in fact realized this absolute art. But unlike the philosopher, she saw its limitations. For she had never lost the desire to contain reality in her work, to mediate through her art between her readers and the world. As she put it, abstraction is pornography. Thus, absolute art, the 'truth,' was itself a failure since it ignored the fundamental issue to be solved through writing—the need to reconcile lived experience with aesthetic experience, to create and communicate with the immediacy of life itself. This conflict, essential to the portrait genre, was not resolved but only dramatized by Stein's artistic progress. Where other absolute artists were content to explore the possibilities of their new aesthetic approach, Stein saw it as a necessary contradiction which placed the artist in a futile struggle. Identity versus entity, human nature versus the human mind, the self for living versus the 'self' for creating—these pairs could not be reconciled for either the portrait subject or its creator. A literalist interpretation of the direction set for western art by the mimetic program could lead only to defeat, and if for no other reason, we must credit Stein with forcing herself to full consciousness of this fact. The demands of artistry and reference makes possible only an uneasy mutual compromise, a compromise in which Stein refused to take comfort. In her unflinching confrontation of this fact, Stein has much to teach us, both as an artist and as a theoretician of art.

Appendix 1

Identity: A Tale

Since there are no men in existence anywhere except here on this earth being men is not an easy thing to happen.

Sweet William had his genius and so he did not look for it. He did look for Lilian and then he had Lilian.

A poem

It is natural that there are many
It is natural that there are few
A city says how do you do
And sometimes one or two

Now Sweet William had his genius and so he could tell a careful story of how they enjoyed themselves. But he did not have his Lilian, he looked for Lilian and so he could not tell a careful story of how they enjoyed themselves.

A conversation

Well well who is a genius he said and she said well well. Well well who is the genius.

What is a genius she said and he said what is a genius. And they both answered at once who is a genius. When they both answered at once they answered well well what is a genius.

Then there was a pause and Sweet William looked for Lilian

He says oh no she says oh no it is so.

Sweet William forgot nothing. To forget is not to remember but to remember is not to forget.

And so Sweet William said that he thought

A motto

Why should alas be near to nothing
And so Sweet William was nervous as was his habit.

An aphorism

It is always well to tell what it is that is done.

No story is interesting although I always listen to it and they have to make up the ending and if it does not make you cry and now nothing makes them cry because no one can try to make them cry. And so there is no ending. That is what makes stories what they are and now I will tell one.

Identity a story

There is any day not what they say there is a man there and it is well done. If he likes it or not it is well done. They like to know that it is well done. That is what a man is they like to know that it is well done. What is it that a man is a man is that they like to know that it is well done. If it is not well done he is dead and they like to know that he is dead if it is well done. That is the one thing that there is that there is now that he is dead and that it is well done.

Since there are no men in existence anywhere except here being men is not an easy thing and therefore master-pieces are so rare.

I wish words of one sylable were as bold as told.

Anybody can like words of one sylable here and there but I like them anywhere.

I will tell in words of one sylable anything there is to tell not very well but just well.

Appendix 2

A List of Stein's Portraits

The list of portraits which follows is based on appendix C of Richard Bridgman's study, *Gertrude Stein in Pieces,* which is a compilation of all of Stein's works as listed in Part 4 of the *Yale Catalogue* and in Julian Sawyer's extension of this list to those works written after 1940. The rationale for the division of the portraits into three phases is discussed in chapter 3 at some length, as is the occasional arbitrariness of the decision as to which works are actually portraits. The dates under which items are listed are the dates of their composition, and the number appearing in parentheses to the left of the titles is the number of each item in Bridgman's list. Following Bridgman's practice, I give only the page number on which a given item begins. In addition, any manuscript comments of Stein's indicating the identity of subjects have been included with the appropriate entry.

The First-Phase Portraits

1. (3) A Man. *Two,* 235. Front inside ms. cover, vol. 1: "David & Mrs." (probably David Edstrom).
2. (4) Five or Six Men. *Two,* 253. Front inside ms. cover, vol. I: "The four and me./Leo Friedman/Derain/Hans Purrman/ Maurice Sterne/& Piot." Others indicated in the portrait: "Sarah Matisse & Mme. & Margot, [illegible] , Bruces, . . . the Derain gruppe [sic] " and "Pablo" (Picasso) and "Alice" (Toklas).
3. (5) *Two Women.* Front inside ms. cover: "Cone Sisters"; Claribel Cone is "Bertha"; Etta Cone is "Ada."
4. (6) Italians. *Geography and Plays,* 46.
5. (7) Orta or One Dancing. *Two*, 286. Front inside ms. cover: "Isadora" (Duncan).
6. (8) Four Protégés. *Two,* 305.
7. (9) Men. *Two,* 310. Front outside ms. cover, vol. 1: "Hutch & David & Sterne" (Hutchins Hapgood, David Edstrom, and Maurice Sterne).
8. (10) Elise Surville. *Two,* 316.
9. (11) A Kind of Women. *Two,* 319. Front inside ms. cover: "Making of an old maid./Dora & Mirtle."

10. (12) A Family of Perhaps Three. *Geography and Plays,* 331. Front inside ms. cover: "Mildred & Edna." Others mentioned in portrait notations: "Dieter," "Jiress," "Clare," "Myra," "Gracie," "Dean of women [illegible]," "Bridget."
11. (13) Ada. *Geography and Plays*, 14.
12. (14) Julia Marlowe. *Two*, 328.
13. (15) Frost. *Two*, 330.
14. (16) Purrmann. *Two*, 333.
15. (17) Russell. *Two*, 336.
16. (18) Pach. *Two*, 338.
17. (19) Chalfin. *Two,* 341.
18. (20) Harriet Fear. *Two*, 343.
19. (21) Hessel. *Two*, 347.
20. (22) Roche. *Geography and Plays*, 141.
21. (24) Rue de Rennes. *Two*, 349.
22. (25) Bon Marché Weather. *Two*, 351.
23. (26) Flirting at the Bon Marché. *Two*, 353.
24. (27) Miss Furr and Miss Skeene. *Geography and Plays*, 17.

1909

25. (28) Matisse. *Portraits and Prayers*, 12.
26. (29) Picasso. *Portraits and Prayers*, 17.
27. (30) Manguin A Painter. *Portraits and Prayers*, 54.

1910–12

28. (34) Harriet Making Plans. *Portraits and Prayers*, 105.
29. (35) Two: Gertrude Stein and Her Brother. *Two*, 1. Front inside ms. cover: "Complete sound and then a bit of what they did and how. Then do Alice and me what we did and how. use the introduction for Alice about babies./Leo and Sally . . . " Others mentioned: "Jane" and "May."

1911

30. (37) Nadelman. *Portraits and Prayers*, 51.
31. (38) Four Dishonest Ones. Told by a Description of What They Do. *Portraits and Prayers*, 57. Between third and fourth paragraphs: "~~Maddalena~~."
32. (39) Storyette H.M. *Portraits and Prayers*, 40.
33. (40) Galeries Lafayettes. *Portraits and Prayers*, 169.

1912

34. (43) Jenny, Helen, Hannah, Paul and Peter. *Two,* 143. Front
     inside ms. cover, vol. I, consecutively under each name in the
     title: "Laura Miriam Adele Ben & Joe." Others mentioned (vol.
     4): "S. Wolfe" and "O. & L. Friedman" in connection with
     Cambridge life.
35. (44) Mi-Careme. *Portraits and Prayers,* 173.

1913

36. (46) A Portrait of One. Harry Phelan Gibb. *Geography and
     Plays,* 201.

The Second-Phase Portraits:

c. 1911–12

37. (23) Portrait of Constance Fletcher. *Geography and Plays,* 157.

1911

38. (41) Mabel Dodge at the Villa Curonia. *Portraits and Prayers,*
     98.

1912

39. (45) Monsieur Vollard et Cezanne. *Portraits and Prayers,* 37.

1913

40. (49) A Portrait of F. B. *Geography and Plays,* 176.
41. (50) Portrait of Prince B. D. *Geography and Plays,* 150.
42. (53) One. Carl Van Vechten. *Geography and Plays,* 199.
43. (56) Braque. *Geography and Plays,* 44.
44. (57) Marsden Hartley and So Forth. *Marsden Hartley Exhi-
     bition,* Little Gallery of Photo-Secession, January-February
     1914.
45. (59) Susie Asado. *Geography and Plays,* 13.
46. (60) Mrs. Th——y. *Soil* 1 (December 1916), 15.
47. (69) Americans. *Geography and Plays,* 39.
48. (72) Guillaume Apollinaire. *Portraits and Prayers,* 26.
49. (75) Simon. "Three Hitherto Unpublished Portraits," *Yale
     University Library Gazette* (July 1975), 42.
50. (77) Irma. *Portraits and Prayers,* 96.

51. (79) Mrs. Edwardes. *Portraits and Prayers*, 97.
52. (80) Preciosilla. *Selected Writings of Gertrude Stein*, 550.
53. (81) Sacred Emily. *Geography and Plays*, 178.

1914

54. (85) Tillie. *Bee Time Vine*, 173.
55. (95) Gentle Julia. *Bee Time Vine*, 178.
56. (99) Mrs. Whitehead. *Geography and Plays*, 154.
57. (100) Lockeridge. *Bee Time Vine*, 177.
58. (101) Mrs. Emerson. *Close Up* 2 (August 1927), 23. Title page:
     "Mrs. Emerson. Mrs. Henry Emerson."

1915

59. (107) Johnny Grey. *Geography and Plays*, 167.
60. (117) David Daisy and Appolonia. *Portraits and Prayers*, 226.

1916

61. (124) Mr. Miranda and William. *Painted Lace*, 274.
62. (125) Henry and I. *Painted Lace*, 273.
63. (135) Captain William Edwards. *Painted Lace*, 272.

1917

64. (153) Miss Cruttwell. *As Fine As Melanctha*, 173.
65. (155) Marry Nettie. Alright Makes It a Series and Call It Marry
     Nettie. *Painted Lace*, 42.

1920

66. (219) Next. Life and Letters of Marcel Duchamp. *Geography
     and Plays*, 505.

1921

67. (231) B. B. or The Birthplace of Bonnes. *Portraits and Prayers*,
     162.
68. (234) Emily Chadbourne. *Useful Knowledge*, 88.
69. (246) Singing to a Musician (George Leroy). *Portraits and
     Prayers*, 232.
70. (247) Finish Constance. *Painted Lace*, 276.

1922

71. (261) Mildred's Thoughts. *The American Caravan*, 648.
72. (266) Jo Davidson. *Portraits and Prayers*, 194.

73. (271) A Valentine to Sherwood Anderson. Idem The Same. *Portraits and Prayers*, 151.
74. (275) Erik Satie. *Portraits and Prayers*, 27.

1923

75. (281) Harold Loeb. *Portraits and Prayers*, 208.
76. (282) Fourteen Anonymous Portraits. *Portraits and Prayers*, 227. Title page: "Anonymous Portraits I/Harold Stevens"; in Portrait 5 after "They tell us so": "Portrait of a female stone breaker who has a rope attached to a mountain. She is not the wife for Michael."
77. (283) Cezanne. *Portraits and Prayers*, 11.
78. (284) An Indian Boy. *The Reviewer* 4 (January 1924), 104.
79. (288) Jonas Julian Caesar and Samuel. *Painted Lace*, 286.
80. (294) He and They, Hemingway. *Portraits and Prayers*, 193.
81. (296) Van or Twenty Years After. A Second Portrait of Carl Van Vechten. *Portraits and Prayers*, 157.
82. (299) If I Told Him. A Completed Portrait of Picasso. *Portraits and Prayers*, 21.
83. (304) My Dear Coady and Brenner. *Painted Lace*, 291.

1924

84. (313) Mildred Aldrich Saturday. *Portraits and Prayers*, 111.
85. (314) And So. To Change So. (A Fantasy on Three Careers) Muriel Draper Yvonne Davidson Beatrice Locher. *Portraits and Prayers*, 143.
86. (317) Pictures of Juan Gris. *Portraits and Prayers*, 46.
87. (318) The Brazilian Admiral's Son. *Portraits and Prayers*, 216.
88. (320) A Description of the Fifteenth of November. A Portrait of T. S. Eliot. *Portraits and Prayers*, 68.
89. (325) Man Ray. *Painted Lace*, 292.

1925

90. (330) Sitwell Edith Sitwell. *Portraits and Prayers*, 92.

The Third-Phase Portraits:

1926

91. (338) Jean Cocteau. *Portraits and Prayers*, 80.
92. (340) Edith Sitwell And Her Brothers The Sitwells and Also To Osbert Sitwell And to S. Sitwell. *Painted Lace*, 293.
93. (341) Allen Tanner. *Useful Knowledge*, 86.

94. (343) Pavlik Tchelitchef Or Adrian Arthur. *Portraits and Prayers*, 213.
95. (244) Lipschitz. *Portraits and Prayers*, 63.

1927

96. (347) Duchess de Rohan. A Writer. *Painted Lace*, 310.
97. (351) Two Spaniards. *Painted Lace*, 309.
98. (355) One Spaniard. *Portraits and Prayers*, 65.
99. (361) The Life of Juan Gris. The Life and Death of Juan Gris. *Portraits and Prayers*, 48.

1928

100. (365) Dan Raffel A Nephew. *Portraits and Prayers*, 86.
101. (369) J. H. Jane Heap. *Little Review* 12 (May 1929), 9.
102. (370) The D'Aiguys. *Portraits and Prayers*, 108.
103. (373) George Hugnet. *Portraits and Prayers*, 66.
104. (374) Christian Berard. *Portraits and Prayers*, 73.
105. (375) Virgil Thomson. *Portraits and Prayers*, 198.

1929

106. (379) Bernard Faÿ. *Portraits and Prayers*, 41.
107. (381) Basket. *Portraits and Prayers*, 181.
108. (384) More Grammar Genia Berman. *Portraits and Prayers*, 185.
109. (386) Kristians Tonny. *Portraits and Prayers*, 212.
110. (387) G. Maratier. *Portraits and Prayers*, 183.

1930

111. (393) Absolutely As Bob Brown Or Bobbed Brown. *Painted Lace*, 311.
112. (394) Eric De Haulleville. *Portraits and Prayers*, 211.
113. (395) Madame de Clermont-Tonnerre. *Portraits and Prayers*, 89.
114. (396) Bravig Imbs. *Portraits and Prayers*, 210.
115. (397) Madame Langlois. "Three Hitherto Unpublished Portraits," 44.
116. (402) Grace, or Yves de Longevialle. "Three Hitherto Unpublished Portraits," 45.
117. (408) To Kitty or Kate Buss. *Portraits and Prayers*, 103.

1932

118. (441) A Play Without Roses Portrait of Eugene Jolas. *Portraits and Prayers*, 200.

119. (450) Margite Marguerite and Margherita. *Stanzas In Meditation,* 269.
120. (453a) Preface. *Picabia, Chez Leonce Rosenberg* (Paris, December 1932).

1933

121. (462) Lucy La Fontaine. *Painted Lace,* 315.
122. (464a) Or. And Then Silence. A Portrait of a Frenchman. *Portraits and Prayers,* 241.

1934

123. (473) Sir Francis Rose. *Notice of Wildenstein and Co., Ltd.* (London, February 1934).
124. (474) Stieglitz. *America and Alfred Stieglitz, A Collective Portrait,* ed. Waldo Frank *et al.* (New York, 1934), 280.
125. (476) Preface. *Recent Paintings by Francis Picabia* (New York: Valentine Gallery, November 1934).

1935

126. (491) Introduction to Paintings by Elie Lascaux. *The Arts Club of Chicago* (February-March 1936).

1937

127. (510) La Baronne Pierlot. *Painted Lace,* 316.

1938

128. (514) *Picasso.*
129. (517) Arthur and Jenny.

1941

130. (534) Francis Picabia. *Exposition Francis Picabia* (3 et 5 rue Commandant-Andre, Cannes, 11 April 1941).
131. (538) Sherwood's Sweetness. *Story* 19 (September-October 1941), 63.

1946

132. (568) Raoul Dufy. *Harper's Bazaar* (December 1949), 93.

Bibliography

Volumes and Collections of Gertrude Stein Used in This Study

Three Lives. New York, 1909.

Tender Buttons. New York, 1914.

Geography and Plays. New York and Boston, 1922. Foreword by Sherwood Anderson.

The Making of Americans. Paris, 1925; condensed version, New York, 1934.

Composition As Explanation. London, 1926.

Useful Knowledge. New York, 1928.

Lucy Church Amiably. Paris, 1930.

How to Write. Paris, 1931.

Operas and Plays. Paris, 1932.

The Autobiography of Alice B. Toklas. New York, 1933.

Matisse Picasso and Gertrude Stein With Two Shorter Stories. Paris, 1933.

Four Saints in Three Acts. New York, 1934.

Portraits and Prayers. New York, 1934.

Lectures in America. New York, 1935.

Narration. Chicago, 1935.

Everybody's Autobiography. New York, 1937.

Picasso. London, 1938.

What Are Masterpieces. Los Angeles, 1940. Foreword by Robert Bartlett Haas.

Four in America. New Haven, 1947.

Blood On the Dining-Room Floor. Pawlet, Vermont, 1948. Foreword by Donald Gallup.

Last Operas and Plays. New York, 1949. Introduction by Carl Van Vechten.

Things As They Are. Pawlet, Vermont, 1950.

The Yale Edition of the Unpublished Writings of Gertrude Stein (general editor, Carl Van Vechten; advisory committee, Donald Gallup, Donald Sutherland, and Thorton Wilder):

Two: Gertrude Stein and Her Brother and Other Early Portraits (1908-1912). New Haven, 1951. Foreword by Janet Flanner.

Mrs. Reynolds and Five Earlier Novelettes (1931-1942). New Haven, 1952. Foreword by Lloyd Frankenberg.

Bee Time Vine and Other Pieces (1913-1927). New Haven, 1953. Preface and notes by Virgil Thomson.

As Fine As Melanctha (1914-1930). New Haven, 1954. Foreword by Natalie Clifford Barney.

Painted Lace and Other Pieces (1914-1937). New Haven, 1955. Introduction by Daniel-Henry Kahnweiler.

Stanzas in Meditation and Other Poems (1929-1933). New Haven, 1956. Preface by Donald Sutherland.

Alphabets and Birthdays. New Haven, 1957. Introduction by Donald Gallup.

A Novel of Thank You. New Haven, 1958. Introduction by Carl Van Vechten.

Selected Writings of Gertrude Stein. Edited by Carl Van Vechten. New York, 1962.

Gertrude Stein: Writings and Lectures 1909–1945. Edited by Patricia Meyer-
ovitz. Baltimore, 1967.
A Primer for the Gradual Understanding of Gertrude Stein. Edited by Robert
Bartlett Haas. Los Angeles, 1971.
The Geographical History of America. New York, 1973. Introduction by William
Gass; introduction from 1936 edition by Thornton Wilder reprinted.
Reflection on the Atomic Bomb. Edited by Robert Bartlett Haas. Los Angeles,
1973.
How Writing Is Written. Edited by Robert Bartlett Haas. Los Angeles, 1974.

Selected Secondary Sources

Abrams, M. H. *The Mirror and the Lamp.* Oxford, 1953.
Anderson, Sherwood. "The Work of Gertrude Stein." In *Geography and Plays,*
by Gertrude Stein. New York and Boston, 1922.
Apollinaire, Guillaume. *Calligrammes.* Paris, 1925.
——. *The Cubist Painters—Aesthetic Meditations.* Translated by Lionel Abel.
New York, 1944. Originally *Les Peintres cubistes [Méditations Ésthétiques].*
Paris, 1913.
Arnheim, Rudolf. *Visual Thinking.* Berkeley, Los Angeles, and London, 1969.
Auerbach, Erich. *Mimesis.* Princeton, 1953.
Baldanza, Frank. "Faulkner and Stein: A Study in Stylistic Intransigence."
Georgia Review 13, (Fall 1959): 274-86.
Bense, Max. "Was erzählt Gertrude Stein?" In *Probleme des Erzählens in der
Weltliteratur,* edited by Fritz Martini. Stuttgart, 1971.
Bernstein, Leonard. "Music and Miss Stein." *New York Book Review,* May 22,
1949.
Boyce, Benjamin. *The Theophrastan Character in England to 1642.* Cambridge,
Mass., 1947.
Breckenridge, James D. *Likeness: A Conceptual History of Ancient Portraiture.*
Evanston, Ill., 1968.
Bridgman, Richard. *Gertrude Stein in Pieces.* New York, 1970.
Brinnin, John Malcolm. *The Third Rose.* Boston, 1959.
Brontë, Charlotte. *Shirley.* London, 1908.
Brophy, John. *The Face in Western Art.* London, 1963.
Bruns, Gerald L. *Modern Poetry and the Idea of Language.* New Haven, 1974.
Burke, Kenneth. "Engineering with Words." *Dial* 74 (April 1923).
——. "The Impartial Essence." *The New Republic* 83 (July 3, 1935).
Cassirer, Ernst. *Substance and Function.* Chicago and London, 1923.
Colby, Alice. *The Portrait in Twelfth-Century French Literature.* Geneva, 1965.
Collingwood, R. G. *The Principles of Art.* New York, 1958.
Copeland, Carolyn Faunce. *Language & Time & Gertrude Stein.* Iowa City,
Iowa, 1975.
Culler, A. Dwight. "Monodrama and the Dramatic Monologue." *PMLA,* May
1975.
Dijkstra, Bram. *The Hieroglyphics of a New Speech: Cubism, Stieglitz, and the
Early Poetry of William Carlos Williams.* Princeton, 1969.
Empson, William. *Seven Types of Ambiguity.* New York, 1947.
Fäy, Bernard. Introduction to *The Making of Americans,* by Gertrude Stein.
New York, 1934.

Flanner, Janet. Foreword to *Two: Gertrude Stein and Her Brother and Other Early Portraits (1908-1912)*, by Gertrude Stein. New Haven, 1951.

Friedländer, Max. *Landscape, Portrait, Still Life*. New York, 1963.

Fry, Edward. *Cubism*. New York, 1966.

Furst, Herbert. *Portrait Painting: Its Nature and Function*. London, 1927.

Gallup, Donald, ed., with Robert Bartlett Haas. *A Catalogue of the Published and Unpublished Writings of Gertrude Stein*. New Haven, 1941.

———, ed. *The Flowers of Friendship: Letters Written to Gertrude Stein*. New York, 1953.

Gass, William H. "Gertrude Stein: Her Escape from Protective Language," *Fiction and the Figures of Life*. New York, 1970.

———. Introduction to *The Geographical History of America*, by Gertrude Stein. New York, 1973.

Golding, John. *Cubism: A History and an Analysis*. New York, 1959.

Gombrich, E. H. *Art and Illusion: A Study in the Psychology of Pictorial Representation*. Princeton, 1956.

Guiney, Mortimer. *Cubisme et Littérature*. Geneva, 1972.

Haas, Robert Bartlett. "Gertrude Stein and the Twentieth Century," *A Primer for the Gradual Understanding of Gertrude Stein*. Los Angeles, 1971.

Haines, George, IV. "Forms of Imaginative Prose: 1900-1940." *Southern Review* 7 (Spring 1942): 755-75.

Hoffman, Frederick J. *Gertrude Stein*. Minneapolis, Minn., 1961.

———. *The 20's: American Writing in the Postwar Decade*. New York, 1962.

Hoffman, Michael J. *The Development of Abstractionism in the Writings of Gertrude Stein*. Philadelphia, 1965.

Howe, Irving. *The Decline of the New*. New York, 1963.

———. *The Idea of the Modern in Literature and the Arts*. New York, 1967.

Jakobson, Roman. "Poetry of Grammar and Grammar of Poetry." *Lingua* 21 (1968).

James, Henry. *The Art of the Novel*. New York, 1962.

James, William. *Principles of Psychology*. New York, 1890.

Judkins, Winthrup. "Toward a Reinterpretation of Cubism." *The Art Bulletin* 30 (December 1948).

Kahnweiler, Daniel-Henry. Introduction to *Painted Lace and Other Pieces (1914-1937)*, by Gertrude Stein. New Haven, 1955.

Kamber, Gerald. *Max Jacob and the Poetics of Cubism*. Baltimore, 1971.

Katz, Leon. "Matisse, Picasso and Gertrude Stein," *Four Americans in Paris: The Collections of Gertrude Stein and Her Family*. New York, 1970.

Langer, Suzanne. "A Note on the Film." In *The Oxford Reader*, edited by Frank Kermode and Richard Poirier. New York, 1971.

Lee, Vernon. "The Portrait Art." *Euphorion*, vol. 2. Boston, 1884.

Lemaître, George Edward. *From Cubism to Surrealism in French Literature*. Cambridge, Mass., 1941.

Lessing, Gotthold Ephraim. *Lessing's Prose Works*. Edited by Edward Bell. London, 1913.

Levinson, Ronald Bartlett. "Gertrude Stein, William James, and Grammar." *American Journal of Psychology* 54 (January 1941).

Linschoten, Johannes. *On the Way toward a Phenomenological Psychology*. Pittsburgh, 1968.

Loran, Erle. *Cézanne's Composition: Analysis of His Form with Diagrams and Photographs of His Motifs*. Berkeley and Los Angeles, 1963.

Macdonald, Hugh, ed. *Portraits in Prose*. New Haven, 1947.

McMillan, Samuel Herbert, Jr. "Gertrude Stein, the Cubists, and the Futurists." Ph.D. dissertation, University of Texas, 1964.

Mellow, James R. *The Charmed Circle*. New York, 1974.

Miller, Rosalind. *Gertrude Stein: Form and Intelligibility*. New York, 1949.

Mohanty, J. N. *Edmund Husserl's Theory of Meaning*. The Hague, 1964.

Morris, Charles. *Foundations of the Theory of Signs*. Chicago, 1938.

Mukařovský, Jan. *Estetická funkce, norma a hodnota jako sociální fakty*. Prague, 1936.

———. "Dialectic Contradictions in Modern Art," *Structure, Sign, and Function*. New Haven, 1977.

Peirce, C. S. *Collected Writings*, vol. 4. Cambridge, Mass., 1966.

Pope, Alexander. "Epistle to Cobham." In *Prose and Poetry of Alexander Pope*, edited by Aubrey Williams. Boston, 1965.

Pope-Hennessy, John. *The Portrait in the Renaissance*. New York, 1966.

Reid, B. L. *Art by Subtraction*. Norman, Okla., 1958.

Reynolds, Sir Joshua. *Portraits*. London, 1952.

Riding, Laura. "Hulme, the New Barbarism and Gertrude Stein." *transition* 3 (Paris, June 1927).

Rogers, W. G. *When This You See Remember Me—Gertrude Stein in Person*. New York, 1948.

Rönnebeck, Arnold. "Gertrude Was Always Giggling." *Books Abroad* 18, no. 4 (October 1944).

Rose, Sir Francis. *Gertrude Stein and Painting*. London, 1968.

Russell, Bertrand. "On Denoting." In *Meaning and Knowledge*, edited by E. Nagel and R. B. Brandt. New York, 1965.

Sainte-Beuve, C. A. *Portraits of the Seventeenth Century*. Translated by Katherine Wormeley. New York, 1904.

Sawyer, Julian. "Gertrude Stein: A Bibliography, 1941–1948." *Bulletin of Bibliography* 19 (May-August, September-December, 1948): 152–56, 183–87.

Shapiro, Meyer. "On Some Problems in the Semiotics of Visual Art: Field and Vehicle in Image-Signs." *Semiotica* 1, 3 (1969).

Skinner, B. F. "Has Gertrude Stein a Secret?" *Atlantic Monthly* 153 (January 1934).

Smith, David Nichol. *Characters of the Seventeenth Century*. Oxford, 1918.

Stauffer, Donald. *The Art of Biography in Eighteenth-Century England*. Princeton, 1941.

———. *English Biography Before 1700*. Cambridge, Mass., 1930.

Stein, Leo. *Journey into the Self*. New York, 1950.

Steiner, Wendy. "The Steinian Portrait." *The Yale University Library Gazette*, July 1975.

Stewart, Allegra. *Gertrude Stein and the Present*. Cambridge, Mass., 1967.

Stieglitz, Alfred. "Editorial." *Camera Work*, Special Number, August 1912.

Sutherland, Donald. *Gertrude Stein, a Biography of Her Work*. New Haven, 1957.

———. "Gertrude Stein and the Twentieth Century." In *A Primer for the Gradual Understanding of Gertrude Stein*, edited by Robert Bartlett Haas. Los Angeles, 1971.

———. Preface to *Stanzas in Meditation and Other Poems (1929-1933)*, by Gertrude Stein. New Haven, 1956.

Sypher, Wylie. *Rococo to Cubism in Art and Literature*. New York, 1960.

Thomson, Virgil. Preface and notes to *Bee Time Vine and Other Pieces (1913-1927)*, by Gertrude Stein. New Haven, 1953.

Toklas, Alice B. *Staying on Alone: Letters of Alice B. Toklas*. Edited by Edward Burns. New York, 1973.

———. *What Is Remembered*. New York, 1963.

Vannier, Bernard. *L'Inscription du corps: pour une sémiotique du portrait balzacien*. Paris, 1972.

Weininger, Otto. *Sex & Character*. New York and London, 1909.

Wilshire, Bruce. *William James and Phenomenology*. Bloomington, Indiana, 1968.

Žirmunskij, V. "K voprosu o 'formal'nom metode.'" *Voprosy teorii literatury*. Leningrad, 1928.

Index